Where There's WILL, There's A Way

REFLECTIONS ON MY SON AND HIS CANCER JOURNEY

By Tom Canan

TABLE OF CONTENTS

Printed in the United States of America

 rookbooks, llc

Library of Congress Control Number: 2013941061

ISBN 978-0-9843319-1-8

Will and "Dr. Jack" – Olmsted County American Cancer Society Relay for Life – Rochester, Minnesota – July 2006

Prologue

It's early morning at the beginning of fall, 2009. Once again, sleep is elusive and abbreviated, coming late and leaving early. I toss in my bed before the sunrise. It's pointless to try to sleep anymore so I drag myself down to the computer to try to vent the torrents of words and memories coursing through my head. With all that has happened, it's so hard to remember exactly from where we have come. I feel the need to try to reduce it all to words in an attempt to bring some clarity and meaning to it all.

I want to share Will's story with others in the hope that his short life will not have been in vain.

This is the story of my son Will and his epic struggle against an insatiable monster known as childhood cancer.

FOREWORD

I never in my wildest dreams thought that I would have a career in Pediatric Oncology. During my nursing training, the two areas I said I would not work in were Pediatrics and Oncology. But someone had other plans and I have been fortunate to have spent the last 39 years working in Oncology, with most of those years spent in Pediatrics.

In that time, I have seen patient survival rates jump from 20-30 percent to over 80 percent, but of course we will not be satisfied until they reach 100%. I have had the privilege of working with many special children, adolescents, and their families. Each child has taught me about life, grace, strength and so much more. They have shown me what is important, and how to love and share life with others. When people find out where I work, they often look sad and ask, *"How can you work there?"* I think, *"How could I not?"* It is always a privilege and honor to travel the diagnosis and treatment journey with the children and their families, even though the outcome is not always what we would like. That brings me to the journey we recently took with Will and his family, which ended in the fall of 2012. In some ways, it seems like a long journey—on the other hand, it was way too short.

Will's bright blue eyes twinkled when he shared his day-brightening smile. It lit up his whole face and always made those around him follow suit. I think the saying "live, love and laugh" is a motto Will lived by. Everything Will did, he did with gusto. He was always thinking and planning, and asked lots of well-thought-out questions about his care. He used his index finger to say "Hi" or to indicate that a question was coming your way. Once when his friends were visiting him, he allowed them to paint one of his fingernails blue, for fun. The symbolism of it ignited, and soon many in the community, including those who read about it on Facebook, were painting a fingernail blue out of support for Will.

When Will started treatment, he was a young boy with questions who let his parents lead the way. His honesty and caring nature showed through even at a young age. He was comfortable directing questions through his parents initially, but soon began asking his own. As he grew and got to know the staff, he became more active in his care and wanted to participate in all discussions. He asked questions and wanted to discuss his treatment, but once his questions were answered he would move on to other topics, while respecting that his parents might have more questions.

Will loved life and everything about it—his family, friends, his dog, and school. Will made friends wherever he went. When he came to Mayo Clinic for care, he knew everyone by name and would ask how everyone was, including their pets, family and grandchildren. He remembered what was going on in their lives and what was important to them. Almost every time I saw Will, he asked how members of my family were doing. What a gift. He had each of us on his care team figured out. One of our secrets was that I was only 29 years old, but had had many anniversaries of that particular birthday. If anyone ever said I was old, Will said with a twinkle in his eye and a smile that I was only 29.

One time Will asked me what my plans were for the weekend. When I told him that another nursing colleague and I were going to a place in a neighboring town for supper, Will declared that he had never been to that restaurant. I said if he wanted to go with a couple of old nurses he was welcome to join us. He was interested. So, we had the most handsome escort at the restaurant and I think we were the envy of many of the women there. Will mentioned afterward that he had a good time but the food wasn't the best. We later tried some other restaurants. The company was always good, but we didn't always agree on the quality of the food!

Will was quite knowledgeable about sports. He could give you all the statistics on the Minnesota Twins and the Green Bay Packers. He didn't rank the Minnesota Vikings quite as highly, but followed their season nonetheless. He got the opportunity to see the Packers in the Super Bowl, which he couldn't stop talking about. Along the same vein, Will had sports names picked out for some of the staff, like "V-rod," and "D-Juan." Not being a sports aficionado, I wasn't sure of the significance, but I know they were given with humor, always with that twinkle in his eye. We all enjoyed talking sports with Will. I always received new data on his teams, which made me look smarter around others.

Will had the chance to spend lots of time and create many memories with his family. He loved them dearly, and wasn't afraid to show it. He had plenty of stories to tell about his family adventures. At one point, when his family had gone on a cruise, Will helped the captain by mapping out where the Bermuda triangle was located to make sure they avoided that area.

My compliments to Will's entire family for supporting him and letting him grow into the delightful young man he was. He was a mature and thoughtful young man who always reached out to others and made sure that those around him were doing well. I remember Will for his good nature and warm personality. Although we have lost him physically, he will forever be among those of us who had the privilege to know him, with his bright, twinkling blue eyes, and a smile that lit up the room.

Donna Betcher, RN, MS, PNP
Associate Professor, Department of Pediatrics,
Mayo Clinic, Rochester, MN
Will's Nurse Practitioner

Will and Donna Betcher – After Will meets the King and
Queen of Norway – Mayo Clinic
– October 2011

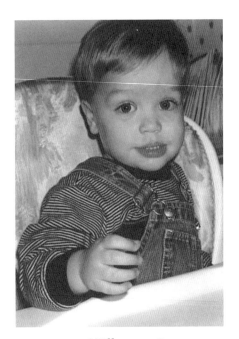

Will at age 2
– February 2000

Will in Rochester Youth Hockey
– Winter 2003-2004

Chapter 1 – Diagnosis and Surgery

Cancer is a word, not a sentence.
– John Diamond

If children have the ability to ignore all odds and percentages, then maybe we can all learn from them. When you think about it, what other choice is there but to hope? We have two options, medically and emotionally: give up, or fight like hell.
– Lance Armstrong

Will Canan came into the world in the Midwestern town of Rochester, Minnesota, on February 19, 1998, a cold winter morning. He joined his sister, Katherine, who was two-years-old, to round out our little family. Will's challenges began early on in his life. As a six-week-old baby, he went through a period of intense colic. Every evening after dinner, for several weeks, his little tummy would get firm with gas and he would cry inconsolably for an hour or two. We tried everything to comfort him – walks, stroller excursions, rides in the car, even putting him on top of the dryer while it was running on the misguided theory that the warmth and the vibration would cure that nasty colic – but nothing seemed to work. Eventually, he grew out of it by about three months and our lives moved on.

At 14 months, Will came down with a sudden illness. He developed an extremely high fever of 104 and his breathing became slow and labored. This was new territory for us as parents. My wife, Liz, and I were very concerned and tried everything to knock that fever down. Then early in the morning, Liz and I both woke suddenly when we heard him gasp and stop breathing and start banging against the sides of his crib as he went into convulsions due to the high fever. We immediately called 911 and the paramedics soon arrived. They crouched down next to Will on the floor in the living room in our old house on 9th Street S.W. and got him breathing regularly again and took him to the ER for observation. Will seemed fine when they got his fever under control and life again returned to "normal," though now with two hyper-vigilant parents. Every time after that when he spiked a high temperature, we remained on guard against a foe that we did not want to return. Perhaps this was a sign of things to come.

Will was a joy of a child to parent. He loved trains, especially Thomas the Tank Engine. He enjoyed zooming high on the swing set in the back yard. He relished trips to the neighborhood park with his sister Katherine. Our Sheltie, Thoreau, was a close and personal friend. Many a spring and summer day were spent outside with Will romping with Thoreau, throwing him sticks (though Thoreau was really only good for about 2-3 stick returns, he had no delusions of becoming a lab or a golden retriever), feeding him scraps from meals in the breakfast nook (Thoreau was partial to Bruegger's Bagels especially), scratching him behind the ears and rubbing the super-soft fur on his belly. Thoreau wasn't always the sharpest tool in the shed. The kids taught him to "shake," but he always growled on those occasions; getting him to lie down and "roll over" was a chasm too wide to cross. Thunderstorms were a personal torture and Thoreau would run in circles around the house barking at each drum roll of thunder, which made for some sleepless summer nights, but we wouldn't have had it any other way.

When he wasn't chasing the dog, Will was a Lego child prodigy. Early on in life, he discovered the wonders of those colorful boxes stuffed with little plastic pieces that bore the raw materials for great feats of imagination. Each new box became a personal challenge and slowly his room filled with bumpy sculptures of fantastic racecars and helicopters and Star Wars characters. I marveled at his skills in this area; when God was dispensing Lego construction skills back when I was a kid, I wasn't even in the right line. Will was always able to figure out how impossibly small Piece 167 fit into Figure 3 while I turned it every which way and still couldn't puzzle it out. His room became a treasure trove of Lego creations and proof of personal obstacles in the small-scale building world overcome.

Will loved his bike. He learned to ride a two-wheeler at age four and I have vivid memories of his elation the summer after he turned five as he raced the other neighborhood kids in the cul-de-sac down the slight incline in front of our "new" home on Tremont Lane again and again. We enjoyed weekend camping trips. One especially memorable occurred when Will was five-years-old at Big Island State Park near Albert Lea, Minnesota. We enjoyed our paddle out onto the lake on a warm sunny day gazing at the dark green turtles clinging to the shore until we realized, out in the middle of the lake, that the canoe had developed a leak and we were sinking. Will bailed as quickly as his small hands allowed and I paddled furiously and somehow we made it back. It was an adventure to remember. His was a normal childhood, so ordinary in so many ways. We did not know then what lay ahead.

In the winter of 2003-2004, Will joined a hockey class. Liz and I were excited as any proud parents following his slow progress in learning to skate and handle a puck from week to week. But suddenly, about halfway through the season, Will wasn't himself any more. He stopped making progress in his skating and puck handling and started to be very fatigued in a way not normal for a typical rambunctious six-year-old. We started to be concerned and took him to his pediatrician who tried without success to pinpoint the source of Will's fatigue. Will's kindergarten teacher, Pam Pappas, also noticed that Will was not feeling well in class. We anguished with her at his spring parent-teacher conference as we were starting to realize that something was horribly wrong and we did not know how to fix it.

– The Terrible Truth

In early March 2004, Will started having some problems with his balance and he began to bump into things repeatedly. On March 14, 2004, Will went to Sunday School class with Liz. All he could do upon his arrival in class was to curl up in a ball on the floor and put his hands over his head. We then took him to the Emergency Room at Saint Marys Hospital where they finally gave Will an MRI that exposed the terrible truth. Will had a tumor growing in the cerebellum, at the rear of his skull, which had been pressing on his brain. Because this part of the brain controls balance and motor commands, the tumor was responsible for the symptoms we had noticed. It was diagnosed as a medulloblastoma. The doctors decided that they would keep Will in the hospital overnight and then they would operate in the morning. Liz and I had a few private moments where we clung to each other at the Emergency Room. Liz sobbed and I was stunned: our child, our little boy Will, couldn't have cancer. He was only six-years-old. Cancer was something that older people were supposed to get. I did not even know where to begin or how to wrap my head around this diagnosis.

We decided that Liz would stay in the hospital with Will, and I would go home with Katherine for the evening. It was a very lonely night. Katherine crawled into bed with me for some comfort and we tried to sleep. Sleep did not come for a long time as this was the first night that Will had ever spent out of our house, away from us. Even Thoreau knew that something was not right. He usually slept next to our bed, but that night, for whatever reason, he slept in the doorway to Will's room, silently keeping watch over the empty bed and waiting for his little master to return.

On the day of surgery, Liz and I sent him off to the operating room and Will understood little about the obstacles that lay before him. He was in surgery for over eight hours. We got updates from the nursing staff periodically on the progress of the surgery, but the wait for bits of information seemed interminable; the news and the progress excruciatingly slow. Finally, the word arrived that the doctors were finished and little Will arrived at his room in the Pediatric Intensive Care Unit (PICU), his head swathed in bandages. He returned to consciousness slowly, and it was obvious that his head hurt a great deal. We fed him ice chips that night and very slowly he improved. Liz and I agreed that I would spend the nights with Will "sleeping" in the PICU and Liz would spend the time with him there during the day. I remember the first night in the PICU distinctly: very alien surroundings, Will's small bandaged head on the hospital pillow, the persistent beeping of the various machines, the flashing lights on the monitors, the low hum of the nurses and the doctors consulting outside in the hall, the swish of the door when it opened and closed for yet another check or poke or prod of our little boy lying there motionless in that bed, Will's slow breathing, and the morning light creeping in after a long, sleepless night that gave no renewal to face the difficult next day.

I had to pull myself together after that night and go to work. At that time, I was the owner of a solo law practice, which meant I was effectively a tightrope walker doing my routine without a net. There was no one to catch me if I fell, though Vicki Johnson, my legal assistant, did her best. While most of the clients would be sympathetic to my situation, in a one attorney law firm there would be no one else who could accomplish the necessary legal actions, no one to seek temporary custody of the children in divorces, or write the briefs for litigation cases, or answer the questions from the mayors in the small cities I represented. There would always be another law firm down the street waiting eagerly to pick up the business if I could not be there to meet the needs of my clients. It became crystal clear that the law practice and the livelihood I had worked so hard to build for my family might be lost in a heartbeat. Disability insurance only prepared for the possibility that *my* body or mind would give out and not for an extended absence to be with my son. And so I sucked it up and tried to pretend that I could be both an advocate for my clients and for my son. Liz has had the good fortune to be working for the Mayo Clinic. They immediately put her on a family leave and told her that her work was taken care of and that she should not come back until Will was well. We were blessed that she worked for an employer that put family first; it gave us some badly needed peace of mind right then.

The next two weeks in the PICU were a blur as the days fell into a routine. I went to my office after nights of little sleep. Clients would bring problems to me in search of a solution; suddenly, their problems seemed petty in comparison to my child's as he lay in the intensive care unit. Our family life had been thrust into uncertainty, and thus the cunning manipulation going on in the family law practice I had became less tolerable. The fights between estranged husbands and wives and the game-playing that sometimes used children as pawns for total control of their marriages seemed more absurd than it had been before. I did my time and left the office and went home for a quick change of clothes and then it was back to the hospital for the "night shift." I remember driving to and from the hospital at that time in utter silence; there was no way I could tolerate the radio. The airwaves were filled with songs about inane things: ending a relationship with a girlfriend, how unsatisfied they were with life, etc. Hearing people complain about such "inconsequential" things was like fingernails on a blackboard. What did they know about pain? I would eat my meals alone in the hallway outside Will's room; sometimes the food came from home, mostly I ordered out. Going through the motions of sustenance. The rest of the family would go home for a meal and some time off from the battle. Liz's parents came and helped us out and my Mom and Dad and my extended family were there at those crucial times as well. Their presence and moral support did sustain us in those very difficult times.

About a week after Will entered the hospital, we did have one moment of levity. Our friends, Chris and Marne Gade, knew I would be spending my 40th birthday at the hospital and they were determined to not let that milestone pass unmarked. Chris made a wonderful chocolate cake and brought it up to the Intensive Care Unit to share it with us. He placed some candles on the cake (mercifully not all 40) and was just about to light them when we realized that there was pure oxygen being used in Will's room, and many of the other rooms nearby for the children, and one open flame could have triggered an explosion that would have likely sent the PICU into orbit. Luckily, we figured this out just in time so that we are all still here to relay this story.

Will slept a lot those first weeks and those were very lonely times. It was apparent that the surgery had affected Will's motor skills and that it was going to take him some time to learn to use his left arm and leg again. I recall sitting in the hospital's beautiful chapel one morning with tears streaming down my face, looking up at the crucifix over the altar and asking God what we had done to deserve this. I begged God to heal Will so that he could be a normal kid again, so that he could grow up with two arms and two legs and a mind that would be attractive to another girl so that he could have his own children to enjoy some day. Then I sat in silence, finished my prayer and scraped some semblance of myself together in order to continue moving forward.

I recall the large get-well card with homemade artwork sent by the kids in his kindergarten class, which we affixed to the wall of Will's hospital room where he could see it. Liz and I were so moved by the outpouring of support by the teachers and the children at school. What a caring extended family at St. Francis of Assisi School who took the time from their busy days to remember us and to think of Will.

After spending a month in the hospital, Will was released on Good Friday, a day laden with the symbolism of death and the promise of rebirth after great hardship. He was in a little red wheelchair, and had lost a good deal of weight after his surgery as his appetite waned. But he was home and that made all the difference! We still did not really grasp then the enormous journey that lay ahead.

On April 19, Will began the first of what would become 31 fractions (separate sessions) of radiation to the cerebellum area of his brain where the tumor had occurred. On April 20, Will began a daily chemotherapy regimen for six weeks. A week later, Will received a drug that would help his body stimulate production of red blood cells to counteract the effect of the radiation on his hemoglobin counts. At the same time, Will took on the added challenge of months of rehabilitation. His surgery and his month-long stay in the hospital had left him weakened, particularly on his left side. The rehab staff at Saint Marys Hospital worked tirelessly to help him relearn how to walk, how to use his left arm and hand. He did stretching exercises on a small blue mat we had for him at home. Very slowly, despite the surgery and the radiation and the chemotherapy treatments, his strength returned and we began the slow climb back toward some semblance of our previous lives.

Will's 7th birthday party at Leo's Pizza Palace in Rochester
– February 2005

Chapter 2 – Recovery from Initial Diagnosis and Treatment

This diagnosis is a reminder that this is the life you've got. And you're not getting another one. Whatever has happened, you have to take this life and treasure and protect it.
– Elizabeth Edwards

Will had months of radiation and chemotherapy that first year, but he got a break in early June of 2004 and so we packed the kids into the car and headed off for a long car trip to Mackinac Island in the Upper Peninsula of Michigan. The hotel in Mackinaw City was nestled back in the trees, right on the beach. Watching Will holding Katherine's hand as they walked on the sandy beaches of Lake Huron made me smile inside. As we checked into the hotel, the owner became aware of Will's illness and all that we had been through. He upgraded our room to one of the best in the hotel, a large corner room on the second floor that looked out over the deep blue waters of Lake Huron, which eased our pain somewhat. The unforgettable memories and highlights from that first trip after his diagnosis come coursing back: I can see the Hydro-Jet Ferries we rode back and forth to Mackinac Island with the large water spouts streaming off the stern that fascinated Will. I recall the nightly sight of the giant towers of the Mackinac Bridge lit up against the sky and reflecting on the bay in the distance out our window. I remember the time spent at Romanik's Ranch where Will and Katherine anxiously fed the eager goats by hand, and stuck their heads through the farm boy and girl cutouts with delight to get their pictures taken. Most of all, I can see Mackinac Island itself, a new world to the kids where the only modes of transportation were horse-drawn buggy and your own two feet. We sat in the cool green park by the water's edge enjoying our freshly made ice cream cones. The day was capped off by a visit to the butterfly sanctuary where the sunlight streamed in through the clear panes of glass above and around us and dozens of our multi-colored little winged friends alighted on our hair and shoulders to say hello before flitting off to work their magic on the fragrant, blooming flowers nearby.

Not long after we returned home to Minnesota from Mackinac Island, we headed north to where my sister, Kathy, has a home on Lake Wissota, near Chippewa Falls, Wisconsin. For as long as Kathy and her husband, Tom, have lived there, my siblings and our respective families have piled into our cars and descended on her house for a long weekend of water sports, sun, food and fun. My brother-in-law Tom is the quintessential fisherman, and knows all the tricks about where the fish hide and how to coax them out to bite on just the right bait. During that summer of 2004 visit, there was one particular evening that Tom took Will and me out fishing. The fish weren't biting much, but at one point – when Will's attention was drawn elsewhere – Tom hooked a good-sized largemouth bass on his line and switched his pole with Will's before he could notice. Suddenly, Will noticed that his bobber had plunged underwater and his line began playing out rapidly off the reel. Will was thrilled when he felt a strong tug on his line and with some difficulty, and a little help from Uncle Tom, he reeled in this squirming fish. Tom hoisted it up, dripping out of the water and into the boat, a 17-inch, 3.5-pound largemouth bass, quite a catch for a boy. Uncle Tom had it mounted for Will and it has proudly occupied a spot on the wall in Will's bedroom ever since.

– First Grade

In the middle of July, Will started a 48-week chemo maintenance regimen, consisting of eight six-week cycles. The regimen started off fine and Will's two inpatient hospital stays for treatment went well. The rest of the summer flew by quickly and suddenly first grade had arrived. Will started off attending part-time for the first few weeks, gradually working up to full days, and even commenting that the school lunches were better than the ones Mom made (he would later feel otherwise ☺). Will's first grade teacher, Robin Erickson, was great at reaching out and going the extra mile to make sure that his transition back to school went smoothly.

It was around this time that Marcia Fritzmeier and Jack joined our cast of characters in Will's cancer story. Jack, a miniature pinscher, is a therapy dog, specially trained to provide loving comfort to patients. With gentle guidance from Marcia, Jack came to the children's ward at Saint Marys Hospital, providing a distraction, soft fur and lots of patience, things sorely needed when the oppression of an illness gets you down. Dressed in his "therapy dog" jacket, Jack would sit on Will's lap when he was getting chemotherapy or resting in his hospital bed. You never heard a bark when Jack had his Saint Marys "game face" on; he was there to please and lick your hand and cuddle up to you and be your friend at a time when you desperately needed one. Jack and Marcia's visits became more frequent. Over time, Jack, Marcia and her husband, Gary, became like members of the family, joining us for First Communions, Christmas concerts and every other important event where nary a canine is ever seen. An event was not an event if Jack wasn't there, hoping to nestle a place on Will's lap and get a pat on his head.

A routine soon evolved during Will's treatment. I would rush home from work, change my clothes and hop in the car to join Liz and Katherine at the hospital. Liz would bring me up to speed on the treatment steps taken that day, and then she would take Katherine home and to bed. Liz, tired after another day of being Will's advocate, would continue her mothering role at home with our daughter. Sometimes Will and I would play video games at the hospital. He would put me to shame at video golf. I can still hear the stilted voice of the announcer on the Nintendo golf game say "Nice Shot" when Will whomped another drive straight down the fairway while I headed off for familiar territory in the cyberspace rough. Sometimes our quiet time was spent watching a movie; other times, I would climb into his hospital bed and read him a book to try to soothe his mind and get him ready for bed. Sometimes he could not get out of bed and I would help him get his PJs on and brush his teeth before snapping off the light and slipping out into the hall to read the newspaper and ponder our fate. The hospital corridor was always quietly humming with some activity and identifying sounds: the maintenance staff swishing past me in the hall with ponderous mops, the rattling of food trays being deposited into the tiered stainless carts, the persistent beeping of doctor's pagers begging their attention to the next pressing need, the whispering of a TV set from a room nearby, the steady gentle gurgling of the decorative duck fountain down the hall, nurses gliding in and out of rooms on rubber soled shoes to check on their charges. The best nurses felt the pain that emanated from those rooms and dispensed care like they were ministering to their own children.

Eventually, it was time for me to go to bed but sleep often did not come easily. The room was usually only semi-dark: dark enough for Will to sleep, but light enough to orient the nurses when they came in for their periodic checks. The IV infusion pump beeped periodically as if to reassure that it remained alive and needed to be fed. Every two hours, the IV fluids flowing into Will's body filled his bladder. Despite the fact that Will was a sound sleeper, he woke up just in time to have me thrust a urinal jug in front of his pelvis to empty out his poor bulging bladder; sleep would come again for him, for awhile. And then there was my bed, which only a sadist could appreciate. It was like sleeping on the ground on a vinyl sheet. I learned quickly that only with the added padding of a camping mat would the nights become somewhat tolerable. Those long nights rolled into longer days as sleep deprivation took hold. But, compared to what Will was enduring, it was nothing. His progress was slow, but it came. I started to feel like somehow, some way, Will would be able to master this terrible disease and we would be able to put it behind us.

It was not only Liz and I who were being affected by Will's cancer: Katherine was also bearing the burden of his illness. The little brother she had grown up chasing around and roughhousing with was now not the same. He was ill and weakened and not able to keep up with her as he had in the past. It was hard to be fair in doling out our precious time to make sure that enough time was spent with Katherine, meeting her needs, as well as Will's and his serious challenges. Will received dozens of gifts from people near and far. Sometimes the gift givers thought to bring a surprise for Katherine so that she would not feel left out; often they did not. This led to hard feelings as to why so many gifts were being "lavished" on Will and so few on her. Katherine came to the hospital after school most days and spent time with Will and Liz. The presence of his sister invariably cheered up Will if he was having a down day. She did her homework at the hospital, which was challenging at times. When I arrived for my night shift at the hospital, she went home with Liz; I missed her presence at the hospital with me a great deal, but that was the way it needed to be. At school, well-intentioned questions about Will's condition were undoubtedly distracting to her. Katherine weathered it well and she found a "new normal," coping with the impact of this disease on her young life.

Late summer soon turned into autumn. On October 13, 2004, we enjoyed a trip down to the city of Lanesboro with Liz's friend, Cheryl Commerford, to take in the beauty of the Root River Bike Trail. I unloaded Will's little bike and he was able to pedal it a short distance down the trail before his stamina gave out. Liz and Cheryl instead pushed Will in his wheelchair along the trail. Katherine and I took our bikes and headed off down the trail for some father-daughter time. God had gotten out the palette of His most brilliant colors to paint the trees hugging the bluffs along the trail in delicate shades of gold and orange that day; it felt great to inhale deeply the cool, clear air rising from the Root River running alongside as we glided down the path. We finished off the wonderful weekend with a trip to Tweite's pumpkin patch to pick out a special pumpkin to carve for Halloween. The following week, Will attended his first Cub Scout meeting as he joined the boys from school in Tiger Cubs. It made me very proud that he would be getting involved in Scouting since it had done so much for me when I was young.

– *Sunflowers*

As fall drew to a close, we had our first sunflower seed harvest. Will's kindergarten class had been given sunflower seeds and Liz and Will had planted them in the front yard next to the garage. In a few months, Will had grown a monster sunflower plant that towered over 10 feet high and the head weighed 7.5 pounds – plenty of seeds to share with his 1st grade class for growing a bumper crop next year. It brought back memories of the Parable of the Mustard Seed from the Bible, a reminder that even though a seed may be small and insignificant, it can grow to become large enough that it can provide shelter for the birds of the air. Is this a metaphor for what is possible for Will, the small boy, to become something mighty enough to overwhelm his cancer? I pray it is. It brought memories of something similar I had done, a young boy planting sunflower seeds next to my garage, with dreams of Jack and the Beanstalk.

On November 9, 2004, Will had an appointment with the Physical Medicine and Rehabilitation Department to check on his progress. The therapists found that Will's strength and agility in both hands had significantly improved from six weeks prior, which was a good sign. That same week, Will had a re-check with the eye doctor. Will had been wearing a patch over his left eye about two hours a night in order to try and strengthen the vision in his other eye. We were happy to hear from the eye doctor that Will's vision in both eyes had improved. Given his progress, the doctor gave us the go-ahead to reduce the time Will wore the patch to about one hour a day. Eventually, Will was going to need surgery to realign his eyes, but there was no harm in waiting to do this. Will's pediatric oncologist, Dr. Cynthia Wetmore, wanted to wait to do this until he was finished with his chemo, which projected the surgery to sometime in the summer of 2005.

Dr. Wetmore was a true godsend as Will's cancer journey got

underway. We needed so many things from Will's doctor: We needed someone who was a great clinician who stayed abreast of the latest developments in brain tumor care so that Will would receive the treatments most likely to lead to a cure. We needed someone who knew their way around the ins-and-outs of Mayo, who could cut through red tape and get Will timely appointments so that his care could proceed as swiftly as possible. But we also needed a friend, someone who had the compassion to understand the stresses being placed on Will, and on us as his caregivers, and offer a soothing word so that we would not become paralyzed with fear and would be able to assure Will that he would eventually come out of this all OK. Dr. Wetmore was all of those things and more: brilliant, capable and caring. She later would even attend some of Will's baseball games. We could not have been placed in better hands, which helped to give us hope as we moved forward.

On November 15-16, 2004, Will had another MRI of his brain, the first one in four months. Much to our relief, his MRI came back normal! His renal clearance test also showed that his kidneys were functioning properly, so they could clear the chemo out of his system once it had done its intended job of killing cancer cells. We did learn at this time, however, that Will had experienced some high frequency hearing loss in his left ear. Cisplatin, one of the chemo drugs that he received every six weeks, was the cause of the hearing loss. The doctors would continue to closely monitor his hearing and we would have to hope and pray that he didn't experience any more hearing loss.

Christmas 2004 was a special day. Will woke up Katherine around 3 a.m. on Christmas morning to go downstairs and check out the stockings and see what Santa Claus had brought them. He then came up to our bedroom and excitedly recited everything that had been left in his stocking. We finally persuaded them to go back to bed until about 7 a.m. Will got several Lego and Playmobil sets to put together, which he and Liz enjoyed working on very much.

Will went into the hospital on December 28th to start his fifth of eight chemo cycles. The medical staff found that he had additional high frequency hearing loss in both ears since November, so they decreased the dosage of the stronger chemotherapy drugs. Fortunately, his kidneys continued to function normally to rid his body of the chemo agents.

That hospitalization was also cause for celebration as Will "graduated" from Rehab. The strength on his left side had become equal to that of his right side! While we were so pleased for Will, it was emotional saying goodbye to his wonderful team of Stacy and Michele who had cared for Will since March and got him to this point through their patient work with him.

2005 brought the promise of a new year and turning the corner on a difficult 2004. On February 19, 2005, Will celebrated his 7th birthday. He woke up at about 6 that morning and couldn't wait until 11:00 a.m. when the birthday party at Leo's Pizza Palace started! The kids had a great time, playing arcade games, eating pizza, and getting their picture taken with Leo the Lion. Will was playing a particular game and hit the jackpot; this caused about 100 tickets to come spewing out of the machine, bringing a huge smile to his face!

This reminded me of a funny story that Will's teacher had shared with me. The kids in her class were talking about feelings. Mrs. Erickson asked Will if he had anything to say about this and he said, "I love chemo because they have great snacks and they give me things." This said a lot, not just about Will's great attitude, but more about the wonderful and caring people who took care of him and tried to make it as pleasant an experience as possible, despite difficult circumstances.

– Sadness and Sunshine

On March 2, 2005, Will had to be admitted to the hospital. He had contracted a form of the chicken pox, which caused him to have shingles on the right side of his face and the back of his head. He also developed a fever and his blood counts were very low. The hospital staff started him on an anti-viral IV right away to help clear up the shingles. He received a blood transfusion and he got daily shots for three days to stimulate production of his white blood cells. All those treatments, as well as IV antibiotics, really helped him improve. Fortunately, the shingles were not painful for him, although they were itchy and it was hard to keep from scratching them.

On May 17, 2005, Will completed a grueling 14 months of radiation and chemotherapy following his original surgery in March of 2004. Just prior to completing his chemotherapy, our pet Sheltie, Thoreau, passed away, at the age of 12. Thoreau had been very instrumental in helping Will cope as he struggled through the multiple rounds of treatments, being there to snuggle with him and be petted after a hard day. Early in 2005, Thoreau had repeated trips to the vet for a variety of ailments. One day he was simply semi-conscious and unable to get up to lick our hands any longer. We gently put him in the van. It was a long drive to take the kids to school, where they said their last goodbyes to our trusty friend. Then Liz and I took him to the vet to end his pain. We held him gently, stroked his fur and held his paws as they put him to sleep; we made an imprint of his paw, and took a lock of his fur to remember him. He had held on just long enough to see that Will would finish treatment. It was one of those small ironies in life when the vet told us that he thought Thoreau likely died of cancer; another sacrifice in the cancer war as he helped Will with his battle. A very hard day.

Just as Will was ending treatment and desperately needing a break, my Mom told us about a camp out in Maine called Camp Sunshine that held sessions for seriously ill kids and their families. As it turned out, they had a week specifically for children who had been battling brain tumors. We put in our application and were overjoyed to find that it had been accepted; soon we were on our way to join the others on beautiful Lake Sebago near Casco, Maine in June of 2005. It was our first real experience being surrounded by other families who had been struggling with the same dire circumstances. The kids went off to activities each day while the adults had an "AA-style" session. We bared our souls about our child, his or her diagnosis and treatment, and the heartaches of being the parent of a child who was seriously ill. The stories told by some of the families were gut-wrenching and heart-rending: stories of children who were not properly diagnosed for months or even years as they grew sicker, stories of children who were teased or bullied at school because their illness made them different from the rest and less able to protect themselves. Lots of tears were shed in those first few days. Liz found sharing these experiences with others to be helpful. For me, however, it got to be too much soul-baring; by the third day, I retreated for some time in a kayak out on the water instead. The caring staff treated the families to wonderful nighttime activities, including a costume dance, a talent show, and a candlelit dinner just for the parents, capped off by a karaoke singing competition. On the second to last day, the kids created beautifully decorated "wish boats" with a small candle, which they set free on a small pond at the camp as soft music played in the background and the sun set on the lake nearby. You could feel the immense power of those wishes as the boats glided away silently on the pond under the watchful eyes of their creator captains. If only those wishes all came true.

We felt that Will had been cancer-free long enough that we decided to hold a party to celebrate the end of his treatment in July 2005. We were moved beyond words as more than 100 people came out to join us in the park behind our house on that hot summer day to celebrate this milestone.

Many doctors had recommended Taekwondo as an activity to improve balance and self-confidence, and build upper body strength. By the end of summer, Will was ready to take on this sport. He really enjoyed it, although we had to make him promise his parents that he wouldn't use his new moves on his sister!

In the fall of 2005, Will was entering 2nd grade. Will's success as a kindergarten and 1st grade farmer had come with sunflowers. Second grade inspired him to venture into new gardening areas and grow pumpkins. At the end of 1st grade, he had planted a few pumpkin seeds in rich black dirt in a small paper cup; a single pumpkin plant emerged, and he carefully transplanted it in the ground next to our house. From these humble beginnings, Will was able to coax three huge orange pumpkins to grow, as well as five other smaller pumpkins, by Halloween. His goal was to supply our entire cul-de-sac with pumpkins! Indeed, he inherited his mother's green thumb.

– *Wishes*

Our bedtime routine also brought some wonderful memories that fall. Will and I enjoyed reading books together on the queen-size bed in Liz's and my bedroom. At first, I was the one doing the reading. Arthur the Aardvark was always a reliable favorite, as well as books about cars and planes and rockets, like most other boys enjoyed. Will, though, seemed to like Dr. Seuss the best. I found a collection of all of Dr. Seuss's best stories and we spent many an evening curled up with that book. *Yertle the Turtle, Gertrude McFuzz, the Big Brag, To Think That I Saw It on Mulberry Street, Horton Hears a Who.* But the best one had to be *The Lorax*, that classic tale of greed and environmental catastrophe. Will always wanted to read the part where the machine that made the products spit out "Gloppity Glopp" and "Schluppity

Schlupp"; he thought those words were very funny. As time went on, he read them to me. Though with the passing years, this routine lost some of its "cool factor" and it became a greater challenge to get him to make time for me, it just made each time he did that much sweeter.

The Make-A-Wish® foundation contacted us in the summer of 2005 about giving Will a Make-A-Wish trip. What a profound blessing it was to have this organization approach us with the offer to make Will's dream a reality. Will wanted to go to Walt Disney World and Sea World in Orlando, Florida. We were given the privilege of going there over the Christmas holiday in December of 2005. It was a trip filled with a lifetime of memories. We were picked up in a limousine and whisked to the airport. When we arrived in Florida, we were welcomed at a wonderful resort called "Give Kids the World." If the world of Willy Wonka really existed on earth, it would be his inspired vision that took shape in Give Kids the World. We stayed in a lovely, sunlit two-bedroom villa. A small train transported families around the grounds of Give Kids the World to take us anywhere we needed to go. Will and Katherine were able to order pizza and ice cream from early in the morning until late at night. The resort also housed a huge game room with one of the largest model train sets I have ever seen. There were radio-controlled boats to pilot through a moat as well as a secluded miniature golf course to navigate. By special arrangement, the Disney characters even made a private appearance on the stage in the Give Kids the World movie theater. Freed from the tyranny of long lines of impatient children and distracted adults at Magic Kingdom, the costumed characters were there just for the families. There is nothing like that magical moment when a larger than life Mickey Mouse takes your child by the hand and you believe that indeed, all things are possible.

At the Magic Kingdom, we enjoyed everything from races on the go-kart track to the scary plunges in the semi-dark roller coaster, Space Mountain. We enjoyed "Soaring" at EPCOT, suspended in the air as we swooped over the Golden Gate Bridge and smelled the oranges as we roared over orange groves in Southern California. We screamed at the sickening 15-story drop on the Tower of Terror (except Mom) and tried our hand at "Who Wants to be a Millionaire" at Disney/MGM Studios. We marveled at the live animals on the safari at Animal Kingdom. By the end of each day, we needed to carry Will, who was still not fully recovered from his last round of treatments. But the smiles I saw from Will and Katherine were genuine and heartfelt, and brought joy to us all.

On our last day in Florida, we were fortunate to visit a place called Discovery Cove, which gave our family the chance to have an up-close encounter with dolphins. We were assigned to work with a dolphin named "Roxie" who was happy to "talk" to us, provide kisses to the kids, and even allow us to hang onto her dorsal fin to pull us across the cove for a short ride. We all thoroughly enjoyed this unique experience.

2006 started out on a positive note and, looking back, it was such a big year. So many really important things first took shape then. On March 3, 2006, Will had progressed sufficiently with his Taekwondo training that he advanced from the lowest ranking, white belt, to the next rank, white belt/yellow stripe. To achieve this, Will also had to learn how to count to 10 in Korean and to recite the Taekwondo pledge from memory. We were all very proud of him! One week later, Will had his first experience with the Cub Scout Pinewood Derby. Will enjoyed this activity right away. It took some time to sit down and figure out what sleek car was lurking under that block of wood in the package of materials. Will went with a rounded bomber with camouflage markings. Dad ended up doing most of the sculpting work, but Will and Mom made the car beautiful with that special camouflage paint job. I owe everything in our short Pinewood Derby career to our friend Dr. Suzanne Viggiano who gave me the invaluable tip that if you sanded off the edges of the nails, which made up the axles of the cars, they rotated much more smoothly and the cars moved much faster as a result. Who knew that an ophthalmologist was so savvy about balsa wood cars? With her help and help from other friends, Will's cars placed in the top three in his pack for the three years that he raced, and his not-so-mechanical Dad enjoyed a rare moment of competency in the mechanical field. In the photo after his first race, Will looks proud as he shows off his trophy; I look kind of stunned. I know that I was overcome with emotion at the winning result. Will so rarely got the chance to excel that it was a very sweet moment for all of us to savor.

Will and Katherine at Camp Sunshine, Casco, Maine
– Summer 2005

Will – The Pumpkin Farmer after harvesting the crop, Rochester
– September 2005

Chapter 3 – Will's First Relapse

During chemo, you're more tired than you've ever been. It's like a cloud passing over the sun, and suddenly you're out. You don't know how you'll answer the door when your groceries are delivered. But you also find that you're stronger than you've ever been. You're clear. Your mortality is at optimal distance, not up so close that it obscures everything else, but close enough to give you depth perception. Previously, it has taken you weeks, months, or years to discover the meaning of an experience. Now it's instantaneous.

– Melissa Bank

April of 2006 also started full of promise.

It had been nearly a year since our beloved Thoreau passed on and our house had been too quiet without the pitter-patter of little paws following us around. Liz and I decided it was time to welcome another dog into our home. Liz did some research and found a breeder at a farm just east of Rochester that raised Sheltie puppies. We all went out to the old wooden barn and followed the little yelps into a metal pen filled with sawdust where the puppies were playing. After looking them all over for a long time, one cute little puppy seemed to take a shine to us and so we paid our money, piled back into the van and, of course, fought over who got to hold him for the trip to his new house. As soon as we got home, we had to take him outside and have him sniff the yard and the neighbor kids and everything else in his new surroundings. The kids had decided some time before that "Scout" would be his name. Housebreaking him wasn't as easy as we remembered it for Thoreau. Scout could not sleep through the night and seemed to sense the tension in our household as we struggled to try to train him. Worse than that, three days after Scout came home with us, Will was diagnosed with his first relapse. The stress of dealing with that challenge and trying to housebreak a new puppy was simply too much. With heavy hearts, we took Scout back out to his former home and the breeder was kind enough to refund our money. We wonder sometimes what happened to Scout. I hope that he found another good home with a loving family. He was fun while it lasted.

Most kids with medulloblastoma – up to 80% of them, in fact – are cured of their cancer after the first round of treatment. This encouraging statistic had given us hope. After each clear brain scan that Will had, we started to believe that he had turned the corner. It felt as though a normal life was just within our reach. We grasped for it anxiously, began to feel the warmth of its promise, but then it slipped through our fingers.

On April 17, 2006, our slow climb toward the light of hope was halted when Will was diagnosed with his first relapse. I distinctly remember sitting in my office that day, bright sunshine was slanting in through my south-facing window. Will was with me. Liz called me on the phone, her voice breaking, to tell me that the cancer was back. I was speechless. It couldn't be, it just couldn't be. After over two years with no sign of any cancer cells, we were convinced we were victorious, that we had beaten the monster. I glanced over at Will and he was drawing me a picture of rainclouds over a rainbow, with a pot of gold at the end, and a caption reading "April Showers Bring May Flowers." A relapse was certainly "April Showers." How long was it going to be before we saw the flowers and the rainbow after the storm?

The MRI scan showed that Will now had a tumor roughly the size of a pencil eraser growing in an area different from the location where the cancer first appeared. Whereas the first tumor had been in his cerebellum, a new lesion had formed in the right ventricle of the brain. The ventricles contain the cerebrospinal fluid and provide a "cushion" for the brain. They are located in the cerebrum, the most highly developed part of the human brain that is responsible for functions such as learning and memory.

On May 3, 2006, Will underwent endoscopic surgery to remove as much of the tumor as the surgeon dared to remove without cutting into vital brain tissue. Who knew that there was brain tissue that you could spare and brain tissue that you had to have in order to function? This type of surgery would be less invasive than his first operation, and would utilize small incisions through which a lighted tube with a camera would make the tumor visible; specialized tools would then be used to carefully remove the lesion. After the surgery, Will was out of the hospital the next day. He was even able to attend the St. Francis School Carnival only two days later, a fact we marveled at.

As with everything in parenting, there was no script, no road map emblazoned with "True Path," on this cancer march. As with everything for Will, he trusted us. He knew we were attempting to do the right thing, no matter what he was forced to endure – surgery, radiation, chemotherapy. And he handled it bravely, rarely complaining.

The doctors' next plan of attack would involve high-dose chemotherapy in hopes of destroying the cancer cells. These same medications, however, would effectively wipe out Will's bone marrow. In June, Will underwent a procedure to harvest stem cells that would be stored until after the rigorous chemotherapy, then subsequently reintroduced to regenerate his bone marrow. Will patiently endured having a catheter line placed in his neck to withdraw blood. A machine extracted the stem cells from his blood, and then returned the remaining blood back into his body. The harvesting procedure went well, but the harvest was not great. Unfortunately, Will's bone marrow was so depleted after all of the previous treatment that there were not enough stem cells that would be able to regenerate his bone marrow. This latest chemotherapy plan had to be abandoned. In the end, it was decided to hope that the prior treatment regimen had done its job, and the cancer would not recur.

– For Love of The Game

Late spring of 2006 brought Will in contact with one of the true loves of his life: baseball. Will was paired with several other classmates from St. Francis School and two of the dads of classmates offered to help coach the team. His team was the Grasshoppers; their team jerseys were orange, Will's favorite color, which seemed to fit perfectly. Every kid on that field was eager to learn the game and played with enthusiasm. You'd never know that Will had endured as much as he had as he chased that ball around the diamond. There wasn't the stress of tryouts for the traveling or "the majors" teams at this simple time in their lives. It was America's pastime played with joy by energetic kids. We showed up for every game, setting up our folding chairs along the sidelines, rain or shine, to cheer them on. It was a great experience for Will to become part of a team, something larger than just himself, and being able to make a contribution to help the team. His happiness is evident in his picture on the day of his first game. Will went 3 for 4 and had two RBIs!

The arrival of summer in 2006 meant it was time for Will's first

Cub Scout Day Camp at Gamehaven Scout Reservation just south of Rochester. He had been looking forward to camp for some time, even though it meant a lot of activities that would have been tiring for the average boy who hadn't been through chemotherapy. Once there, he enjoyed the obstacle course, and making shields as an art project, but he really seemed to shine when he got to learn how to shoot a BB gun on the range and especially learning to make arrows fly through the air on the archery range. I watched the beads of sweat grow on his forehead as he worked hard to grip his bow correctly, knock an arrow and send it soaring toward the red painted circles on the hay bales down range. He enjoyed time in the pool with his buddies, although the fact that he had never learned to swim meant he had to stay in the shallow end of the pool. By the end of the day, he barely made it out to the parking lot for the drive home, but I never heard him complain once.

Will and Dad at Cub Scout Day Camp, Gamehaven Scout Reservation near Rochester – Summer 2006

Once Cub Scout Day Camp was over, we returned to treatment as Will underwent a Gamma Knife procedure on June 29, 2006. Gamma Knife is a special surgery whereby super-fine beams of radiation are delivered directly to a tumor; the small beams converge on their target to create a high dose of radiation. It does little damage to the surrounding healthy brain tissue. This procedure is well suited to wipe out a small group of tumor cells in a specific location. We checked into Saint Marys Hospital about 6:45 a.m. that day and by about 7:30 a.m. Will was asleep and they started fitting him with the head frame as part of the procedure. Liz and I were able to be with him until he went to sleep. They delivered radiation to the exact tumor location for about 15 minutes.

Will was back in the Recovery Room by about 10:00 a.m. When we walked in and saw him, he smiled at us and wanted to get up into a chair and watch a movie. His head was wrapped in gauze to help minimize swelling; however, this was removed within an hour. The only evidence that he had the procedure were four marks that looked like mosquito bites: two on his forehead and two in the back of his head where they put pins to secure the head frame. He did not have a headache or experience any pain from the procedure. The success of the operation would not be known until another MRI was done, several months down the road.

In July of 2006, Will was selected as the childhood cancer representative for the American Cancer Society "Relay for Life." Leading up to this event, we were asked to ride on the float in the local Rochesterfest parade. Will rode on the Relay for Life float; Liz, Katherine and I walked along side. Periodically, Will got off to throw candy to the crowd gathered along the curbsides.

Will got a haircut in preparation for the Relay. The chemo he had received in June was causing his hair to come out in clumps; it was hard to watch this precious boy of ours lose his hair. With a crew cut, his hair was much easier to manage and Will felt better about himself. Paul Dallman, Will's barber, is a wonderful guy. Knowing why Will needed a haircut on this occasion, he cut Will's hair free of charge, gave him a stick of bubble gum and a quarter to keep or buy some candy. With that grand send-off, Will was ready for the Relay for Life, which was held the evening of July 14, 2006.

We had never been to this event, and did not know for sure what to expect, though we knew supporters carried banners for the cancer patients they were pulling for. Will and Mike and Margaret Dougherty's kids worked for about three hours on the "Fishing" banner that was to be carried by his supporters at the Relay. The neighborhood kids, Will's baseball team, and St. Francis School also collaborated on banners for Will; Mayo Health System Administration created a "Chess" banner for

Will, the chess player. Our good friends, Laurie and Anna Sutherland, also made about 35 visors, and painted them orange with the words "Will's Warriors" on them to hand out to friends at the event. Will's orange visor had the words "Canan the Man" inscribed on it. Katherine worked hard on "Will's Warriors" buttons to hand out as well. It had all of the trappings of a political campaign by the time the preparation was done. The camaraderie and the outpouring of support were a great honor, to be sure, but a "race" in which you had to have cancer in order to participate was a course no one really wanted to run.

From the moment we arrived on that very warm evening, Will was given the royal treatment. He had his picture taken by the media with one other adult and one child cancer survivor, Jessica Van Horn. Many of our neighbors, Grasshopper baseball team players and families, Jack and Marcia, and other friends and colleagues had gathered there in supporting Will as the Honorary Chair for the 2006 event. Liz gave a very moving speech about all the wonderful support that many in the community had given us throughout Will's illness; she also encouraged others to provide support for those in need. Then it was time for Will and Jessica, the Honorary Chairs, to cut the ribbon and start the Relay for Life. It was quite poignant to see the two of them walking hand-in-hand. Jessica was often dependent on a wheelchair for mobility, but she didn't use it for that initial lap! Her tremendous determination shone through. They were followed by our family and Jessica's family, as well as other survivors and supporters carrying their wonderful, colorful banners.

On our walk, we passed numerous people who had set up tents because teams walk throughout the night as part of this event. Many of the campsites were decorated with homemade signs and banners, both in honor of loved ones lost and for those currently battling cancer. Hundreds of luminarias, dedicated to survivors and those who had lost their battle, lined the track that the walkers take during the event. At sundown, every individual's name is read and their luminaria lighted as part of the ceremony. Many people clapped and cheered Will and the other survivors as we slowly made our way around the parking lot and back to the start. As night fell, shimmering luminarias lighted the way for those who continued the Relay for Life. The heat had tired out Will, so we needed to go home. But the memories of all the people who were there to support us really helped to buoy our spirits and continue on with the fight.

On July 19, 2006 Will was excited to receive a package from the Green Bay Packers. Inside was a 2005 signed football and stand, a Packers pen, an authentic jersey, a puzzle, a shirt with a coloring kit, a Frozen Tundra hat, and a card signed personally by quarterback Brett Favre! Will's face literally beamed once he saw what the Packers had done for him, as he and I are big fans. We have Marcia and Gary Fritzmeier to thank for this. Marcia wrote a heartfelt letter explaining Will's situation to the Green Bay Packers organization; within two weeks, Will received this wonderful package.

Will goes knee boarding for the first time – Lake Wissota,
Wisconsin – Summer 2006

On August 8, 2006, we returned to my sister Kathy's house for the annual Canan summer reunion. This get-together was noteworthy because Will learned how to kneeboard behind a speedboat and loved it. He was able to get up on the board and out of the water right away and went around a big area of the lake two times. We tried to get him to stop at the dock after the first time around, but he had a huge smile on his face and wanted to keep going! He also went tubing with Katherine and was always the one giving the thumbs up sign to the driver of the boat to go faster!

– 3rd Grade

The summer came to a close with another week with the cancer kids and siblings at Camp Jornada. The highlight of the week was making

27

attire for a formal Homecoming Dance out of duct tape. Will was voted runner-up for Homecoming King. Will also told us he got to ride in an antique car that went 125 miles per hour, but we'll just hope this was a real tall tale and let it go at that.

Throughout the summer and fall of 2006, Will's gardening skills continued to expand. His garden included basil, zinnias, pumpkins, sunflowers, morning glories, and moonflowers. By the time the fall harvest arrived, Will had a total of 25 pumpkins to share with the neighbors on our street and the kids at school, an amazing number given the small area he had to work with next to our garage.

Fall 2006 meant the start of 3rd grade for Will, but it also meant the start of a new treatment regimen. On September 5, 2006, Will started chemo treatments. The schedule required that he would get chemo via IV infusion for four hours each day from about 1-5 p.m., for five days. Then, he would get a three-week break. Dr. Wetmore wanted to start out giving him one chemo agent for the first several cycles to see how his body tolerated the treatment. Will had to go to the hospital for the treatments, but would not have to stay overnight. This schedule would allow Will to attend school in the morning, and eat lunch and have recess with friends, before going for treatment. Will's white blood cell counts dropped so low after a couple of weeks that they had him come into the hospital twice a day for IV antibiotic infusions. In the end, he spent six nights in the hospital related to this issue before being released to come back home. After that, he still needed to receive daily GCSF (granulocyte colony-stimulating factor) shots intended to help his bone marrow produce more stem cells. Despite this grueling schedule, Will signed up to play in a fall soccer league run by the YMCA on Saturday mornings. I was happy to serve as one of Will's assistant coaches. It was all he could do most days to try to run and keep up with the other kids, but he never stopped trying or enjoying himself.

On September 25, 2006, one of Will's 3rd grade teachers had a great story to tell us about Will. He was giving Will a makeup Phonics test and gave him the first word. He then got distracted and didn't give Will another word for about 3-4 minutes. All of a sudden, Will looked at him and said, "I'm not getting any younger." Mr. Krenik (affectionately known around the school as "Mr. K.") could not stop laughing and had no comeback, which is rare for him! Considering all Will had been through, we are forever thankful that he never lost his sense of humor!

On October 3, 2006, Will and Liz got a special opportunity to attend a Minnesota Twins playoff game, along with his friend Cate Arendt and her dad Joe. One of Liz's colleagues, Dr. Eric Edell, made arrangements for us to meet some of the Twins players prior to the game. It was a very gracious gesture on his part, which we deeply appreciated! Our dear friend, Chris Gade, provided Will and Liz with great seats for the game. Katherine and I drove up in the morning to meet the players. When we arrived at the Metrodome, many fans were already gathering. We all got our faces painted at the Qwest booth prior to going to the Twins Executive Offices to meet our designated contact at 10 a.m. The offices were very impressive, with paintings of Kirby Puckett and the future Target Field, as well as past World Series and ALC trophies and World Series rings on display. It was also interesting to see the different people coming into the offices.

While we were waiting, we were introduced to Tony Oliva, a former Twins All Star. He took time to autograph baseballs for Will and Cate. Our contact then greeted us and handed Will a bag with Twins baseball caps for him and Katherine, a baseball signed by Torii Hunter (one of Will's favorite players) and a very nice player book. He then took us all down to the area right outside of the Twins Clubhouse – the locker room. We saw several players come out, most of whom stopped to say hello to the kids. Matt Garza autographed their baseballs and we saw Boof Bonser and Matt Perkins. Ron Gardenhire, the Twins Manager, also came out and spent a lot of time with us. He was very personable and took individual pictures with Will, Katherine, Cate and all of us. That was impressive, considering the pressure of the playoff game that his team was about to play. Will and Liz, Cate and Joe all had a wonderful time at the game.

By October 16, 2006, Will's condition had deteriorated. He developed a cough, which lasted for several days. It gradually worsened, keeping him awake and causing his chest to hurt. He also was running a fever. His white blood cell counts became quite low and a chest x-ray indicated that he might have the beginnings of pneumonia. The doctors admitted him to the hospital and put him on an IV antibiotic that covers pneumonia and other infections. He was discharged from the hospital to return home three days later.

By Halloween 2006, Katherine's 11ᵗʰ birthday, Will was feeling much better and he got to pursue the other love of his life, Star Wars. Somewhere along the way, with those countless hours of downtime in the hospital and the Clinic, he got exposed to Obi-Wan Kenobi, Darth Maul, Darth Sidious, Emperor Palpatine, Yoda, and all the other characters that other Star Wars nerds carry around using "the Force." He opted to dress as Darth Vader for Halloween that year – a great costume, although the breathing hole probably worked a whole lot better on the $50,000 costume Darth got to wear in the movie. The Viggiano kids came over to go trick or treating. They are special friends, former St. Francis students who were then home-schooled. I don't know if it was the home-schooling or just their nature, but somehow the cynicism of the world did not seep into them as quickly as it seemed to with other kids. They took to Will readily, shared his love of Star Wars and video games; they seemed to appreciate him for his abilities and not for his limitations, a rare gift in this journey and a trait Will thrived on. The Halloween candy came in droves that night, and was mostly tossed after a few weeks, but it was yet another great memory tucked away for other less happy times.

November 12, 2006 was a rough day for Will in the hospital; he had been admitted a couple of days earlier because he was neutropenic (his white blood cell count was too low). He developed hives while receiving a red blood cell transfusion. He'd been given a preventive dose of Benadryl before getting platelets; however, he wasn't given another dose of Benadryl during the red blood cell transfusion that followed. This caused him to break out in hives on his face and torso and they itched terribly. To see him in such pain and discomfort made us feel so helpless.

The following day, Will was dismissed from the hospital. Since his white cell count had risen dramatically over the night, and his platelets had increased too, the doctors said he could go home. He was cracking jokes with the nurses before being dismissed. When one nurse was in his room, he opened up a vanity mirror on the bed stand, looked into it and said with a straight face, rubbing his bald head, "How's my hair today?" It made everyone in the room double over with laughter! It was Classic Will.

On December 2, 2006, Will finished his fourth round of chemo treatments. An MRI was scheduled for December 5, which would tell us whether all of the treatments he was enduring so patiently were helping. It was pure anguish waiting those days, hours and minutes until the results were back. Hallelujah! The MRI showed no signs that the tumor had recurred. Maybe, just maybe, Will could fight this thing and win! Three more months to breathe easy before the oppression of worry made it difficult again.

December 2006 also meant the annual St. Francis of Assisi School Christmas Concert. No "holiday" concerts here: "Christmas" is still a word said with love in our grade school. By tradition, the students, families, and friends gather to see what Ms. Judge, the flamboyant St. Francis music teacher, has put together for the annual concert. Will had lost his hair by then, but was all smiles when Marcia and Jack the Dog showed up to hear those heavenly voices. Jack sat quietly on the bleacher next to Marcia and didn't make a peep the whole time, more than you could say about the kindergartners. Will and Katherine sang their little hearts out – a little off key, but touching nonetheless. Those concerts always put me in the mood for Christmas, and the best gifts are the ones you don't see under the tree.

December 12, 2006 was also a noteworthy day; Will was recognized for his popcorn sales in his St. Francis Cub Scout pack. The Cub Scouts sell popcorn in order to help raise money to offset the cost of activities, including summer camp. Normally when sales of items by school kids comes up, the eyes start rolling because the promotions never seem to end once the school year starts: pizzas for hockey, cookies for the Girl Scouts, etc. Will had a knack for selling Cub Scout popcorn, however, when he was feeling well enough to go door-to-door with Mom or Dad. It's hard to resist when a little boy shows up at your front door, shivering in the cold, dressed neatly in his Cub Scout uniform, his little head bald as a cueball, asking if you could use a few bags of popped goodness. People's defenses seemed to melt and they'd start reaching for their wallets and pocketbooks to help – and that was just with people he didn't know! The ones he did know were an even easier mark. Will's final sales total was $805, which amazed us all. He took third place in the entire Pack and he won a nice trophy to commemorate his accomplishment. This warmed my heart because it was one of those few activities that a boy did not have to have special athletic skills to really excel – and Will excelled! That trophy, and later ones, sit proudly on the shelf in his bedroom.

On December 19, 2006, it was Pep Fest Day at school, a day that I somehow missed. This was an "out of school uniform" day, and Will (and Katherine) went all out. Will dressed up as a punk rocker and looked very much like Gene Simmons from the band "Kiss." He wore a long black wig with spiked bangs, and a bandana with skull and crossbones on it; a black T-shirt with swords and flames, black pants, a magnetic skull earring and finally a black leather bracelet completed the ensemble. Katherine dressed as a '60s hippie (flowered flared pants, a hipster belt, and a peace necklace). I don't know if Will won any prizes, but I laughed so hard I cried when I saw them come home in their outfits. He was every mother's nightmare for their teenage daughters in that outfit! A bright spot in the long regimen of cancer treatment.

Will at Cub Scout Pack Popcorn Sales Award Ceremony, St. Francis School, Rochester – December 2006

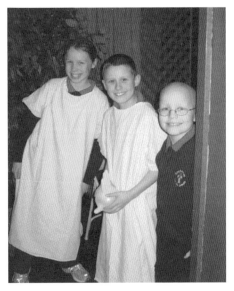

Will, Katherine and classmate Isaac Plager at Will's class "End of Treatment Party" – February 2007

– New Year

With the arrival of 2007, Will reached another milestone on January 31, when he finished his last chemo cycle! We were so proud of him for bravely enduring five straight months of chemo with six cycles of Topotecan. This was a total of over 120 hours of treatment and time spent in the Pediatric Infusion Treatment Center! Although he never complained, we're sure he had many days when he felt lousy; he had to have no energy due to his very low counts caused by the chemo targeting his bone marrow. Will didn't really react much to finishing chemo, although when Katherine came home one day and said, "you're done with chemo, Will," he smiled; they hugged and she rubbed his head as she had done so many times during all of this. Will's 3rd grade classmates were also pulling for him throughout the long ordeal and wanted to do something to mark this momentous occasion. They came up with the brilliant idea to have an "End of Treatment" party on February 9, 2007. They surprised us when we arrived: they were all dressed up in medical scrubs. 36 little doctors and nurses! The bigger hit at the party was blowing up surgical gloves with helium for the kids and letting them draw faces, etc. on them! It warmed our hearts to see how much they cared for Will and were so happy for him that he was finished with treatment.

On February 12, 2007, Liz and Will made the short trip north to meet with the complementary medicine staff at Minneapolis Children's Hospital to see if there were any nontraditional therapies Will could do that could complement the conventional treatment he was receiving. We wanted to explore any option that was going to give Will the best opportunity to be cured, even if it was a little unconventional. As part of this appointment, Will was given a biofeedback session; he was asked to close his eyes and visualize something. After awhile, the doctor asked him to open his eyes and share what he envisioned. He quickly said, "A dead person." Then, he went on to say that he was playing baseball with Babe Ruth. It made everybody smile to hear that; the creative wheels were always turning in Will's head. I found myself wondering what that encounter would have been like. Would it have included the Great Bambino waiting patiently for gentle pitches from Will delivered from the pitcher's mound, Will's jaw dropping in awe as he watched Babe slug pitch after pitch over the weathered outfield fence? Or would it have included the final years of the Babe's life when he, too, fought a cancer inside in his head and he and Will would have swapped stories about their treatments and finding the strength to carry on each day in the hopes of getting to play some baseball just a few more times? We'll never know.

February 19, 2007 was Will's 9th birthday. Will had been interested for some time in learning how to ski like big sister Katherine, so we headed to a nearby ski resort, Welch Village, to do some downhill skiing. Al Southwick, the husband of a close friend of Liz, is a ski instructor there and so we met up with him to get lined up with gear and some instruction for Will. We left Will in Al's capable hands. When we returned about an hour later, he and Al had already gone up on the chair lift and down a green run several times! Will skied beautifully, albeit a little on the fast side … but what 9-year-old boy doesn't?! Fortunately, Al also taught him how to stop.

At lunchtime, we took a break and Al had reserved a table in the ski chalet; he had it decorated with balloons and confetti and a birthday cake. After lunch, Will was back out on the slopes as fast as he could get his skis back on. He absolutely loved it and we had to drag him off the lifts at about 6 that evening to head back to Rochester. Al called him the "Energizer Bunny" because he just kept going and going!

Later that night, as Liz was tucking Will in, she was hugging him tight and telling him how proud she was of his skiing that day. She asked him if he would dream about going down "Annie's Alley" (a Welch blue level run) that night. He quickly said, "No, Mom. I'm going to dream about going down a black diamond run called 'Chicken' at Welch Village!" That summed up the day. It was incredibly heartwarming to watch him succeed with yet another aspect of his life, knowing what he had already endured. Will never ceased to amaze us – so we learned to never underestimate him. It was symbolic in many ways watching Will ski down the hills and having complete control over his actions and the freedom to ski fast or slow or whatever speed he wanted. The choice was his. It was one of the best days that our family had had in a long time and we didn't want to see it end.

By March 2007, winter was slowly winding down. We lost our first fellow warrior in the cancer wars at this time: Will's friend, Bryce Breuer, was only 8-years-old when he lost his battle with leukemia. His mom, Susie, had worked tirelessly trying to find treatments that would save him, but in the end, Bryce went back to be with God. All of us fighting the cancer battles felt his loss, knowing that someday it might be our turn if we could not find the right treatments.

In an effort to fight the winter doldrums, Will wanted to try something new, so he opted for basketball at the YMCA. We signed him up and took him down to the Y on Saturday mornings; the season lasted from January through March. He was unmistakable out on the basketball court, his slight body and beads of sweat on his smooth round head as he worked to learn the skills. His coach was friend Mark Hayward, a fine basketball player himself back in the day and just the person with oodles of patience to help Will along. Will hustled and tried so very hard. In his best game of the season, he had three passes/assists to teammates, one rebound and a shot that rimmed in and out. It was hard for Will to run up and down the court and dribble the ball at the same time, but he did not quit and his determination shines through the end of season photo with Mom and Dad. We were so very proud that he persevered.

We were also thrilled on March 7, 2007 when Will's MRI came back clear. Could it be that all those treatments were behind him forever and we could just work on building up his battered body so he could try to catch up with his peers? Time would tell.

March 10, 2007 was the Pinewood Derby for Will's Cub Scout Pack. He made a red, white and blue car with painted stars that year, complete with a Lego boy driver. Will and I did most of the work together, shaping the car, fitting on the axles and the wheels. Mom assisted in the painting category. When the dust had settled at the end of the race, Will won a 3rd place trophy in his Den! We were thrilled for him: another rare activity in which he could hold his own with his peers and boost his self-confidence.

On April 21, 2007, the four of us joined Liz's family in Houston, Texas where Liz's niece, Sarah Levy, was getting married to Scott Hatch. Will was chosen to serve as the ring bearer. He looked great dressed in his little tuxedo and Katherine served as a junior bridesmaid. It was a beautiful outdoor wedding under a gazebo at a mansion next to the Brazos River. Will did a great job as ring bearer and it meant a great deal to all of us to join together, all dressed up, for a multi-generational family picture before the bride and groom departed and we all left for home.

Will, Scott Hatch

Will, Scott Hatch and Mom's extended family at Scott and Sarah Levy's wedding, Houston, Texas – April 2007

– Buddy, Baseball, and Brighter Tomorrows

On April 28, 2007, "Buddy" entered our lives to brighten our days. The kids had been on the lookout for another dog ever since Thoreau passed away and after our trial run with Scout had not worked out. Buddy turned up at the Rochester Animal Shelter in the spring of 2007. The kids spotted him first and took me down there to check him out, though I could see even before we left home what the outcome of this encounter was going to be; our dog-expert friend, Marcia, made the trip with us. Ironically, Buddy had been owned by the ex-husband of a former divorce client of mine; he had good intentions, but kept Buddy tied up outside all day which, if you know Buddy, is about the worst thing you could do to the poor animal. He ran off repeatedly until he finally became a "guest" at the Animal Shelter. Buddy quivered when we first met him and was very timid, but Marcia could tell he had good potential and so after paying the princely sum of $5.00, home with us he came that day. Buddy was a lifesaver for Will. The first hug of the day, as well as the last one at night, was for Buddy. He'd tear around the living room with Will till you thought there wouldn't be any fluff left in the rug. Buddy would stare at you and nudge your hand until you'd take him for a walk; his ball would have to be thrown until he lay on his side, gathering strength till he was ready for the next round. He was a constant companion for Will and Katherine; he was a welcome distraction for all of us. He helped lighten the burdens we had been carting around for so long.

May of 2007 also meant the start of something important, Brighter Tomorrows. Liz and three other moms who had children battling various forms of cancer, Sherrie Decker, Teresa Carlson and Bridget Dahle, all realized that there was a definite need for an organization that would help support families going through treatment. They started small, with monthly meetings at the Ronald McDonald House where families going through treatment would get together to share a meal provided by McDonald's. Then the kids would leave for a creative or fun activity giving the adults a chance to update the other parents on the battles won and lost and to console each other and share information about treatments. In time, it would grow beyond all the expectations of its founders.

May also meant the start of another baseball season for our little slugger. His team for the 2007 season was the "Mudcats." The season started with Will getting hit in the hip by a fastball; and then a bloody nose during practice thankfully stopped quickly because his blood counts were good. He told his coach, "this is just like what happened to Justin Morneau" (the Minnesota Twins star first baseman, although Justin actually got a concussion from his encounter) and then he smiled and proceeded to go back out on the field. That's one tough boy. They won their first game of the season by the amazing score of 21-0 and Will went 1 for 3 with a single. They also won their second game and Will hit a triple! Miracles do happen!

June 2007 was a big month. On June 20, Will had another MRI. To our great relief, his scans came back clear: a cause for great celebration! June also brought our encounter with the special folks at an organization called "Hunt of a Lifetime." They grant hunting and fishing wishes for seriously ill children since the Make-A-Wish organization does not grant wishes of children who would like these types of experience. Ever since he was little, Will had always enjoyed fishing on trips with Dr. Steve Adamson on the "wild waters" of nearby Lake Pepin. Now he wanted to go salmon fishing in Alaska. Stacey Hildebrandt, the camp director at Camp Jornada, nominated Will for the trip; to our surprise and amazement, he was selected. Mindy and the other wonderful staff at "Hunt of a Lifetime" made it happen at the end of June 2007. Our family flew in to Juneau, Alaska, where there was a floatplane water landing strip right next to the main runway at the airport. None of us had ever been on a floatplane before. The pilot gunned the engine and we hurtled down the narrow waterway and with a slight lurch we climbed into the air over the deep green pine trees and headed south over the mountains. The views were glorious! Rugged mountains and the deep blue waters of the Gulf of Alaska slipped by beneath our windows; above, the sun climbed higher into the sky as we made our way south to Angoon. We landed at our fishing camp at Whaler's Cove Lodge, perched among the trees, hugging the water, the snow capped mountains of Admiralty Island visible in the distance. There were no roads leading to it; you could only get there by air or by water.

For the next five days, we were blessed to participate in the fishing equivalent of the US Open or the Super Bowl. Each day we ventured forth with a different fishing guide in a different boat, loaded with gear and know-how. The aroma from the salt water drifted through the air as we headed out each morning in search of ocean treasure: halibut, salmon, rockfish, crab. We learned that salmon loved herring, so our salmon fishing started with lines containing fish guts and multiple hooks trolling for herring. Will caught a 41-pound halibut and Katherine caught a 32-pound salmon, with a little help from Dad and the guides. These finned foes fight a little harder than the "big" fish on Lake Pepin! Will got to pull up the crab pots with assistance from our guide and was careful to avoid the pincers as he grabbed the salmon-hued crabs. We marveled at a large, brown bear we spied on the shore contentedly eating berries and soaking up the summer sunshine. We hiked up to a crystal clear trout stream one day and learned how to gracefully arc our flies into the rushing stream and to present them until a pastel striped Dolly Varden trout came up for his lunch. At the end of each day, we had a great meal back at the lodge and shared stories of our conquests with the other families. Needing a short break from all this fishing, we took a boat ride across the straits one day to Baranof Island where we enjoyed the magnificent beauty of a huge waterfall; we hiked up to mineral springs where a small pool invited us to soak our sore tired bodies in the steamy warmth. We remember the glistening brown seals who clung to the bobbing, bright red buoys in the strait that weren't afraid of us and entertained us with their "ark, ark" noises. Will bonded with "Kita," a tiny lovable Springer mix at the resort whose tail never seemed to stop wagging as Will followed him up and down the rocky beach searching for unique things washed up from the edge of the ocean. It was a trip we will long remember, including taking off from Anchorage at 12:45 a.m. and seeing the midnight sun just getting ready to set in the west as we raced east for Minnesota on the "red eye." Soon after we arrived home, 200 pounds of expertly fileted fish we had caught in Alaska showed up on our doorstep, neatly wrapped and frozen. I asked Will when we were back home how he rated the trip on a 1 to 10 scale, and without hesitation, he rated it a "10."

I digress from Will's story for just a moment here. Looking back on those trips to Alaska and to Florida, when I began writing my memoirs in 2009, I reflected briefly on another oddity in this incredible journey we were on. Will was blessed with the chance to partake of amazing trips through both Make-A-Wish and the Hunt of a Lifetime organizations, trips that created memories that will live on forever in our hearts and minds. But these organizations operate from the mostly sound premise that the trips are being offered to children who are either 1) cured and are being rewarded for putting the hell of surgery and treatment behind them once and for all, or are 2) dying and therefore want to be given a few pleasant memories to try to blot out some of the pain in their last days on the Earth. Where do the rare kids like Will fit in? By 2009, he was not cured and we did not know if he ever would be at that point. He was not dying and hopefully would not be any time soon. Those trips were so wonderful because they gave Will something great to focus on to stick it out through treatment and they were great to look back on once they were behind us. What do we do now, five years out in this battle, when neither of those two reasons really applies to us anymore? Is it fair to hope for more trips for Will to look forward to, despite these awesome past experiences, or has his chance come and gone and the resources of these organizations should now be devoted to helping other kids in the fight? There was no easy answer to this question.

Returning to Will's story upon our return from Alaska ... August 2007 meant the return of another favorite event of the summer, Camp Jornada. Stacey Hildebrandt, a cancer survivor, had always had a dream of starting a camp for kids with cancer and their siblings as a way to help with the healing process. In the summer of 2004, Camp Jornada was launched at Ironwood Springs Christian Ranch south of Rochester with the help of lots of volunteers to make it possible. We had some apprehension that first year Will and Katherine attended in 2005 whether Will was really ready for a week at camp without Mom and Dad. I think we lost sight of the fact that, with all the trials he had already faced in his young life, being at camp without Mom and Dad around was probably a walk in the park and we needn't have worried. Camp meant freedom from so many worries and cares. Camp in 2007 meant a special Frisbee-catching dog show, an Elvis impersonator who came out and crooned songs for the kids and led a dance, a special field trip to the water park in Stewartville and, of course, the Jello war – that 15 minutes of organized insanity when you get to pitch as much Jello at your neighbor as you can handle. It takes quite a while to get that strawberry gelatin scent squeezed out of your hair, but it's worth it.

Earlier in the year, the American Brain Tumor Association had solicited drawings from children with brain tumors; they wanted to include the artwork in their annual calendar. Will drew a great baseball scene with the caption, "Happiness Is ... hitting a grand slam in baseball." In August, Will learned the results of the contest: his drawing was chosen to be featured as one of the month's pictures in their 2008 calendar! What an honor for Will!

September 2007. A hint of fall was in the air when Will and I headed east to Wildcat Mountain State Park in Wisconsin for a weekend of camping and canoeing with my old high school friend, John Van Herwynen and his son Luke. That was a weekend "match made in heaven" because Luke was just as big a Star Wars nerd as Will was. They made us spend three hours one lovely afternoon sitting in the camper playing Star Wars Monopoly, but I remember the weekend best because of our float trip down the Kickapoo River. John and I rented a couple of canoes. I settled into the stern of one to steer, Will took the bow seat to serve as lookout, we grabbed our paddles and off we went with John and Luke paddling along side. It was an amazing feeling of freedom for a couple of hours – bright sunshine, clear water, the unspoiled beauty of the Wisconsin bluff country and abundant laughter. Maybe it was that brief feeling of being in control of your destiny, if even for the shortest time – knowing where you were headed, with people who made getting there a joy.

In mid-December 2007, Will was excited to receive a "care package" from the University of Kansas Athletic Department. Liz attended KU and was a rabid basketball fan who never missed a game. Will shared his Mom's passion for KU basketball, watching the games together on TV. A family friend of ours contacted the KU Athletic Director and shared Will's story with the basketball team. The package from KU contained a basketball signed by the team, a picture and jersey autographed by Brandon Rush (Will's favorite player), a Jayhawk key chain, license plate, cup and hat. Will loved the basketball and wanted to sleep with it! Will and Mom hoped to go in person to Lawrence in 2008 for a game.

Around this time, Will also "got" a very large check. In October 2007, families from the area who had loved ones affected by brain tumors joined together for the first annual "Brains Together for a Cure" walk to raise awareness and money for brain tumor research. Liz was fortunate to be asked to assist the Planning Committee, and our family participated in the event. The group raised close to $40,000! Will, and other adult brain tumor survivors, signed and presented the large symbolic check to Mayo Clinic. He loved it. He took the check to school afterward and shared it with his class. His comment was, "I really want to cash it." When Liz asked him what he'd do with that amount of money, he said, "Buy a Wii for each of my classmates, and add on to the school." Thinking of others first has always been one of best parts of Will's character. It is reassuring to know that organization's money will be put to good use right here at Mayo Clinic and lead to some real progress in the fight against brain tumors.

Will and the Camp Jornada kids learn "Elvis" moves, Ironwood
Springs Christian Ranch, Stewartville, Minnesota
– Summer 2007

Will, Dad, and friends John and Luke Van Herwynen – Canoeing
the Kickapoo River near Wildcat Mountain State Park, Wisconsin
– September 2007

Chapter 4 - Will's Second Relapse

That is the beauty of cancer, it tells you that your days are limited, that you could die at any point. It is that perspective that allows you to live a better life while you're here.
– Shelley Hamlin

– A Change of Venue

On December 11, 2007, we learned that Will had another relapse of his cancer. Two small new tumors were found, one in his right ventricle and one in his left ventricle. In the short term, it was decided that on December 21 Will would have another Gamma Knife procedure. In the longer term, however, a second relapse lessened our chances of prevailing in this terrible fight and so we needed to cast a broader net to consider other treatment options. We spoke with Will's doctors at Mayo Clinic, followed up by research on the Internet about where the best brain tumor experts practiced and some of the treatment options they could offer, before deciding the East Coast was where we needed to go.

Our travels took us first to Washington D.C. to see a specialist at Children's National Medical Center on January 3, 2008. There, Liz's friend Lindsey Hutter opened her home and her heart to us. When we had time for the sightseeing part of our trip, we drove by the White House and Jefferson Memorial. Katherine, Liz and I made a short pilgrimage one frigid afternoon up the steps of the Lincoln Memorial. We marveled, as people often do, looking down the length of the National Mall toward the dome of the U.S. Capitol shining on the horizon in the distance. When in Washington, you have to "do the Smithsonian" and take in its wealth of treasures. We took Will and Katherine to the wonderful Air and Space Museum at the Smithsonian, which also contained several items temporarily on loan from the American History Museum that was under renovation at the time. Will, the consummate baseball fan, did tell us when we finished that the best part about the Air and Space Museum was Carl Yastrzemski's batting helmet and glove. At the time, I was a bit frustrated to think that Will wouldn't realize these items were not normally a feature at the museum devoted to air exploration, but now this observation makes me smile.

After consultation with Dr. Roger Packer at DC Children's Medical Center, it was determined that the program offered there would not be the best treatment option for Will. So, on January 8, we headed to New York City where Memorial Sloan-Kettering Cancer Center (MSKCC) and Drs. Ira Dunkel and Kim Kramer awaited us. It was there that we met Chuck and Meryl Witmer, a couple with twin sons Will's age, Andrew and Ian. Andrew had a medulloblastoma like Will, but had been successfully treated at Sloan-Kettering. The Witmers were wonderful hosts. Their high-powered positions in the financial industry on Wall Street gave them resources the likes of which we have never seen; it was like entering another world. They owned a huge, gorgeous condominium on the Upper East Side of Manhattan overlooking the East River. They even had a doorman, a dog walker, and a cook who had delicious dinners awaiting their arrival every night and a chauffeur who sat in the family vehicle day and night like man's best friend just waiting to be called.

After meeting with Dr. Dunkel and Dr. Kramer, we decided to pursue a Phase 2 study at MSKCC called "targeted radioimmunotherapy." In simplified terms, the protocol called for them to place an Ommaya Reservoir (similar to a Port-a-cath) under the skin in Will's scalp; a tube would extend into a lateral ventricle of his brain to deliver injections directly to the affected area of the brain. In Will's case, this would involve the lining of the brain and cerebrospinal fluid. Will would receive four injections, several weeks apart, of radioactive iodine and an antibody. The hope was that the antibody would target any remaining tumor cells expressing a certain receptor, attach on to these and kill them. This was good because it meant the injection did not have to go through the blood stream and cross the blood/ brain barrier, which created a hurdle for all chemo drugs intended for delivery to a brain tumor. The injection was low toxicity and wouldn't remain in his system for very long. Will would still need to receive chemotherapy in addition to this treatment, either between the second and third injections or after we'd completed the MSKCC study. While MSKCC hadn't treated a large number of kids with recurrent medulloblastoma, the ones they had treated did experience some success: one child had survived five years, others were still alive two years following treatment and were supposedly doing well.

On January 21, 2008, Will had surgery at Mayo Clinic once again to place a port-a-cath in his chest, his third time for this surgery. On

January 26, 2008, Will got a nice surprise. Friends Mike and Shelly Kuhlmann had arranged for Will and Mike to meet Joe Mauer, the star catcher from the Minnesota Twins, one-on-one, as part of Twins Fest in Minneapolis. Mike was also battling a brain tumor at this time. Joe came walking down the dimly lit tunnel at the Metrodome where we were to meet him. Katherine, who prior to this time had never shown the slightest interest in boys, suddenly demonstrated a huge interest in a handsome adult male; she swooned as Joe drew near and stuck out his big hand to say hello. Will and Mike were both thrilled and we snapped a number of precious photos with Joe. Joe also signed Will's red Twins cap, a cap that he wore often throughout the remainder of his cancer journey as a reminder of that important day.

Liz, Will and Liz's Mom travelled to New York the week of January 28th to begin the treatments at Sloan-Kettering. On January 29, Will had another surgery, this time on his skull to make an incision and carve out a recess where the Ommaya reservoir could be placed. As was typical for many of Will's procedures, they had him report for surgery at 5:30 a.m., but did not call him back for surgery until 11:30 a.m. for a procedure that took only 30 minutes. Patience is indeed a virtue when you are a cancer patient waiting for care. Will spiked a fever after the procedure and was not released from the hospital until January 31.

While he remained in the hospital, Will was visited by two clowns from the Big Top Circus; they performed a twenty-minute act that was very funny! They had Will giggling and smiling, which made Liz very happy. The lead clown was a woman married to a guy from Austin, Minnesota, only 50 miles away from where we live, so it was truly a small world. The Big Top Circus clowns visited pediatric units at various New York hospitals two days a week, entertaining the children and their families.

Will was released from Sloan-Kettering at about 4 p.m. What Liz didn't know at the time was that this coincided with shift change for the NYC taxi drivers. The two innocents from small town Minnesota were mystified why there wasn't a cab to be had in a city usually crammed with taxis, but they were adjusting to life in the big city. After a long wait, they were finally able to hail a cab and return to the Witmer's residence. Following that lengthy adventure with transportation issues, the Witmers graciously offered them the services of their driver. Phinlay (although Will called him "Fenway" – he must of thought he was a Red Sox fan!) was very kind to take Will and Liz to and from their subsequent appointments, waiting in between until his services were needed once again.

On January 31, Liz and Will met with Dr. Kim Kramer, the MSKCC physician leading the I3F8 study. She was very knowledgeable and a caring physician. Will seemed to be comfortable with her. Will had blood work done and had to get thyroid prescriptions filled; he needed to take this medication during the entire time in the study to "coat" his thyroid and protect it from the radioactive antibody medicine. Will was to receive an injection of contrast dye into the Ommaya reservoir in his scalp. He didn't even want EMLA cream to numb the site and amazingly didn't flinch a bit when a long needle was introduced into his scalp. Next, the medical staff withdrew spinal fluid and analyzed the cells and then they injected the contrast. For the next hour or so it was Will's job to lie perfectly still while they used sophisticated camera technology to trace the dye flow throughout his brain and spinal fluid. This was called the "CSF flow test," and Will had to be able to pass this test in order to participate in the study. The following day, they would see how much of the dye had cleared his system by taking further pictures.

On February 2, Will, Grandma Levy and Liz visited the 86th floor of the Empire State Building. It was breezy up on the observation deck, but the visibility was an amazing 15 miles. Will was very excited when they got to the top and he could see many landmarks he had heard about in school: the Statue of Liberty, Brooklyn Bridge, Chrysler Building, and Central Park. On February 3, they watched the New York Giants win the Super Bowl and heard lots of New Yorkers out hooting and whistling in the streets following the big victory as they packed up to move from the Witmer's residence to the Ronald McDonald House for the remainder of their stay in New York.

On February 4, Will had a brain and spine MRI to give the staff a baseline of what his tumors looked like before the therapy; to our great relief, it came back clear. On the evening of February 5, assuming Will passed the CSF flow test, he would be admitted into MSKCC. All systems were "go" and on February 6, he received the test dose of the antibody therapy. If this "test" went well, the full dose of antibody would be given in a week. The medical staff had to access his Ommaya reservoir twice that morning, which was a little painful for Will. His head was wrapped in gauze to hold the needle and tube into his scalp in place; they took samples of his cerebrospinal fluid from there about every hour, so thankfully he didn't need to be re-stuck each time.

Dr. Cramer indicated that the first 24 hours would be rough – headache, nausea and vomiting. Liz decided not to tell Will about this until shortly before the side effects could be expected to lessen any anticipatory dread, even though she and I both knew he could handle that and so much more. As it turned out, only 30 minutes after the dose Will developed a severe headache and vomited; the medical staff gave him anti-nausea and pain medications, which allowed him to sleep some.

Liz was impressed by the caring people at MSKCC, who went the extra mile to make a child's stay there as comfortable as possible. These included Nuclear Medicine techs who got warm blankets to cover Will for his return trip to his room because they overheard him say he was cold; another person brought Liz a chair as she was waiting in a hallway with Will for a test; a desk attendant asked if she could go and get Liz and Will lunch one day, as they had to wait so long for an appointment. "Minnesota Nice" doesn't exist just in Minnesota. These people were as kind as anyone could be.

Will was dismissed from the hospital on February 7 and returned to the Ronald McDonald House to convalesce. It was a difficult night. Will spiked a fever and vomited several times, just seconds after taking six Tylenol chewables and liquid Zantac. There was also a bit of humor too when Will woke up, sat up on the side of the bed and promptly peed on the floor and narrowly missed Liz's shoes, without ever waking up!

On February 8, Will had his final PET scan as part of the study. This was used to assess the distribution and clearance of the radioactive antibody. The scan data would be studied by the medical team and used in calculating further doses for Will. They also accessed Will's Ommaya and drew a cerebrospinal fluid sample to be analyzed.

Upon their return to the Ronald McDonald House, Liz and Will got the webcam link to his class back in Rochester established. Will was able to see and hear his classmates; they were able to see him, but could not hear him. Will was able to gather that they wanted him to webcam the Empire State Building for them, which was going to be a little hard to do. Nevertheless, this contact with lots of familiar faces from back home really lifted Will's spirits.

On February 11, Liz and Will and Grandma went to the Westminster Kennel Club Dog Show at Madison Square Garden. They got to watch the Herding Group show and saw Smooth and Rough Coat Collies, Shetland Sheepdogs (like our former pup Thoreau) and German Shepherds. After watching the Herding Group, they went back to the "bench" area, where all of the dogs in the show are kenneled, groomed, etc. Will got to pet and interact with many dogs including a Smooth Coat Collie; an Australian Shepherd named "China," who loved Will; "Cappuccino," a beautiful St. Bernard; "Salty Dog," a huge Yellow Lab; an extremely tall Great Dane; and, of course, several beautiful Shelties. Will was even fortunate to have a small part in a commercial TV segment about the "Angel on a Leash" program, which featured James, the Springer Spaniel, who won Best in Show 2007, and had just visited the Ronald McDonald House. Will was in dog heaven after this experience.

Then, on February 14, the hospitalization at Sloan-Kettering was repeated and Will received the first real injection. He did experience a slight headache (less than the first time) and received more pain and anti-nausea meds, which made him very sleepy. He slept until about 11 p.m. when Liz had to wake him to give him some pills and drops to coat his thyroid, which tasted terrible and, of course, he threw them up immediately. The nurses gave him more anti-nausea meds through his IV, which settled his stomach enough for him to take his other meds later and keep them down. Liz and Will were finally able to return to Rochester on President's Day, February 18. Katherine and I were there to greet them as they got off the plane in Rochester – along with 40-50 smiling friends, classmates, neighbors, and of course, Jack the Dog. It was very emotional to see the turnout and to see Will and Liz after being away for three weeks.

Three weeks was a long time for Katherine and me "holding down the fort" in Minnesota. We were stuck inside on the cold dark nights of winter and the days dragged on. We were able to see and hear Will and Liz in New York via webcam, but there were so many things that physical separation made difficult. I sorely missed my time with Liz while she was so far away, the many small things that a spouse can do to make shared lives together special; my inability to be with Will in person and hug him and tuck him in every night was very hard. I know that Katherine struggled to have her Mom half a country away, despite my best efforts to "wear both hats" in her absence, and missed the humor and smiles that Will brought to our lives.

On February 19, we celebrated Will's 10th birthday. As a surprise for Will, I had purchased a recumbent bike. My good friend, Jack Decker – who is much handier than I – did most of the work to assemble it. Before his original surgery robbed him of the necessary balance and coordination to ride his bike, Will had loved riding his two-wheeler. I now looked forward to the warm, sunshiny days of spring when Will could get back out on the sidewalk on his new blue, low-slung, flamed, three-wheeled bike and recoup some of the joy that he lost when bike riding became no longer possible.

That would have to wait, however, as just a few days later, on February 25, Will and Liz needed to return to New York to get the second injection. This was scheduled to occur on February 27; however, the medication used for the injection did not pass quality assurance testing and so Will could not receive the shot until the next day when an acceptable batch had been obtained. He got the second injection on February 28. No nausea this time, only a slight headache and fatigue and a low-grade fever the next morning on February 29. The night after the injection wasn't too restful, though, as Liz was awakened at 2 a.m. by a Sloan fire alarm: blinking strobe lights in the hall and faucets automatically going off due to sensors being triggered by fire alarms! Fortunately, it was a false alarm and Will didn't wake up.

On March 1, Will awoke and was very thirsty and drank a lot of water and then some OJ. He started to eat breakfast and then vomited. He was somewhat shaky and complained that his head hurt when he was upright, but after getting plenty of fluids, seemed to feel much better. Will started working on a paper for school in the Computer Room at the Ronald McDonald House. He was reading the Laura Ingalls Wilder book *Little House in the Big Woods* and had to pick an animal in the book to write about. What did he choose? The bulldog, of course – that symbol of tenacity that personifies Will so well.

On March 8, after returning to Rochester, Will participated in his second Pinewood Derby, with a car done up in KU colors with some help from Dad and Suzanne Viggiano. He placed second in his den and we were thrilled when his name was called to go to the front of the room to collect his trophy.

On March 23, 2008, it was Easter Sunday. Will apparently still believed in the Easter Bunny, though he had some doubts about its authenticity, which meant that the fun of preparing for the Easter Bunny and Santa Claus and even the Tooth Fairy was about to become a thing of the past. It isn't quite the same when none of the kids believe in the magic any longer – another milepost of childhood about to pass us by. Our family gathered at church, joined by my parents, and my sister Kathy, brother-in-law Tom and their son Ben; Will and Katherine had the opportunity to serve Mass together. To have them serve together on such a special day to remember the resurrection of our Lord, with my extended family present, made me very happy and proud as a parent.

Will and Katherine serve Mass together for first time at St. Francis Catholic Church, Rochester – Easter 2008

–Hope Springs Eternal

On March 28, we were also lucky to have the class hamster, JoJo, stay the weekend at our house. The kids were constantly holding him and putting him in mazes that they built. Will even constructed a Lego wagon that he put JoJo in and pulled her around. I kept thinking of all of the things that a hamster loose inside a house could do if we lost track of it; she was no doubt glad to have some rest and peace and quiet when taken back to the class on Monday morning. We also learned at this time that Will's teacher, John DeRouin, whom he loved, was diagnosed with a melanoma under this thumb; however, after amputating part of his thumb to remove the cancer, they were satisfied they had gotten it all. Very good news for John, his family and all of his devoted students. On that evening, Will and I were invited to attend a Minnesota Wild hockey game as guests of HopeKids, a great organization that provides special events for kids with serious illnesses and their families. We got to sit in star player Marian Gaborik's private suite with several other HopeKids families to watch the game. After the game, Will got to go down on the ice and shoot a puck into the goal, which was absolutely thrilling for him!

On March 27 and 28, Will had MRIs of his brain and spine. On April 1, we were filled with glee when we got the results: the brain and spine MRIs showed no signs of any tumors! After discussions with Dr. Wetmore regarding the chemo regimen Will should pursue, we decided he would take an oral chemotherapy agent called Temodar. He would take one pill nightly for five days and then be off about 28 days. The Mayo medical staff said it would impact his counts, especially his platelet levels, which they would monitor closely. The plan was to do two cycles of Temodar and then go back to New York City for the remaining two I3F8 treatments.

On April 6, Katherine and I ran in the annual Fool's Five Race in Lewiston, Minnesota. Proceeds from the race benefit cancer research at Gundersen Lutheran Medical Center in LaCrosse, Wisconsin, as well as Mayo Clinic. There were over 1800 racers. Will wanted to run the one-mile race so much, but because it was rainy and potentially slick, and the fact that he was in active chemo, we decided it was best not to have him run. It broke our hearts as tears welled up in his eyes, but we hoped there would be future opportunities when he could join us out on the course and take an active role in helping raise money to find a cure for him and so many other kids like him.

On April 7, there was lots of excitement at our house because the University of Kansas was playing for the National Basketball Championship!!!! Will, who loved KU basketball as intensely as his Mom, wore his KU hat (part of that wonderful care package received from the KU Athletic Director and team in late autumn) during the game, but he had to go to bed at the three-minute mark when KU was down by 9 points. Will was very emotional during the game, cheering when they led and even breaking into tears when they were down. The game went into overtime and, unbelievably, KU ended up winning.

Katherine and Liz made a big sign and posted it in Will's room so he could see it in the morning when he awoke. Will was thrilled when he heard the news.

On April 8, 2008, I decided to close the solo private law practice I had owned for nine years. Effective May 12, I started at a new job in the Civil Division of the Olmsted County Attorney's Office in Rochester. There were a number of factors that led to this decision. First and foremost, the stress of trying to be there for my family, physically and emotionally, was taking a toll on my ability to serve my private law firm clients. Second, the Great Recession was just starting to take hold; many people were being laid off and having difficulty paying their bills, including to their attorneys. It seemed that life would be simpler, with more regular hours, collecting a paycheck, and serving the public at the same time, which is my passion. I did it and it was the best employment decision I have made since leaving law school nearly 20 years ago.

Katherine, Liz and Tom at the Minnesota Make-A-Wish Ball – the Depot Hotel, Minneapolis – April 2008

On April 11, 2008, Holy Spirit School in Rochester hosted their 2nd Annual Walk-a-Thon. The school chooses a family in need that can benefit from funds raised during the event. Over 250 people showed up to participate in the event that, because of bad weather, was held inside the school. The school decided that a portion of the funds raised would be used to assist our family in offsetting some of the expenses incurred during Will's treatments in New York. It was a very kind gesture, but not uncommon for the generous people who make up the Rochester Catholic School system; they have repeatedly

Will at Camp
Jornada on the
Mayo Clinic
Blood Donor
Center Calendar
– May 2008
(Photo Courtesy
of Mayo Clinic)

Will's story

Will was diagnosed with medulloblastoma, a malignant brain tumor, in March, 2004. The six weeks of radiation and year-long chemotherapy regimen that followed his surgery were extremely hard on his young body and required him to have a number of red blood cell and platelet transfusions. After a year in remission, another small lesion appeared in Will's brain in April, 2006. He underwent another six months of intensive chemotherapy with an agent that was especially hard on his counts and required many more transfusions.

"These blood products were vital to restoring Will's health and the vitality that he is experiencing today! Our family will be forever grateful to those who donate blood and want them to know how they helped my son during his cancer treatment." — Liz Canan, Will's mother

Will and Team
United Rentals at
the St. Baldrick's
Day Benefit for
Cancer Research,
Whistle Binkie's
South, Rochester –
May 2008

opened their arms and their hearts to help us when we were in need without ever expecting anything in return. We were deeply thankful for their efforts.

On April 19, 2008 we headed to Minneapolis for the Make-A-Wish Ball. We were invited as guests of Dr. Wetmore, who was a member of the Board of Directors of the Minnesota Make-A-Wish Foundation. The evening started with an auction, which was an incredible event to watch. Many very wealthy people in attendance thought nothing of bidding $7,000, $10,000, or $17,000 on auction items! The items up for bid were stupendous: a private plane to fly four people to Napa Valley for a vacation at a chateau; use of a VIP suite at a Boston Red Sox game; use of a suite at a Twins game for you and 24 of your friends; the list went on and on. In only an hour, over $200,000 was raised in the auction! Make-A-Wish holds a very special place in the hearts of many Minnesota philanthropists. After the auction, we danced to live music performed by '80s and '90s pop star Richard Marx.

While Liz and Katherine took great pleasure in dressing in formal attire, Will had little interest in the Ball. He been in the hotel pool with the kids of a grad school friend of Liz's for most of the evening and had no desire to come out. Toward the end of the evening, Dr. Wetmore insisted that Will should come to the Ball, so Liz went to get him. She proudly escorted him in, with wet hair, swimsuit and bare feet! She heard a few men (most of whom were wearing tuxes) say as we passed by, "Boy, he sure looks a lot more comfortable than me." Will came over to the table, got a huge hug from Dr. Wetmore and was introduced to the other table guests before retreating back to the hotel room for the rest of the evening. It was a wonderful event and a lasting memory. We were very grateful to Dr. Wetmore and Mayo for sponsoring a table and inviting us as guests.

On April 30, Will started a second cycle of Temodar and the dosage was increased to the maximum for Will's height and weight. It caused him to be fatigued, but we fought that by trying to get him to bed earlier. He finished the second cycle on May 4 with a stomachache, but no other obvious complications.

Liz had a surgical procedure on May 8 to remove a benign uterine fibroid. It was minor surgery; however, she had to have to have general anesthesia. She was a little anxious because she'd never had surgery before. Will said, "Mom, do you want me to come with you?" When we thought about the major surgeries that Will had on his brain that put her small operation into perspective. She was calm after that.

On May 9, Will's picture and story were featured during Mayo's Blood Donor Center's *Precious Gifts–Precious Life* photo display. The display celebrated the important connection between those "precious gifts" made by blood donors and the "precious lives" of kids like Will that blood donors have helped to save. We're grateful for the many people who have given blood to help Will along his journey.

Will's baseball season got underway once again on May 15, 2008. His team was the "Mini-Mets," which was a little ironic given his new ties to New York City and the fact that his doctor there is a big Mets fan. On

May 17, we gathered at Whistle Binkie's on the Lake Pub for the annual St. Baldrick's event. Katherine and Will perfected their barber skills as they shaved the heads of several volunteers who raised money for the families of kids fighting cancer. We owe a huge thank you to Marv Corsbie and his colleagues at United Rentals for organizing a team, raising funds in Will's honor and learning that bald really is beautiful.

On May 18, Will had a marvelous day. He played in the Kid's Cup golf tournament in Byron, Minnesota, which raises money for pediatric cancer research at Mayo Clinic and Gillette Specialty Healthcare in St. Paul. With a limited amount of playing time prior to this, he was still able to shoot a 51 for 9 holes and even hit one 150-yard drive! As a result, he won First Place among all other 4th graders competing! He was also the top fundraiser ($500, and $1,400 with Mom's pledges included). This accomplishment was all the more special due to the fact that Will was the first patient actively undergoing chemotherapy to have played in the tournament and won! Will was very humble in accepting the awards, though he had a huge smile on his face. We were so proud and happy.

Just before school got out for the summer, the Mini-Mets won a memorable game. Will played great! The first three grounders went to him at shortstop and he fielded all three very well. Liz and I both took deep breaths as the ball rolled to him. He threw out a boy at second base and almost got two others out at first, but those throws from short to first base are a long way. He also got a walk and an RBI. Way to go Will!

On May 30, Will had his 4th grade class picnic at Mr. DeRouin's farm near Dover, Minnesota. "Mr. D" had a full day of jobs assigned for the kids to do, like tree planting, mulching, washing clothes, making ice cream the "old-fashioned" way, planting the garden and, of course, shoveling manure and hay. Will said he really liked shoveling manure. Go figure! Mr. D. had 60 newborn chicks that all the kids could hold. Will loved that. He also had goats, two-week-old kittens, a horse, chickens, and a one-year-old St. Bernard named "Lucy." After chores and lunch, Will and the kids played various games, including the annual water wars with squirt guns/super soakers! All in all, it was a highlight of Will's school year.

Will had another MRI done on June 2 of his brain and it came back clear. This one was unusual because he told us the night before we got the results that his scan was going to be clear. He just had a premonition about it. We were left feeling full of hope that the treatments and chemo were really working.

On June 9, Will and Liz, Katherine and Grandma Levy returned to New York City for Will's third injection. They got settled in at the Ronald McDonald House once again. The Ronald McDonald House on East 73rd St. became their "home away from home." This large House was full of caring people who set up warm meals and visits to Central Park. Will had always enjoyed the stories about "Lyle the Crocodile" who was a lovable crocodile who lived in a bathtub in a flat on East 88th Street. I made Will smile when I told him that I always imagined, as we moved about on the streets near the Ronald McDonald House, that we might run into "Lyle" out playing with the neighborhood kids someday, but he never wandered by. On June 10, Will, Liz and Grandma Levy made their way to Shea Stadium where they took in most of a game played by the New York Mets.

On June 11, Will received the third I3F8 injection at Sloan-Kettering. He slept for several hours afterward due to all of the pain and anti-nausea medications he was given during the process. He spiked a fever of 102.5 degrees, even though the medical staff told us not to worry since his body's immune system was reacting to something foreign being injected into the spinal fluid. He complained that his head was hurting, too. His temp ended up peaking at 103 degrees, the highest so far during treatments, and he vomited three times. Will being Will, he did not complain at all, despite the hardships. His fever did not fully abate until June 14, a full three days after receiving the injection.

Liz was able to witness a unique event while at the hospital with Will. They had a commencement ceremony honoring all of the graduating high school seniors who were cancer survivors and had been Sloan-Kettering patients. Their names were displayed on a board and they had a formal ceremony for the young men and women. Liz was quite touched to witness this and to see delight in the kids as they recognized their former caregivers. The staff was equally gratified to see these survivors since death is an all too frequent occurrence for them. Liz found herself looking into the future and holding on to the hope that, one day, Will's name would be on that board as well. She reflected on the sick children she saw as she walked the halls there, from as young as six months to as old as 21 years, and asked herself why do all these kids get cancer? She also felt joy when she saw some kids who had been so sick during their stay in February, but who were now growing hair again and were up and about, and even out of the hospital. It gave us hope for Will and proved again how resilient children really are.

On June 15, after a call to Dad back home to wish him a Happy Father's Day, Will, Katherine, Mom and Grandma headed out for a three-hour Circle Line Cruise around the entire island of Manhattan. The light rain cleared off shortly after leaving the dock. They all loved the cruise. Will and Katherine's favorite parts were seeing the majestic Statue of Liberty soaring 300 feet above New York Harbor, Ellis Island, Yankee Stadium, and the former site of the World Trade Center. The kids got Statue of Liberty foam hats and wore them the entire trip. Shortly after this, Liz and Will were able to return home to Rochester for a brief visit.

On June 23, Liz and Will flew out to New York City for his last I3F8 injection. They were fortunate to fly out there at no cost, courtesy of an organization called "Operation Liftoff" that helps pediatric cancer patients reach their appointments in distant places. I joined them a day later. Before dinner that night, the kids at the Ronald McDonald House built and decorated ships and sails made of styrofoam. Will, our little creative artist, called his ship, "Will Power." Once they were constructed, all the kids placed them in a swimming pool and raced their boats across, blowing on the sails through drinking straws. Will won in the 10-year-old division. "Will Power" prevails!

On June 25, Will received his fourth injection. He slept from that afternoon until the following morning, vomiting only once, and again spiking a fever of nearly 103. With the right meds, they were able to bring the fever back down and he was discharged from Sloan-Kettering on June 26. It was an emotional parting because we did not know when Will might be back there, if ever. They took great care of Will, but still there is no place like home. That evening, the Ronald McDonald House arranged a picnic for the kids and their families in Central Park, sponsored by the New York City Police Department. We rode in a NYPD van, and what a trip that was! Our NYPD driver drove at top speeds; he used his sirens at red lights so that we could speed through them without stopping. He particularly enjoyed blowing the siren when he got behind a taxi and loved to watch them scurry out of the way! He also drove faster than any New York cabbie, but the kids loved it. When we arrived at Central Park, we played baseball and football, and enjoyed a picnic lunch before hopping in with our crazy escort again and getting the same wild ride back home.

Katherine had been away at a YMCA camp in northern Minnesota but would soon be coming home, and I had to get back to work, so I returned to Rochester on June 29.

On June 30, Will, Liz, Liz's brother David and sister-in-law Karin had an evening to remember in New York when they were invited to Yankee Stadium as guests of the New York Yankees, for a game against the Texas Rangers, because Will was a patient at Memorial Sloan-Kettering. It started with a subway ride to Yankee Stadium in the Bronx, which was a first for Will and an experience that he enjoyed. They were warmly greeted in the front office lobby by their own personal tour guide, Alyssa, from Milwaukee, Wisconsin; they all received gracious attention. Alyssa gave them "special guest" lanyards to wear before they went out directly onto the field to watch the Yankees take batting practice. Will, the baseball guru, was able to identify a number of the players, both Yankees and Rangers. Following batting practice, they got to go into the Yankees' dugout and sit on the players' bench. There, Alyssa also presented Will with an official "New York Yankee" baseball. Next, they went on a "behind the scenes" tour of the stadium, taking in the broadcast booth, interview room, and the Yankees' and opposing team's clubhouses (from a distance). They also went into the old Yankee clubhouse, and the players' cafeteria/restaurant.

Then their tour went to the outfield area, to the "monument" section, where a number of great Yankee players have their uniforms/numbers retired. Some of the greats enshrined there include Babe Ruth, Lou Gehrig, Mickey Mantle, and Thurman Munson. As every team has, the Yankees have retired Jackie Robinson's number 42, even though he never played for them. This same area of Yankee Stadium also has a section of beautiful monuments honoring many of these great players. In fact, Alyssa told them several of these monuments, including Babe Ruth, Lou Gehrig and Mickey Mantle, used to be located directly in the outfield and players would have to navigate around them during games to catch fly balls, etc. Interestingly, during this tour, a woman was dumping ashes from an urn onto the retired number plaques of some of the greats, presumably fulfilling the last wishes of a Yankee fan!

After this, Will and the rest of the family went back down to an area right outside of the Yankees clubhouse, where many of the players were starting to emerge and go out on to the field as game time approached. Will was given a special, cushy Yankees chair to sit in and he had his brand new Yankees ball gripped tightly in his hand.

Then the real magic part of the evening began. The players could not have been more gracious: they took time to shake Will's hand, sign his ball and take a photo with him, with Alex Rodriguez being the first to approach him. Other players trickled in and Will got to meet and get photos with several of them, including Jason Giambi, Jose Molina, Melky Cabrera, Hideki Matsui, and Derek Jeter. During all of this, Will remained his usual calm, unassuming, polite and respectful self. Jeter was the last player out of the clubhouse to sign Will's ball and take a picture with him. We didn't know that he happened to be Will's favorite Yankee player, so the night was complete when this happened. As Jeter walked away, Will turned to Liz, pumped his fist and said, "Yes!" with a huge, beautiful smile on his face. The Yankee players will probably never know the impact that just a few minutes and kind words had upon Will and how much happiness it brought that evening. It was very emotionally moving for Liz, David and Karin to witness this.

Then, when one couldn't possibly imagine the night could get even better, it did. Alyssa escorted them to their seats, which were one row directly behind home plate. Mr. Randy Levine, President of the Yankees, donated his four tickets frequently to Sloan-Kettering families in similar situations to ours. We want to publicly thank Mr. Levine for his incredible generosity toward our family and the joy his simple donation has brought to so many families fighting cancer.

The seats were positioned such that the Yankees on-deck hitters were literally only about six feet away. What a great image: Will, sitting next to Liz's brother David, both watching the game intently and happily on a beautiful night in the Big Apple. They were also offered all of the food and drink that could be ordered off of a menu. Toward the 7th inning, Alyssa came down to see them and brought Will a large bag filled with Yankee memorabilia, including a hat, umbrella, water bottle, players guide, frames, light switch plate covers, and a 3-D picture of Matsui, among other items.

Will started to get tired and they wanted to beat the rush so they left at the top of the 8th inning with the Yankees trailing the Rangers 2-1. They all rode the subway packed with many other Yankees fans to the 59th Street stop, before David and Karin got off and got Will and Liz a cab back to the Ronald McDonald House. What a joyous, memorable, dream-come-true evening it was. Sloan-Kettering and the Yankees could not have scripted a more glorious way for Will and Liz to spend their final night in NYC, especially considering the circumstances that had brought them there.

– There's No Place Like Home

On July 19, back in Rochester, the mighty Mini-Mets baseball season came to an end. The team was leading 6-4 going into the bottom of the final inning, but they couldn't pull it out. Will probably played his best game ever. He hit two singles, drove in one run, and made several outstanding defensive plays at second base. One play included Will making a diving tag of a runner headed to second. He got a standing ovation from the other Mini-Mets parents who knew his story, which of course brought Liz and me to tears. All this, while still fighting off the effects of his recent treatments and chemo, made his play all that much more remarkable.

On July 29, Will had another MRI and got his hearing tested. The hearing test results showed that his hearing loss, mostly at a high frequency level, was stable in his left ear. He had sustained much more loss, however, in his right ear, both low and high frequency, which oddly enough Liz and I both thought was his better ear. Although not at a level where he would need hearing aids, it was just one more thing taken for granted by most kids that was slowly being stolen from Will. On the much brighter side, his MRI once again came back clear, showing no signs that the cancer had returned.

On August 4, 2008, the "Humor to Fight the Tumor" team started arriving at our house around 9:30 a.m. to set up for the interview and video shoot. Back in April 2008, Liz was approached by Joelle Syverson. Joelle is a Rochester native, brain tumor survivor and founder of a comedy event called "Humor to Fight the Tumor," which raises money for brain tumor research. Joelle was interested in having Will be one of the two pediatric brain tumor kids featured. We agreed and so a team was sent to our house to prepare a short video to introduce Will and tell about his life to the attendees at the event. Mike, "the Video Guy," interviewed Will and the rest of us, and filmed Will and the Viggiano kids playing, and Will playing with Buddy, our camera-shy dog. Aubrey King, age 6 and another 2008 honoree, was also there with her mother, Tracy, for the video. Tracy is also a counselor at Camp Jornada and Aubrey had been a camper there with Will. We looked forward to seeing the finished video at the event scheduled for September 27.

Then on August 6, Will's short career onscreen expanded a bit further when the film crew from Animal Planet arrived! "Jack the Therapy Dog" is a very unusual dog. There are very few Miniature Pinschers that act as service dogs. Somehow a producer for *Dogs 101* on Animal Planet got wind of a local newspaper article about Jack and thought that a story about him on *Dogs 101* would be interesting. Given the close relationship between the two, they decided that they would like to do some video footage of Jack and Will. They filmed Jack with two of his many patients in the Pediatric Infusion Treatment Center at Saint Marys Hospital. One of them was a young woman who walked Jack for the first time on her new prosthetic legs – a very powerful event to witness. When finished with this footage, the cameras were still rolling when they captured an unscripted moment: a 3-year-old boy from Saudi Arabia, who was getting treatment, and his father. The little boy was visibly frightened, but once he saw Will and Jack peek at them from around the corner, a radiant smile appeared on his face and his huge brown eyes sparkled with delight. Will walked Jack over to him and he calmed down almost immediately.

After that, the crew filmed Will on a bed and we reenacted a treatment appointment and Dr. Wetmore came and "examined" him. Jack laid on the bed next to Will and, at one point, started digging into the sheets to try and get under the covers, which left Will giggling and smiling during all of this. After about two hours at Saint Marys, we headed to our house to recreate a birthday party for Will and, of course, Jack was an invited guest. They filmed the kids out on the deck (even though Will's friends and family knew that his birthday was in February when no one in Minnesota celebrates birthdays out on their decks) with Buddy and Jack, and having birthday cake. Jack even wore a party hat! The *Dogs 101* segment with Jack and Will aired on Animal Planet in November. The local newspaper ran a story about it prior to the airing, and we held a party at our house, complete with homemade dog treats for the canines in attendance. Jack was on his way to becoming an international media star with that great exposure on Animal Planet.

On August 12, we met once again with Dr. Wetmore to decide what the next phase of Will's treatment regimen would entail. After much discussion, we decided to restart Will on Temodar, an oral chemo agent, to be taken nightly for five days and then off for about 23 days. He would also start on a low dose of the drug Accutane, best known for its use fighting severe acne; some research indicated that Accutane, in combination with Temodar, was effective against some brain tumors. Will finished his third cycle of Temodar on August 23.

On August 16, we departed for our week-long family vacation to the Black Hills in South Dakota. We stayed in a cabin at Sylvan Lake Lodge. Surrounded by towering pine trees, at an elevation of 4000 feet, the cabin was rustic and cozy (two beds, all in one room); the lake was not far away. We also had a grill at the cabin and the kids had a blast cooking hot dogs and brats; they also made the best s'mores ever, thanks to a nice charcoal fire. We even tried Jiffy-Pop popcorn on the grill, but it burned a hole in the lid area and when we took it in to finish it on the stove (Mom's bright idea), popcorn started flying everywhere. Will yelled, "take cover," as we all laughed uncontrollably! In fact, Liz and I thought the kids enjoyed this part of the trip almost more than anything else.

We also enjoyed a bumpy Jeep safari ride into the remote areas of Custer State Park. This brought us up close and personal with the huge brown buffalo and their calves, antelope, and deer. We marveled at the huge Crazy Horse Memorial and were at Mt. Rushmore for the evening lighting ceremony, which was very impressive. We also squeezed in time on an Alpine slide, mini-golf, and a great waterpark near Rapid City with very steep banzai slides. We capped off our trip with a 90-minute trail ride through the wooded hills, which we enjoyed immensely. It was the first time that Will had ever ridden a horse and he did great!

Upon our return from South Dakota, we learned that several people active in the St. Francis Church and School had taken it upon themselves to organize "Will Weekend," a benefit designed to raise money to offset some of the substantial costs we had incurred related to Will's various treatments, which would take place the weekend of September 13. On Sunday, September 7, after the morning Masses at church, kids from the parish and school handed out 600 small canisters of tiny M&Ms. Each bottle was labeled "Will Weekend" and people were asked to eat the candy, fill the empty bottle with pocket

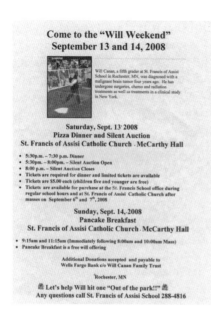

Will, Katherine, Mom and Dad at "Will Weekend" Benefit at St. Francis Catholic Church, Rochester – September 2008

change, and return it to school as part of the benefit. It was a unique fundraising idea. Will and Katherine enjoyed handing them out to people after the 10 o'clock Mass on Sunday. Will took enough for the kids on our street and even put them in his belt loops on his shorts!

On September 10, Will, Katherine, and our good friends Laurie and Anna Sutherland got to be on the *Tracy McCray Show*, on local radio station KROC, to talk about "Will Weekend." The actual festivities began on September 13 with a pizza dinner and silent auction and kids' activities in the church/school cafeteria. Dinner for the evening was donated by several businesses: pizza from Nick & Willy's, salad by the Canadian Honker Restaurant and ice cream treats from Dairy Queen.

Our family stood in line to greet people and thank them for coming and we were astonished when approximately 550-600 people showed up for the event. We were also blessed to have our parish priests, Fathers Reker and Thompson, present. The diners listened to beautiful music by Joe Dearani on saxophone and a friend of his on keyboard. While people were eating, they had a chance to partake in the silent auction set up in a room next door. There were a total of 69 beautifully prepared baskets with a great variety of items to bid on. Will immediately eyed the NERF Gun/Accessories basket and ended up winning it. He also had the high bid on a beautiful charcoal drawing of Twins relief pitcher Joe

Nathan done by the Honorable Joe Chase, an Olmsted County judge.

On Sunday, September 14, the final phase of the "Will Weekend" included pancake breakfasts following the morning Masses. The Knights of Columbus and Will's Cub Scout Pack each had a major part in these activities. There were a total of around 300 attendees for both breakfasts, a record for the Knights of Columbus up to that point.

It was a heartwarming and humbling experience for our family. We knew that we had been able to endure Will's cancer journey because of the love, prayers, and support we had been shown by countless people. And now the financial support and outpouring of friendship would give us the strength to carry on, even through the darkest times.

On September 24, Will started his fourth cycle of Temodar and Accutane. Three days later, we gathered with family and friends at The Depot Hotel in downtown Minneapolis for the "Humor to Fight the Tumor" comedy fundraiser. Will was an honoree, along with his friend Aubrey, age 6, as well as two adult brain tumor patients, at the event. Unlike his attendance at the Make-A-Wish Ball, this time Will would need to wear a tuxedo! Liz rented one for him in black, and he selected a fall orange tie and vest (naturally). He looked sharp! Upon arriving at the event in his formal wear, Will initially told us that he looked like a "doofus" and commented that everyone was staring at him. Liz reassured him by saying he didn't look like a "doofus" and that people were looking at him because he looked so handsome! The honorees had their photos taken and then the cocktail hour and silent auction got underway. Will bid on and won a Twins package complete with an autographed baseball by former players Tony Oliva, Paul Molitor, and Terry Steinbach, a hat, and bag/satchel. However, before we could pay for this unique package, we learned it had already been paid for by an attendee we had not met, Bonnie Bashears. We were privileged to meet her later and personally thank her for doing such a wonderful thing for Will.

The Depot ballroom was elegantly decorated in purple, grays and blacks. We were fortunate enough to have a table in front; friends and families surrounded us at three other nearby tables. Will had a big contingency there: his Uncle David, Aunt Karin, their daughter Sarah with her husband Scott, daughters Anna, and Julia; Granny and Grandpa Levy, Grandma and Grandpa Canan; Aunt Kathy and Uncle Tom; and many other friends from graduate school, Mayo Clinic, Brains Together for a Cure, and Camp Jornada.

The evening started with a delicious meal, served to the 600 attendees. After dinner, the program included a performance by David M. Bailey, a musician, who is a 12-year glioblastoma survivor. He is an excellent songwriter, singer and guitarist. His music and his strong faith reflected his cancer journey. After David Bailey finished, the honorees were recognized. Each of them were featured in a filmed segment shown on a huge screen. All of the videos were quite moving and powerful, and demonstrated the incredible obstacles each of them had overcome. Then all of the honorees and/or their families were asked to come on the stage to be recognized to a standing ovation. It was very emotional to stand on that stage with Will and the other honorees and their families knowing the mighty mountains they had all climbed to be present that evening.

After this, a live auction commenced. It was absolutely incredible the amount of money that was raised during the evening – something close to $100,000. One of the most touching bidding rallies involved our very own table. Unknown to us, Liz's Mom and brother pooled their resources with the goal of winning the auction item "batting practice with Minnesota Twins' catcher, Joe Mauer." They wanted so much to make this happen for Will. We were shocked as they kept answering other's bids with increasing amounts of money. They reached their limit of a whopping $3,000, but in the end the item went for $4,500 to another bidder. Will had tears streaming down his face after learning the outcome of this impassioned bidding war.

The entire evening was emotional and memorable, but mostly a cause for immense respect for people like Tracy King, mother of the other 2008 honoree Aubrey, who not only nominated Will but was a planner of the event, and Rochester native Joelle Syverson, the founder of "Humor to Fight the Tumor." These selfless people give so much to raise awareness and support for brain cancer research.

On October 27, we lent our support once again to help brain tumor research when we attended the second annual "Brains Together for a Cure" walk at the RCTC field house in Rochester. We were happy to see roughly 700 people turn out on a cool, sunny day to help raise money for brain tumor research.

Will and Dad's extended family at "Humor to Fight the Tumor" Benefit for Brain Tumor Research – the Depot Hotel, Minneapolis – September 2008

On October 28, Will had another MRI and, to our great relief, it showed no sign that the tumor had recurred.

Will and Mom's extended family at "Humor to Fight the Tumor" Benefit for Brain Tumor Research – the Depot Hotel, Minneapolis – September 2008

Will, who had decided he wanted to play on the 5th grade St. Francis boys' basketball team, played in his first game on November 8. He had several good plays on defense, but was disappointed that he did not score any points. In our mind, just the fact that he was out there and was able to play about half of the game was a testimony to his determination. He was not about to let cancer hold him back or prevent him from reaching his goals.

On November 21, it was determined that Will was lymphopenic (low lymphocyte levels), which meant that his immune system was compromised in its ability to fight infections. The doctors were especially worried about a particular type of pneumonia. We were pleased to learn that Will could take Bactrim, an antibiotic, on the weekends to, hopefully, provide enough coverage during the week to protect him from infection while waiting for his levels to increase. What amazed the doctors most was that Will's lymphocyte levels had remained relatively strong for so long, considering the effect of chemotherapy on his bone marrow.

We spent the 2008 Thanksgiving break from school with Liz's parents down in Lawrence, Kansas. On November 30, we went to the KU basketball game against Coppin State. We were fortunate that Tom Bowser, a dear family friend and great KU alumni and supporter, had obtained a block of seats for us just two rows behind the Coppin State bench on the floor. KU won the game with relative ease, but it was still fun to be present for the enthusiasm of fans and the electric feel inside the Allen Field House, especially with the rest of our family. After the game, Will and I and Grandpa Levy were granted access into the KU locker room (no girls allowed). We spent 30 minutes with the KU players, coaches and former greats like Danny Manning. The players and coaches were very gracious in spending time with Will. He received an autographed basketball from player Sheron Collins. He also got pictures with Sheron, Cole Aldrich (one of his favorite players who is from Minnesota), and Coach Bill Self. Once again, another unforgettable evening for Will and the rest of our family, this time thanks to the Jayhawks.

Will and University of Kansas Jayhawk Mascot – Allen Field House, Lawrence, Kansas – Thanksgiving 2008

With Thanksgiving behind us and Christmas approaching, Will had begun the full court press on Mom and Dad for a pool table for Christmas. Still a skeptical believer, Will evidently believed pool tables were too big for Santa Claus to pack into his sleigh, and so he wrote us the following letter:

Dear Mom and Dad,

I would really like a pool table. Some reasons that would support the pool table would be many of my friends and family like to play pool, it is interesting to watch, and it is a good game to play when your (sic) bored, Katherine and I could play against one another. We could switch off on teams. Pool is also a good game to play when you have friends over at your house; you can play this instead of video games. If we got a pool table and decided we didn't want it anymore, we could sell it on Ebay for money, we could go to Pawn America, or we could sell it at a garage sale. These are the reasons I think we should get a pool table.

Love,
Will

Already marshaling his arguments, it made me have visions of Will in law school, though he might have to pawn his pool table at Pawn America to be able to pay for it by that time. We enjoyed his letter.

It was also just before Christmas that an essay that Katherine wrote for a book about siblings of pediatric cancer patients was published. The book Day by Day by Christine Frisbee includes Katherine's essay in Chapter 5; it is entitled "Sadness and Helplessness."

Katherine, 12, Minnesota

My brother Will is a cancer survivor. He has been through a rough road, but he is healthy now, thanks to the nurses and doctors and the Mayo Clinic. That's not it, he's had cancer TWICE!

When he was sick, I always felt sad and worried about him at school. But when I was at the hospital and he was there, I knew he was in good hands. One thing I loved to do there was play in the playroom with Will. I felt tired or sometimes energetic when I would get good news.

Sometimes you feel different from the world, but most of the time I think there are always other people with the same kind of illness so you don't have to feel left out or scared because you can know that your brother or sister isn't the only one out there.

Most of the time I am scared because there's something that could always go wrong, right out of nowhere and your brother or sister could be gone forever. But Will is always here with me and I usually don't worry about it. I am confident and I don't fret but know that at this moment he is probably feeling great.

The second time my brother got sick wasn't nearly as bad as the first. It was all because his tumor was about the size of a pencil eraser. But in Kindergarten, when he first got it, it was much bigger. He also got cured much faster in 3rd grade. I feel happy about that.

In 2005, our family got to go on a Make-A-Wish trip! We went to one of the best places ... Disney World. We went over Christmas. That was the best. The weather was awesome, about summer temperature. We stayed at the best village ever. There was free ice cream and pizza whenever you wanted. The food was awesome. All of us went to every theme park. My favorite ride was the Tower of Terror.

This summer we got to go to Alaska for Hunt of a Lifetime Trip. Wow, was that amazing. In all we caught 250 lbs of fish!! There was so much to say about it.

All of this sickness made a whole new me. Now I look at

everything differently and am thankful for what I have.

I am so glad that my brother is well and I thank God for it every day

Enjoy the holiday season and take time to cherish the moments with friends and families.

She is certainly wise beyond her years with what she has endured and seen Will endure in their short lives as evidenced by this essay.

On Christmas Eve, 2008, the four of us attended Mass at 10 p.m. The darkened church was filled with heavenly Christmas music from the choir; the lights rose as Mass was about to begin. The church was resplendent in beautiful decorations and filled with the aroma of pine boughs and incense to celebrate the birth of the Christ Child!

Afterward, we came home and encouraged the kids to go to bed so that we could finish Christmas preparations. Will had been in bed about 10 minutes when all of a sudden we heard sleigh bells ringing outside, beneath his window. We all gathered in Will's room to listen to the bells. Katherine was immediately suspicious and asked, "Where's Dad?" I was standing right next to them in Will's room! It was priceless and, for just a moment, she believed too. Our thanks to our former neighbors, Kate and Monte, for coming through with sleigh bells right on cue.

After that excitement, Will called out about 10 minutes later and said, "Mom, I heard a thump on the roof and I think it might have been Santa." Ah, the magical wonder of Christmas when you have children in the house who still believe. We got to bed quite late, only after making sure that cookies were out for Santa and oatmeal for the reindeer (Will's request). In the end, a pool table did find its way to our basement just after Christmas, much to Will's great joy; he quickly lined up friends to start using it for hours on end. 2008 was drawing to a close.

Our prayer for the New Year was that Will would remain free of cancer.

Will and snowman at Faith's Lodge Retreat near Danbury,
Wisconsin – January 2009

Will and fellow pediatric cancer fighters – Hearts and Diamonds
Benefit for the Ronald McDonald House, Rochester
– February 2009

Will and his 5th Grade classmates at St. Francis School, Valentine's Day 2009

Will getting to know snakes and turkeys with Olmsted County Parks Director and friend, Tom Ryan, at Oxbow Park near Byron, Minnesota – February 200

Will getting to know snakes and turkeys with Olmsted County Parks Director and friend, Tom Ryan, at Oxbow Park near Byron, Minnesota – February 2009

Chapter 5 - Will's Third Relapse

We must embrace pain and burn it as fuel for our journey.
- Kenji Miyazawa

On January 27, 2009, we learned that Will's cancer had returned for the third time. The sensation that the walls were starting to close in became greater than ever. We put off a treatment decision for the time being while the doctors considered the best course of action.

After receiving this news, we spent the weekend of January 30– February 1 at Faith's Lodge in Danbury, Wisconsin with seven other families who have children battling cancer. It was exactly what we needed. It was best to be around people who could support us and truly understand what we'd been going through – they had walked in our shoes. We shared many tears and much laughter that weekend with our "other family." They reminded us to not give up hope for Will; the doctors had not yet exhausted all of the possible treatments. It was an honor and a privilege to share the weekend with these amazing families and children. The cancer kids continued to amaze and inspire us with their hope, faith, strength and ability to deal with adversity and to "live in the moment" – they do not know what tomorrow holds for them. Who does?

On February 7, we started off the day with the Frozen Goose 5K & 10K Walk/Run to benefit childhood cancer research at Mayo. The weather cooperated beautifully; it was 34 degrees at race time, a small miracle for Minnesota in February. Katherine, Buddy our dog, and I ran in honor and support of Will along with about 180 other participants, the largest number in the history of the event! The race generated almost $7,000 toward pediatric cancer research at Mayo.

After the run, we raced home to get Will ready for the local Ronald McDonald House benefit called "Hearts & Diamonds." He and friends Danielle, Hannah, Gustavo and Tim were asked to be greeters for the guests at the benefit. Will was fitted with a tuxedo and looked very handsome with the other kids, who were also decked out in formal attire. The evening began with photos of the kids at the Ronald McDonald House. Then a long, stretch black limo pulled up to transport the kids to Somerby Golf Club for the event. It was like a Hollywood event at Somerby: the limo pulled up to the entrance where a long, red carpet was laid out. Tom Garrett, a local radio DJ and co-host of the event, announced the arrival and introduced each child as they emerged from the limo. They got to walk the red carpet to loud applause from the audience. They spent some time meeting the assembled guests at Somerby, giving the donors a chance to get to know in person some of the special kids their donations would help. They hopped back into the limo for a stop at the McDonald's restaurant drive-thru for fries and the trip back home.

On February 10, Liz and I spent the entire afternoon meeting with Will's medical team at Mayo to discuss the best treatment option. They had decided that this new tumor was in the same area of the brain as the original one, in the frontal part of the left ventricle; that tumor had been partially removed through endoscopic surgery in 2006. Now the plan was to have Dr. Wetjen, Will's pediatric neurosurgeon, surgically remove the tumor with a more invasive procedure. He would do a craniotomy requiring a several-inch incision on the left forward part of Will's head to remove the entire tumor (only 3mm in size) and clean margins around it. He would also put in the endoscope through the incision site and look throughout the ventricles for any other problem areas. We prayed to God he wouldn't find anything further.

Will was not anxious about the surgery, but he did say that he was angry that the cancer was back and that he'd have to go through more treatment. We told him, "you have a right to be angry, Will." During the appointment with Dr. Wetjen, Will asked him what he does with the tumor once it's removed. After explaining that process, Dr. Wetjen told Will that he'd take a picture of the inside of his brain during surgery, as well as a movie of his ventricles. A big, beautiful smile appeared on Will's face: he thought this was cool as it had the potential for a great school science project.

Early on February 11, we drove Will to the hospital to check in for his surgery. The wonderful team of professionals prepped him for surgery; the people who would administer his anesthesia asked Will to choose the scent he would prefer for the gas to breathe him off to sleep – he chose root beer. Liz and I were allowed to accompany him to the operating room to say our good-byes and be with him until he was asleep, which only took moments. Liz and I walked back to the hospital room where they would bring Will after the surgery, which was expected to take several hours. We weren't back in the room 15 minutes when we were called to say that the surgeon needed to talk to us about the MRI. This totally unexpected change in plans left us dumbfounded. I had a huge gnawing pit in my stomach as Liz and I walked back for the conference.

Dr. Wetjen told us that he'd found two additional microscopic tumors in Will's other ventricle. These showed up on the MRI done that morning in preparation for surgery because triple contrast was used. This contrast was not routinely used for Will's usual 90-day scans because it is hard on the kidneys. He said that surgery was too risky to remove the tumors in both ventricles, and that he wouldn't be able to get all of them anyway. He felt that it was too much to put Will through to go ahead and remove what he could. We were completely devastated and asked that he call Dr. Wetmore and make sure she agreed with the decision not to proceed; upon learning the facts, she concurred.

After Dr. Wetjen left the room, Liz and I broke down and sobbed for quite some time and held each other tightly. Thankfully, Pastor Warren Anderson, the hospital pediatric chaplain and our good friend, came right away and spent over an hour with us. He consoled us both and we greatly appreciated his calming presence as we grappled with this devastating news. Katherine arrived before Will had come back from Recovery. We had time with her to explain what had transpired. We shared some very deep, personal time and conversation with her as well and held each other while we cried together as a family for Will. Later in the evening, we told Will what had happened during the day and that we would talk to Dr. Wetmore the next day about the new plan. He seemed to understand and accept the situation, as he had done all along this horrible journey.

With this setback, the focus shifted to a Plan B. We were in uncharted territory now. Because Will had relapsed after the standard treatment regimen, we scoured the Internet for sources and information about promising, innovative treatments. Our confidence remained in Dr. Wetmore and her unfailing dedication to patients like Will. She discussed with us the new plan of action: a chemotherapy regimen involving a new combination of drugs (Avastin and CPT11/ Irenotecan). Will would receive the first infusion right away, and then every two weeks thereafter. The side effects, mainly from CPT11, usually appear 3-4 days later so we would be watching him closely.

Will went to school on February 13 for his class Valentine's Day party. He had a good time and everyone was so glad to see him there. The class gave him a huge stuffed animal dog. They also made him a "Valentine box" in the shape of a heart with stickers and stuffed it full of cards and candy. Nothing could have made him feel better than to be back there with his friends.

Katherine also returned to school that day. When Will was in the hospital, Katherine had taken time off to be with him. She also had been given some TLC of her own: Dr. Wetmore took Katherine out for a Coke and conversation. They talked about Will, his illness, how she was feeling, and many other things. Not only is Dr. Wetmore a competent doctor for Will, but she is also a compassionate woman who realizes the impact that cancer has on an entire family. We are blessed to have Cynthia Wetmore as a physician and friend, who supports us and gives us hope.

February 19 was Will's 11th birthday. It gave us time to verbalize what we'd always thought. Liz said what she had long believed: Will was an easy-going, happy child with beautiful, large blue eyes that twinkled with mischief, and a radiant smile that would light up any room. Chaplain Warren Anderson called him a kind, "life-loving" gentle soul. On this birthday, he'd go to school, like always, and share chocolate chip cookie cakes with his class. His birthday dinner would be at his favorite restaurant, the Mongolian grill, Hu Hot. Dessert would be a Mom-baked chocolate cake with vanilla frosting. A day full of Will's favorites, and time to reflect on this wonderful child.

Will continued to tolerate the first treatment of the new chemo pretty well. Thankfully, he did not have the diarrhea or stomach cramping that the CPT11 can cause. God knows he deserved a break with as much as he has had to endure.

On February 21, we headed out to Oxbow Park and Zoo near Byron, Minnesota for Will's birthday party. Tom Ryan, the County Parks Director and one of my colleagues, offered a "private peek/behind the scenes experience" at Oxbow for Will and his friends, which turned out to be about 15 kids. Tom started the kids with learning to "hold" a rattlesnake with a special pole that kept the snake a short distance away as it shook its rattler. Next, we were taken out to a shed where the possum is caged during the winter. The possum was hissing and baring his front teeth much of the time; he even charged toward Will's friend

Caleb at one point, which got their prompt attention. There were also two turkey vultures housed in a warming hut. We were able to peek into their cage, but very slowly, as they will vomit if they are frightened or feel threatened (the kids thought this was very funny, of course).

After that, we went to another building where dead rodents are housed in freezers and used as food for the otters and other animals. While the smell was a little overpowering at first, the kids all thought that holding frozen dead mice was really cool. Then Tom had the kids glove up and head over to the otter exhibit. On the count of three, the kids hurled dead, frozen mice up, over the fence and into the exhibit, where the otters were patiently waiting for their food.

Next, some of the group headed over to the deer and elk area for feeding time. A male elk, with a heavy rack about 6-8 feet in diameter, slowly approached the fence because he knew he was going to be fed and could hear the kids putting feed into buckets. Three younger female elk followed behind the male. Once some feed was poured into the troughs, the kids were able to hand-feed the females. Elk are incredibly beautiful animals, dainty eaters and very gentle creatures as we watched them eat out of the children's hands.

After those great adventures, we came indoors for birthday cake and ice cream topped with fresh maple syrup made at Oxbow Park. Will opened his gifts. He received a NERF® Longshot and this proved to be a favorite of Tom Ryan's as well. He brought out a stuffed turkey on a cart and Will had a great time using the turkey as a moving target for NERF gun practice. (We now know a perfect gift for Mr. Ryan.) Tom and Mary Ann Ryan were gracious, loving hosts who made the experience and Will's birthday party unforgettable.

February tends to feel like the longest month during the cold Minnesota winters, and this February was no exception. The need for warmth, as well as the need for a distraction following Will's relapse, brought our family to Florida for vacation. On February 25, we headed south to Fort Myers and the Minnesota Twins spring training camp. Through the kind assistance of our friend, Chris Gade, the Twins and the Boston Red Sox both learned about Will's situation and they rolled out the red carpet for us. First, Chris arranged for tickets to a Twins game and a private tour of the spring training facility. It was surreal to see a Twins baseball stadium surrounded by swaying palm trees. The tour was capped off by a private "meet and greet" session with Twins stars Justin Morneau and Carlos Gomez. The two players could not have been more gracious. They spent at least 10 minutes with our family, posed for photos, and signed Will's baseball and baseball cards. Gomez then went into the clubhouse and brought back an autographed 8x10 black and white photo of himself, as well as an autographed baseball card from when he was with the New York Mets, as he was out of Twins cards.

An amazing moment then transpired. Justin Morneau is a very unassuming and soft-spoken man. He came out from the locker room, spent a few moments chatting with Will and then said he had something for Will and slipped back into the locker room. He returned from the clubhouse carrying a bat that he presented to Will. It was one of his bats that he used often, complete with tape around the handle, with his name burned into it, and signed, "Will, Best Wishes to you. Justin Morneau." Will's eyes (and ours) were as big as saucers as he handed over the bat to Will to keep – a "Kodak moment" if there ever was one. Will grasped the bat tightly, and never let go until we got back to our hotel later that day. Justin Morneau and Carlos Gomez were truly great ambassadors for the Twins organization. We got a private tour of the Twins offices, including meeting Bill Smith, the Twins General Manager; Dave St. Peter, President of the Twins; and John Gordon and Dan Gladden, the announcers for the Twins during spring training.

We also got a private tour of the Boston Red Sox spring training facility and a chance to privately meet and greet a few of their players, including "Big Papi" David Ortiz who leaned over and whispered to Will that he wanted him "to get better soon." We enjoyed some time picking up shells, and building sandcastles on the beaches of Sanibel Island and soaking up some badly needed sun before heading home.

Following our return, in the spring of 2009, I first became aware that a small flowering Japanese cherry tree we had planted in the back yard was suffering from some horrible disease. In several spots on the branches, the limbs were swollen grotesquely and the bark was twisted. Before the winter snow had melted and the cold spring sunshine had worked its magic greening up the trees, the suffering of this tree was painfully evident. But when the leaves and the blossoms started to come, the tree literally burst with blooms, bracketed by the elephantiasis-like spots on the branches. It's as if it knew that despite being horribly sick and disfigured, it was determined to shine anyway. It would show the world that it would rise above the limitations placed on it by this dreadful disease. I think of Will when I see that tree. His battles with cancer left him scarred, both physically and emotionally, but his smile and his enthusiasm shone through nonetheless. He never considered it would be otherwise.

Prior to our Florida trip, Will's blood counts had been low, but by March 17 they had rebounded enough that he was able to go to the PITC to receive his third round of chemo. Liz and I realized it had now been five years since Will's original cancer diagnosis. Five years of very hard work and endurance on Will's part. We were grateful that we indeed had those five years with Will, though we couldn't help but wonder what the past years would have been like if he'd never gotten this horrible disease that made us all travel down this very difficult road.

On March 19, we learned that fellow cancer fighter, Tim Bays, was in the hospital and was about to lose his battle with Burkitt's lymphoma, a very rare type of cancer. We got to know 17-year-old Tim and his family through Brighter Tomorrows; the Bays have fought Tim's illness with great courage. Knowing what he was facing, Tim's high school presented him with an Honorary Diploma, which fulfilled a dream for him and his family. Another friend of ours, Axel Johnson, who is a friend of Tim's and about his age, was also battling cancer. He had been in a hospital room just down from Tim's. Axel was well enough to take advantage of the private tutoring that is offered to patients at Saint Marys Hospital. As he was heading out to the classroom in his wheelchair, Tim's dad, Jim, greeted Axel in the hallway. Axel said, "I'm sorry." Jim responded by saying, "God has a plan for everyone and sometimes we don't know or understand what the plan will be. But you go and have the best day possible at school, Axel, and we love you." It's a testament that in the midst of their own sorrow, Tim's family could still have such empathy toward others still wrestling with their own cancer demons.

Tim passed away on March 24. Liz and I, along with our friends, the Deckers, drove to a small town in Wisconsin to attend Tim's funeral. It was a beautiful service held in the high school gymnasium, which was the only space in town large enough to hold the 700+ people who turned out to support Tim and his family. Tim loved music and, as we entered the school, we were given guitar picks with Tim's name on them. Many people spoke, including people from Mayo Clinic who had helped care for Tim. The day ended with his football teammates in their uniforms wheeling his coffin down to the football field. They took one final lap in the sunshine to give Tim the opportunity to be on the field with his teammates where he had previously found such joy. We were glad to attend in support of Tim's loving parents, Jim and Janet, and to rejoice in the fact that he was no longer in pain and free at last from cancer. Again, however, we could not help but wonder, just briefly, if a similar day would someday arrive for us with Will.

On March 19, Liz received a phone call from the school nurse, which immediately made her anxious. Will was running in gym class, tripped and fell, hitting his forehead on the wood floor. He got a "goose egg" the size of a half-dollar above his right eyebrow; he completely bent his glasses, and had a small scrape on his nose. Other than that, he was fine! The school nurse put ice on it right away and asked Will key questions to assess a head injury. Thankfully, he answered everything "right." In the absence of those symptoms, the nurse did not believe he sustained a concussion ... but a hard blow to Will's precious head, which had already seen so much trauma, was the last thing he needed.

On April 6, Will finished his fourth cycle of chemo. The following week would bring the next round of MRIs, which would tell us whether we were gaining or losing ground in the fight. On April 13, we got some good news. The MRI was stable compared to the late January scan. The existing small (3mm or less) tumor in Will's right ventricle was still visible but had not grown, and had maybe shrunk ever so slightly. The microscopic disease in his left ventricle remained unchanged. No new tumors were visible on the MRI. Dr. Wetmore told us that Will needed at least three months, or more, on these chemo agents to see if the tumors would shrink. Because he'd been on this protocol only six weeks, the plan would be to continue Avastin and CPT11 every two weeks. While we wished the tumors had shrunk, we were still hopeful that the new drug combination would have an impact. We had to learn to accept "pretty good" news: the existing tumors had not grown and they appeared to remain slow growing, and there were no additional tumors.

Doctor Wetmore told us that she would be attending a conference in Japan at which physicians and scientists from around the world would gather to discuss treatment of brain tumors. She would certainly have Will in mind as she listened to presentations and met with other experts to discover if there were any additional weapons in the arsenal to fight this vicious monster.

On April 20, Will's counts were high enough to have another cycle of Avastin and CPT11. The main side effect we saw was much more fatigue as he got more chemo into his system. His next MRI was scheduled for mid-July, but we asked if we could move it to June. If the Avastin and CPT11 were not working, we didn't want to subject Will's body to more of these harsh drugs. We also hoped that, if they weren't effective, there would be another course of treatment to offer him.

On April 29, Will received a special envelope in the mail. It was a note from an organization called "Hands of Hope" and a generous check for Will to use it as he/we wished. Started by our friend, Susie Breuer, in honor of her son, "Hands of Hope" is a group that is committed to carrying out Bryce Breuer's legacy of compassion. Bryce lost his battle with leukemia in 2007, but wanted to bring joy to other children enduring their own medical issues. Hands of Hope offers hope and support to children facing difficult challenges. Like her son, Susie Breuer is a compassionate person and incredible friend; we were so grateful for this act of kindness toward Will. We placed the money in Will's college fund in the sincere hope that he would overcome his cancer and be able to go to college someday.

On May 17, Will was blessed to once again participate in the Kid's Cup junior golf tournament fundraiser at the Links of Byron with his friend, Joey Viggiano. Despite being in the middle of a difficult regimen of chemo, Will won 1st place in his age division for the second year in a row! He was also the second leading fundraiser. Liz and I followed him on the last five holes and he made us proud. He never ceased to amaze us with his strength, determination and poise.

Not long after this, we learned that our dear friend, Shanna Decker, who was cancer-free from osteogenic sarcoma for 11 years, found a lump in her breast. She had surgery to remove the lump but would not know the precise diagnosis until the pathology report came back. The preliminary information was that it might be a rare tumor type, which is benign, but grows aggressively and doesn't respond to chemo or radiation. Shanna is yet another cancer warrior who must be forever looking over her shoulder wondering what lurks behind her in the shadows.

When June got underway, Will had his counts checked once again and they had rebounded well. Dr. Wetmore agreed, though, not to give Will an eighth cycle of chemo because of his upcoming MRI, and to give his weary body a little time to rest. Will was very glad and said, "I have better things to do than be here." Truer words were never spoken!

On June 5, we attended "Action for Axel," a fundraiser at the Kahler Hotel for Axel Johnson, our 16-year-old friend mentioned earlier, who was battling rhabdomyosarcoma. It was a tremendous success with hundreds of friends and families in attendance, generously bidding on the many silent auction items to help offset those weighty medical bills. Despite being a beautiful evening of love and support, we only wish we had met the Johnson family under very different circumstances...

Liz had a vivid dream in mid-June that Will was free of cancer and that there were no more tumors. On June 19, Will had MRIs of his spine and brain. Dr. Wetmore, knowing we would be in agony waiting until Monday, emailed us the results on Father's Day. The news was not the Father's Day gift I had been praying for. It was a mixed blessing: Will's spine remained clear of tumor, as it had been. The brain MRI showed that the two small nodules were stable, meaning no growth, but there was also no shrinkage from the seven cycles of Avastin and CPT11. Was this a win, a loss, a tie? According to Dr. Wetmore, there were still treatment options available to Will, but no clear "best option" based on concrete scientific data, which makes any decision terribly difficult. We needed to educate ourselves, to the best of our ability, and surround ourselves with the best medical team to make the most well informed decision possible, with Will's quality of life being paramount. There were treatment options out of state, with a protocol at the University of Vermont that seemed promising. But then we had to factor in other considerations, like more time away from work and the ever-present worry of paying the bills, not to mention the impact this would have on the family: Liz and Will would need to be in Vermont for treatment, and Katherine and I would need to keep things running at home. As always, no easy answers.

On June 20, Will was the unexpected recipient of a monetary gift from the Bob Buckmeier Foundation, an organization that helps local families battling cancer. Bob died in 2004 from a brain tumor. We didn't have the good fortune of ever knowing him personally, but came to know and love his wife Becky, as well as one of her sons and his precious family. Every year they have a big summer bash to raise money for the foundation, which was established to offer resources and financial assistance to families undergoing cancer treatment. We were deeply grateful for the generous gift to Will; we hope that others will support the foundation to help them continue their wonderful work.

On June 23, after a long, anguished meeting with Dr. Wetmore, we decided to stay in Rochester and continue with the same treatment (Avastin/CPT11) for two more months. We all reached the conclusion that this regimen was at least partially successful as the tumors had not grown and no new tumors had developed. We also considered adding another complementary type of treatment, and increasing the dose of CPT11 as well, to see if those measures would have any beneficial effect. There was still hope that the very tiny tumors would shrink, but this can sometimes take a number of months and would be gradual. When tumors are very small to start with, it can be difficult to determine if shrinkage has occurred. Surgery would not be a good option at this point because of the location and tiny size of the tumors, when balanced against the risks.

July 12 was the first annual Staff Appreciation Picnic, hosted by Brighter Tomorrows, for the Mayo Pediatric Hematology/Oncology staff that cares for our kids battling cancer. About 120 families and staff attended and enjoyed a few hours filled with great fun, food, and fellowship. The bond formed between families and the hematology/oncology group is very strong. In many regards, the staff has become like family. They know firsthand each medical mountain and valley, and the roller coaster of emotions the kids and families have faced along the way. Will had an especially good time at the picnic, playing baseball with the other kids starting around 3:00 p.m. and continuing in some fashion until we dragged Will off the field at 8:30 p.m., with only a short break for dinner!

On July 14, Will had a particularly memorable baseball game with his regular team, considering the effect the cancer and treatments had on his hand/eye coordination and his stamina. Even though his team came up short in the end, Will hit two singles, drove in two runs, scored a couple of runs, had a walk and even got hit by a pitch. But the *pièce de résistance* came when Will made a great catch of a high pop fly while playing second base. Liz and I held our breath as the ball arced, came down and Will positioned himself perfectly and caught it! He tried to suppress a big grin, but it shone through as he came back to the dugout!

On July 23-26, we gathered at Chula Vista Resort in Wisconsin Dells with my brother Steve, and sisters Maureen and Kathy, and their families in honor of my parents' 50th wedding anniversary. We enjoyed checking out the resort's two championship golf courses, indoor and outdoor waterparks and pools, the arcade, sand volleyball, and shuffleboard. I had spent many hours putting together a photo montage, with music, for my family; it started with my parents as newlyweds in 1959, continued with their growing family, right up to the present day. As the photos unfolded on the screen and the music from each decade of their years together lingered in the air, I took a moment to look around the room and see all the people who I was so thankful for: they had grown up with me and made me who I am today, they watched me become a father of my own, and then became strong shoulders to lean on after Will's diagnosis and the years of treatment continued. You only truly know how far you have come when you look back and see the humble beginnings from which you have come.

Grandma and Grandpa Canan's 50th wedding anniversary celebration at Wisconsin Dells, Wisconsin – Summer 2009

On August 4, 2009, we lost another brave warrior in the cancer battle, 8-year-old Jackson Schneider. Liz and Will would see Jackson and his Mom or Dad every couple of weeks on the 16th Floor of the Mayo Building. Jackson was always friendly and quick to smile and wave his hand and say "hi" to them. He liked to keep a couple of Batman action figures in his pocket to entertain himself while waiting for appointments. We learned on August 3 that Jackson was fighting for his life. He had developed a lung infection, which steadily grew worse. His lungs weren't moving air in and out as they should be, so carbon dioxide was building up in his body and causing his kidneys to shut down. Jackson had courageously fought neuroblastoma for three years and, until two weeks prior, he had been doing very well. However, his immune system was worn out from all the treatments leaving him susceptible to infections. Jackson passed away the following day in his mother's arms, surrounded by his Dad and two loving sisters.

It was difficult to have to tell Will and Katherine that yet another friend fighting cancer was gone. It was a constant reminder to Will that not all of the warriors survived this battle. It was too difficult emotionally for Will to attend Jackson's funeral as he continued to wage his own battle. Liz, Katherine, and I attended the funeral; over 300 friends and family gathered to say good-bye. The service included the reading of a poignant letter to Jackson, written by his mother MariClair, which was filled with funny stories that made us laugh and cry. Katherine was surprised about this at a funeral, but Liz told her that this was a celebration of Jackson's life and a time to remember the good times, and what made Jackson unique. Will was certainly affected by Jackson's death. After the funeral, he and Katherine both asked many questions, including how the funeral home prepares the body, among other things. It was difficult for Liz and me to try to answer these questions honestly, but we did the best we could. We didn't want to make Will fearful about death; we also didn't want to color the way he approached his life or his fight against cancer. Liz and I both certainly hoped that God spared Jackson much pain and suffering and that he slipped away into the lasting peace of heaven, free from cancer.

On August 18, Will had another routine MRI. It showed that while the original two spots of tumor were being held in check by the chemotherapy, a new third spot had arisen in the brain stem. It was torture to break the news to Will. It broke our hearts as the tears streamed down Will's face when we told him that he'd have to have more chemo. He had high hopes that he would get to stop undergoing chemotherapy if this scan looked good.

As we contemplated this latest setback, we were fortunate to read a post on the CaringBridge site of another cancer fighter, Lexie Williams. Lexie had been battling a brain tumor for several years and her mom, Alice, posted on her progress and shared this gem of a motivator.

1) Attitude is the factor in life we most control. 2) Energy and action spring from a positive attitude. 3) Winners regard a setback as a disappointment, not discouragement or despair – just disappointment. 4) The setback is not the test – the COMEBACK is. 5) Embrace life with passion and compassion. 6) Love and be loved.

"The setback is not the test – the COMEBACK is...." Just the words we needed to hear when our hopes had been dashed and we were still thrashing around looking for the right path to move forward.

Before making a final decision on what the next treatment step would be, we headed west to Liz's family's cabin in the mountains west of Colorado Springs, near Pikes Peak and the red rocks of Garden of the Gods. We gathered for some special family photos including some of Will with Katherine and his cousins at a beautiful spot overlooking these two scenic spots. The highlight of the trip might have come when Liz and Will, her Dad, and brother David were playing golf. Liz had them all loaded in the golf cart and was driving when she managed to launch Will out of the cart, causing him to land on his face. Miraculously, the only casualties were a skinned knee for Will and one very scared mother, and Will continued to play on unaffected. David told Will, "Willard" (one of his many nicknames for him), "you're the only person I know who can dive head first out of a golf cart and then play better."

Upon our return home and before the new school year got underway, Will and I got an opportunity to go camping at Forestville State Park with Mike and Ben Gustafson. Ben, who is Mike's son, is a leukemia survivor and so they get the "cancer world." We had a great time playing catch in a sunny, open field by the campsite, going for a hike along the gurgling South Branch of the Root River and skipping stones across the clear running water. We roasted huge marshmallows in our crackling campfire to make monster s'mores, listened to the coyotes howl and cows moo under a blanket of twinkling white stars before bedding down for the night, and shared a tour underground in the glistening stalactites and stalagmites of cool Mystery Cave. It was a special time away from the cancer wars, if only for one night.

Will, Katherine and their cousins Sarah Hatch, Anna and Julia Levy – Colorado Springs, Colorado – August 2009

Camping with Mike and Ben Gustafson at Forestville State Park, near Wykoff, Minnesota – August 2009

With our camping trip behind us, it was time to address treatment once again. Because the new spot that appeared on Will's MRI had not received Gamma Knife before, it was a candidate for radiation this time. On September 2, 2009, Will underwent the Gamma Knife procedure for the third time. We were with him as they breathed him to sleep for the procedure with his new-favorite anesthesia scent, "Cotton Candy;" he was calm despite the circumstances. Twenty minutes after we had left the procedure room, however, Dr. Link, who was coordinating the procedure, asked us to return to the Gamma Knife suite. Liz and I both immediately felt sick to our stomachs at the request.

For a change, there was some good news. Dr. Link wanted to treat three tiny spots: the new one on Will's brain stem, the one in the right ventricle we were previously aware of, and another new small area of tumor cells right near this existing spot. We agreed and so Will was radiated for about 90 minutes versus the 30 minutes we had originally anticipated. The procedure should have reduced the area of the tumors, the "burden," by about 75% and only one tumor, in the left ventricle, remained.

Will came out of anesthesia pretty quickly and devoured ice cream, freeze pops and pudding within an hour after the procedure! Will also asked Liz if Dr. Link had done his spine worksheet for school, and he asked us when he could get "out of this wasteland." He came home the same day as the procedure. He had some tenderness where they had to screw his head into a metal frame so it would remain perfectly still during the treatment, but felt reasonably well, enough for me to catch a few smiles from him that evening. We let Grandpa Canan know about the outcome of the procedure, but learned that Grandpa's prostate cancer, which he had been battling for about five years, had spread to one of his lymph nodes. Luckily, his bone scan was clear and he would begin hormone therapy injections to try to get a leg up in his own fight.

On September 18, we buried another soldier in the cancer wars. Axel Johnson was just 17-years-old when he lost his brave fight against rhabdomyosarcoma. His loving family was at his side as he took his last breath and "went home." While we had the privilege of knowing Axel for only about 18 months, we got to know a young man with a big smile, and courage and grace beyond measure. We had spent a wonderful weekend with him and his family at Faith's Lodge in January of 2009. His funeral was a beautiful tribute to him, and concluded with the Beatles song, "Let It Be." It was a song that Janet, his Mom, said, "just seemed right to play." When Katherine learned of Axel's death, she asked Liz, "Mom, when will our friends stop dying?" Liz had no answer or response to that question. Why should a 13-year-old have to worry about such things … or about whether her brother will follow Axel? We will never know or understand why.

The latest Gamma Knife procedure was not going to be the systemic treatment we needed to rid Will of all of the cancer cells. We discussed further options with Dr. Wetmore, realizing that this was becoming a narrowing list. We decided to enroll Will in a Sonic Hedge Hog clinical trial at St. Jude's Children's Hospital in Memphis, Tennessee. Before our departure, Liz and Will talked to his 6th grade class about what awaited him at St. Jude. They showed pictures of the hospital at St. Jude, his doctor and nurse there, the Memphis Grizzlies House where we would be staying, information about how long Will would be away, and how to contact him. The kids listened very intently and asked great questions like, "Do you have your own bed and own room to stay in at the Grizzlies House?" "Do you have a schedule to follow for your appointments?" "Do you all eat together in the House?" Then Will tossed out 100 Grand candy bars to all of his classmates and Barb Plenge, the St. Francis principal, closed with a blessing for Will. It really made us feel that school was behind him 100%, the kind of unconditional support that gave us great peace of mind.

On October 4, Liz, Will and I travelled to Memphis, and got Will enrolled in the clinical trial. One of the first steps in the process was for Will to get an MRI of his brain, and I went in the procedure room with him. He asked them to play some music while he was undergoing the scan. One of the very last songs they played was Tim McGraw's song, "Live Like You Were Dying," about a man who is diagnosed with cancer; it tells about the things on his "bucket list" he did in the days before his life came to an end. It's one of those great ironies along this journey that they played this song while my precious son lay strapped inside a huge machine that would tell us whether he would be winning his own battle with cancer; the tears came unexpectedly with my realization of the parallel and they were not quick to stop.

We really enjoyed the facilities at St. Jude's. The staff was very welcoming and more informal than Mayo. We encountered many children – big ones, small ones, tall ones, short ones, kids with hair, kids with no hair and somewhere in between – all wrestling with cancer. Because there are no ill adults treated there, St. Jude's has a different feel to it than a typical hospital. The hallways are filled with art done by the children. You might think that the art would reflect the pain felt by the children, and to some extent, it does. There was one wall that contains the children's thoughts about cancer, each poster keyed to a letter of the alphabet. Will was partial to "V is for Vomet" (sic), which described how chemo made you toss your cookies; he could certainly relate to that feeling. But much of the rest of the art was bright and hopeful; you could feel the determination of those kids to rise above the pain and come out on the other side, cured of their cancer.

The St. Jude staff has a sense of humor, we were happy to learn. During one of Will's appointments, a nurse was examining him and said, "OK, now I need to look at your privates." Will then said, "Which ones?" She responded, "Well, how many do you have?" We all laughed, a light moment that was all too rare.

Once the testing was completed, we met with Dr. Amar Gajjar, Will's oncologist at St. Jude. We reviewed Will's brain MRI with Dr. Gajjar and asked many questions about the study. The one tumor in the left ventricle remained. It may have grown slightly from the images in the MRI from June but, on different images, the tumor looked roughly the same size as it did in the MRI from August. Will would start taking the oral biologic pill for the clinical trial, and remain in Memphis for a week so he could be closely monitored. Weekly blood work and checks could be done at Mayo, but we would need to return to St. Jude's in two months, around December 1, for MRIs of the brain and spine. The MRIs had to be done at St. Jude's because it was the site for this research study.

Dr. Gajjar also explained more to us about how brain tumors function. There are four different molecular pathways of medulloblastomas. They understand two of them, Sonic Hedgehog (SHH) being one. The SHH is a neurodevelopmental pathway that usually shuts off in children early in their development. In some children, the SHH keeps signaling to replicate cells, and tumors form. Shutting down the SHH pathway, therefore, was the purpose of the clinical drug trial that Will was assigned to; it would starve the existing tumor and prevent additional tumors from forming. Dr. Gajjar indicated that the side effects of this drug therapy might be fatigue or change in the taste of food; we hoped they would be minimal and manageable.

On October 8, Will received his first dose of the clinical trial drug. He endured five blood draws and three accesses of the Ommaya reservoir on the top of his head, which meant insertion of a half-inch needle into his scalp three separate times in one day. Initially, he was very quiet and had a concerned look on his face. Will asked if they were going to put medicine into his brain today like they had done back at Sloan-Kettering in New York City. Of course, he remembered how sick he had become for about 12 hours after that. Once he was reassured that wouldn't happen this time, his look of relief was immediate. Will's bravery, once again, made us so full of pride. The long day was made easier with what awaited him at the Memphis Grizzlies House that night. Thanks to his teacher, Mrs. Pankratz, Will's entire 6th grade class had left him a voice mail. He immediately recognized all the voices of his classmates, which brought a huge smile to his face.

Just before Will and Liz returned from St. Jude, Liz received an e-mail from Heather VanKoeverden, a true friend of our family and mother of Ana, also a brain tumor patient. We've shared our stories through Brighter Tomorrows. Heather, ever the eloquent mother of a cancer fighter, wrote this:

You are walking your life journey with the disruption and inconvenience of cancer, not letting it get in your way. You do not choose this path, yet you weather it with bravery and you ooze positive energy toward us as you go ... truly teaching us how to live, how to love, how to embrace the life we have ... We are praying, fervently, for you both to have a peace that surpasses all understanding. We pray you can feel our love, our connection and our support across the miles. Through Brighter Tomorrows, you have become an extension of our family. A spirit of solidarity unites us. Your joy is ours, we share your sorrow, and we are all in God's hands. May our prayers lift you up when you feel weak, reminding you of how far you've come, of how much you've overcome already, and how tightly God holds us to His heart when we call upon Him. We pray for Tom and Katherine, and the many, many, MANY others that continue to be enlightened and touched by your life.

Beautiful words when you are in thick of the fight so far from home.

On October 15, Will saw Dr. Gajjar and was cleared to go home. Dr. Gajjar is a very kind soul; he would reassure Will with a friendly pat on the head or hand on his shoulder. He was also very attentive to detail, for which we were very thankful. St. Jude is unique, and feels like so much more than a medical center. One lady in Registration remarked to Will, "You have such a kind and calming voice." Other staff members took the time to comment on how intelligent, handsome and funny they found Will. We felt some hesitation at leaving this remarkable place, but the pull of home, friends, family and school was strong and so we returned to Rochester to pick up our old lives once again.

The arrival of Halloween coincided with Katherine's 14th birthday. Where have the years gone? Katherine dressed as an angel for Halloween; while that didn't always correlate with her behavior, it was one of those nice ironies. Will was initially undecided about whether to dress up as Michael Jackson or Ozzie Osbourne. Given that both of these guys had their hits long before he was born, we weren't quite sure where he came up with these ideas. Conveniently, however, he did possess a long, black, curly haired wig. Phy Ed teacher Mr. Arvold told Will he would have to do the Moon Walk in Gym if he was going as Michael Jackson. In the end, he went dressed as a hobo, a profession that we hoped he never decided to pursue in earnest.

On November 3, Will injured his left ankle playing dodgeball at school; he could barely put any weight on it after that. X-rays of both his left ankle and hip showed nothing of concern, which was the good news. The doctor gave him a stocking to wear for additional support and wanted him to ice the ankle frequently and stay off it as much as possible. Two days later, Will's left leg started twitching/shaking involuntarily. Will's teacher noticed it right away while Liz was still at school. Will was flushed, on the brink of tears and obviously very scared. This, in turn, frightened Liz. Dr. Wetmore made time to work Will into her schedule right away. His neurologic exam was normal. She believed the twitching/muscle spasm was related to Will favoring his left ankle and not related to the further spread of his brain tumor, as Will had feared. Once she explained this to Will, Liz could see the fear leave Will's face and body because he trusts Dr. Wetmore completely.

On November 19, Liz received the Mayo Clinic Cancer Center Distinguished Service–Patient Advocate award. It was a very humbling and moving experience for her with many staff and friends present to witness this great honor. It was well deserved in light of the great care and advocacy she has done for Will over the years.

Around this time, Will came home from school with a fever of about 100 and complained of a sore throat. His fever eventually went above 101 and so we took him to the Emergency Room. With concern running high about an outbreak of H1N1 at that time, and the disastrous effect it could have on people with compromised immune systems like Will's, they did an H1N1 test, but it ended up being negative. They did give him one dose of Tamiflu just to be safe. They also gave him an IV antibiotic to cover any other potential infections, although a test to determine if his port-a-cath had become infected also came back negative. He continued to run a fever of between 100 and 102.

At this time, Will also started to develop very painful hand, feet and neck cramping. The cramps would last up to 10 minutes and bring him to tears, which was hard for us to witness. The only comfort Liz and I could provide him was to try to keep him calm, breathing deeply and offering some light massage and a warm compress. The medical staff tested his calcium, magnesium and potassium levels to make sure they weren't out of balance; these tests also came back normal. Of course, we were concerned that these were side effects of the new drug he was taking. Complicating this further was the fact that Will also developed a cough; this would need careful monitoring. Because of all the cancer treatment he'd had, Will's lymphocytes chronically ran lower than normal. This made it harder for his body to fight bacterial or fungal infections, like pneumonia. Fortunately, the remainder of his blood counts were in normal range. It appeared that a nasty viral infection was the cause for all his symptoms. It took until Thanksgiving for Will to start feeling better, and even then his stamina was much slower to return to normal.

We returned to St. Jude's for a follow-up visit on November 30, 2009. Katherine was able to join us for this trip. It was obvious Will enjoyed having his sister at St. Jude with him. While at the hospital or at the house, Katherine would randomly scoop Will into her arms. He feigned embarrassment at this, but we think he secretly liked it; it always brought a smile to his face. When Will and I went to the MRI suite, Liz offered to show Katherine around St. Jude. She responded, "No, I want to wait and have Will do it."

The MRI results showed that while the smaller tumor in the right ventricle remained stable, the larger tumor in his left ventricle had increased in size. Thus far, the experimental treatment had not been working. It was another hard blow and it shook all of us. Will became tense and quiet when he heard the news. He undoubtedly knew what it meant. Neither Liz nor I were prepared to discuss his mortality with him. After more discussions with Dr. Gajjar, we opted to keep Will on the drug for another 30 days to see if there could still be some beneficial impact. He was tolerating the medicine relatively well (despite the cramping side effects). Sometimes it takes longer to see changes in the brain due to the need for the drug to penetrate the barrier between the bloodstream and the brain. We would return to Memphis the week after Christmas for Will to be re-scanned and then assess where to go next.

Upon our return from Memphis, I noticed that Will had immersed himself even more heavily in video games, a hobby he had always enjoyed. He had a special talent when it came to video games: master of his virtual universe, whether it be whacking a baseball out of the park or slaying Darth Vader to keep him from destroying another world. Only then did I come to realize that universe was one of the few things he had complete control over, in stark contrast to his physical world, over which he had no control. I was relieved and glad that he had something to bring him peace or at least a diversion from the cares that follow him around with this horrible disease.

On December 10, Liz shared Will's story at the Mayo All Supervisors meeting with roughly 300 people present in person or viewing the meeting remotely. Her heart was pounding in her chest and she thought her legs were going to give out right before she went up to the podium. But despite the need to pause several times to regain her composure, she made it through her thoughts and slide show of pictures about Will's journey. She received a standing ovation, which was overwhelming and so deeply gratifying because it was all about our son, Will the Warrior. She received numerous hugs and e-mails, from other Mayo employees, telling how Will's story had truly touched their lives.

The best part of her presentation was trying to describe the experience of being the parent of a child fighting cancer through the use of a short story called "Welcome to Holland," which was written in 1987 by Emily Perl Kingsley.

When you're going to have a baby, it's like planning a fabulous vacation trip to Italy. You buy a bunch of guide books and make your wonderful plans. The Coliseum. The Michelangelo David. The gondolas in Venice. You may learn some handy phrases in Italian. It's all very exciting.

After months of eager anticipation, the day finally arrives. You pack your bags and off you go. Several hours later, the plane lands. The stewardess comes in and says, "Welcome to Holland."

"Holland?!?" you say. "What do you mean Holland?? I signed up for Italy! I'm supposed to be in Italy. All my life I've dreamed of going to Italy."

94

But there's been a change in the flight plan. They've landed in Holland and there you must stay.

The important thing is that they haven't taken you to a horrible, disgusting, filthy place, full of pestilence, famine and disease. It's just a different place.

So you must go out and buy new guide books. And you must learn a whole new language. And you will meet a whole new group of people you would never have met.

It's just a different place. It's slower-paced than Italy, less flashy than Italy. But after you've been there for a while and you catch your breath, you look around ... and you begin to notice that Holland has windmills ... and Holland has tulips. Holland even has Rembrandts.

But everyone you know is busy coming and going from Italy ... and they're all bragging about what a wonderful time they had there. And for the rest of your life, you will say, "Yes, that's where I was supposed to go. That's what I had planned."

And the pain of that will never, ever, ever, ever go away ... because the loss of that dream is a very, very significant loss.

But ... if you spend your life mourning the fact that you didn't get to Italy, you may never be free to enjoy the very special, the very lovely things ... about Holland.

Mindful of our blessings and with the difficult news from St. Jude, Christmas preparations were extra special in 2009. As we decorated our Christmas tree, we had a little fun tormenting our dog, Buddy; Will placed a small Santa hat (designed as a tree ornament) on his head and took his photo. If ever a dog could look like a deer caught in the headlights, it was Buddy on that cold snowy night as we gathered in the living room around our tree.

The kids also prepared at school for Christmas. During Advent, the students participated in a short play. Will got the fortunate assignment to play the role of Jesus. Mrs. Pankratz, his teacher, was paired up with him as Mary. She told Liz on the day of the play that Will was going to be sure to tell the kids at the end, "I'm the reason you get off the next

10 days." Our son, the comic.

Christmas time also meant the arrival of the annual newsletter from Camp Sunshine in Maine. Nancy Cincotta is a social worker and the Psychosocial Director for Camp Sunshine whom we got to know during our wonderful week at camp back in 2005. Nancy's column in the 2009 newsletter captured well what makes Camp Sunshine such a unique place for kids fighting cancer and their families.

It is about the dialogue, but it is not always about the words.

There is a soul to Camp Sunshine that is not often talked about, not because it is not worthy of conversation, but rather because it is too personal, and maybe too complicated to explain, but it is understood. Perhaps it is what brings people back to Camp.

It is being a child with cancer and coming to camp, and feeling like you don't have to talk about having cancer, because everyone gets it. It is about parents talking with other parents about thoughts and feelings that they do not otherwise share. It is about the dialogue, but it is not always about words. It is really about living with a life-threatening illness, and everything that means. For family members, for volunteers, and for those who do a bit of both, it is about the willingness to participate.

It is about the willingness to become active and connected in a world in which people often pass side by side, never really allowing themselves to be close enough to feel the joy and the sorrow of those on either side of them. Camp Sunshine is about crossing the line by becoming part of a bigger community, a large extended family, something bigger than any individual, any illness.

When you are faced with a life-threatening illness, you come to understand the meaning of life in a more profound way. Camp Sunshine cultivates a climate that allows you to experience the moment, to embrace the illness journey, and to reconnect with parts of yourself that you may have lost touch with. This phenomenon happens campus wide, and is not exclusive to families. There are concentric circles forming at Camp Sunshine, and relationships growing with tremendous energy surrounding them. The circle, the complexity, the honesty, the communication, the joy, the creativity, and the caring are all part of the bigger picture.

For 25 years, Camp Sunshine has been developing the bigger picture. The picture is all about people, thousands of people, those facing illness and those who choose to join in the journey with them, everyone is giving of themselves. The base of Camp Sunshine is expanding. It is the synergy among people that is propelling Camp Sunshine forward. We cannot be more grateful for all of you who have joined the ever-growing network, regardless of which of the three yellow doors you entered.

If only we could have a little Camp Sunshine aura to carry around with us all the time, our world would be a better place.

A trip to St. Jude's on December 27 revealed that the clinical trial drug was finally working. The tumor in the right ventricle remained small and unchanged. While the larger tumor in the left ventricle grew slightly since our November visit, the rate of growth slowed quite a bit and the tumor width may have even shrunk slightly. We'd count that as a battle victory in the ongoing war. Will would continue on the drug and we would return to St. Jude's for MRIs in about 60 days.

We also discussed surgical removal of the larger lesion in Will's left ventricle. The neurosurgeons at St. Jude and Mayo (and even Memorial Sloan-Kettering) would have to weigh in on the best approach, but we learned that surgery to remove the largest tumor was a viable option. Liz and I struggled with whether it was best to have the surgery done here in Rochester or down at a hospital in Memphis affiliated with St. Jude's. In the end, our familiarity with the great care Will has always received at Mayo won out and we decided to have the surgery done in Rochester by Dr. Nick Wetjen.

Will, Dr. Steve Adamson and friend Brendan Sagers at Buena Vista Park, overlooking the Mississippi River near Alma, Wisconsin – April 2010

Chapter 6 – Will Faces a New Decade in the Battle

Oh, my friend, it's not what they take away from you that counts – it's what you do with what you have left.
– Hubert Humphrey

The surgery was scheduled for February 5, 2010. The days leading up to surgery were a predictable pattern at the Canan's. Little issues around the house became bigger issues as the stress of the impending operation bled through. Poor sleep became poorer sleep. Barb Plenge, Will's St. Francis School principal, reassured us that we were doing the right thing, telling Liz, "You are giving Will every fighting chance." What helped the most though was a Chili Feed that the County Attorney's Office hosted on January 29 to benefit our family as a show of support. 250 people attended the event at the Government Center, seven local restaurants offered a pot of their special chili recipes, and over $5,000 was raised to help offset some of the costs of Will's care that were not covered by insurance and for the costs for transportation to and from Memphis. So many people wished us well; it lifted our spirits a bit as we prepared for the operation.

February 1 was "Community Worker" theme day to kick off Catholic Schools Week. It was fitting that Will and Katherine dressed as physicians in lab coats and Will carried a purple squishy brain stress ball, all courtesy of Dr. Wetmore. On February 3, on the way to school, Liz asked Will if he had gotten any homework to work on for next week when he would be out after the surgery. He said, "Well no, I'm only going to be out two or three days!" Will, the eternal optimist, contrasted with his parents, who worried about every move in this story; Liz and I were determined not to crush or dampen his will and fighting spirit.

On operation day, we rose early in the dark and made the short trip to Saint Marys Hospital in silence, each lost in our own thoughts. Will seemed unconcerned, a trait I wished his two parents could learn. We suited up to go back into the operating room with him and gently held his hand as the operating team, with some old trusted friends, coasted him off to sleep. There were tears on the long walk back to the waiting room, fear of the unknown, complications that could lay ahead. We found Will's room in the Pediatric Intensive Care Unit and slowly visitors started making a path to our door: Father Tom Loomis from Resurrection Catholic Church, Father Tim Reker from our own parish of St. Francis of Assisi Church, and Rev. Warren Anderson, the hospital chaplain, who had been there with us through so many previous dark days with Will. Prayers for Will were offered and words of encouragement lifted us as we waited. After about three hours in surgery, Will was set free from the operating room and recovery, and eventually returned to the PICU. Dr. Wetjen was happy with the outcome; there were no unexpected complications, and nearly all of the tumor was removed. The post-operative MRI looked fine, showing no sign of tumor remaining on the scan! The operation was a success. Dr. Wetjen was also pleased at how well Will was doing post-operatively; he had some pain due to the large incision on his head, but it was well managed by Tylenol. After about an hour in his room, Will said, "I'm bored." While these are not typically the words a parent likes to hear from a child, it was music to our ears. To be free from pain enough to feel bored was a great sign.

I spent three nights with Will in the PICU and out on the General Pediatric Floor. It brought back a lot of old memories from his first days in the hospital. As I lay on the "day bed," I could hear the soft tones from an infusion pump down the hall; it sounded just like the turning letters on *Wheel of Fortune.* As I drifted off to sleep, my imagination took flight. Pat Sajak in surgical scrubs, Vanna White garbed in a pediatric nurse smock with little bears on the back and the "Wheel" set squarely in the main hallway of the PICU with our studio audience of severely ill and injured children and their parents arrayed in their rooms watching the action. In my dream, Pat told me to spin the Wheel and off we went. Vanna turned another square each time I correctly guessed a letter in synchrony with the chimes from the infusion pumps. Another spin of the wheel. Now it's time to buy a vowel. I think I can answer the riddle…. "C-U-R-E-F-O-R-C-A-N-C-E-R" it spells. Pat steps over to tell me what I have won. I have won an 11-year-old boy, slightly used, low miles, loves baseball and Star Wars, cancer free. I scream wildly as Will is delivered to me on stage, vibrant and full of life, able to run like the wind and shag the deepest fly ball, no signs of the cancer battle scars on his head. I've won the grand prize. Then I awaken and reality slowly trickles back as I move to try to find at least one somewhat soft spot on that piece of furniture pretending to be a bed.

Will was released from the hospital on February 8 to continue recuperating at home and rest up for the next step in the journey. He was just glad to get a free pass on washing his hair for a few days. We, on the other hand, wanted to clean away the trauma to his precious head. Liz and I were simply savoring the moment; we felt victorious in this war skirmish. A gift from Will's classmates and teachers awaited his arrival home: a Fathead® life-size cutout wall poster of Minnesota Twins player Justin Morneau. Will loved it and could not wait to find a special place for it on his bedroom wall.

The pool table that Will lobbied for a year ago at Christmas served him well as he recuperated. While cancer indeed robbed him of some of his athletic abilities, he was still able to hold a cue and shot a pretty good game of pool. Good enough to join a winter pool league just before his return to school. Our basement playroom was stark contrast to the pool league's venue: a bar, out in the country, complete with dim lighting, loud music, and beat up décor. It reminded me of the kind of establishments I saw as a young man in rural Wisconsin, and we felt a bit like fish out of water upon our arrival there. Will didn't care. He simply got his cue out of the case, screwed it together, and got down to business. He beat some of the other kids and was gracious in defeat. It's a good diversion through the long winter months.

On February 10, Will was up and dressed in his school uniform by 7:15 a.m., thinking he could go to school. Liz had to break it to him that he couldn't return until the following week. That was typical of Will: dedicated to his work and expecting to be back at school only five days after having major surgery. Will was able to go back to school for the last hour of school on February 12 so he could celebrate Valentine's Day with his kindergarten buddy (a tradition for the 6th graders at St. Francis) and be reunited with his friends. His classmates were standing in the hall outside the kindergarten rooms when they saw him. There were shouts of joy, high fives, and hugs as they were so excited to see him back. It warmed Liz's heart and reduced her to tears to see their reaction. Will, being Will, played it cool and just smiled and returned their high fives and hugs. Not long after this, I overheard Will talking to Matthew, one of his classmates, on the phone. Matthew was asking quite a few questions about Will's surgery and Will responded, "It was no big deal." I could only smile and shake my head in disbelief when I heard this. On February 24, Will was back at the Clinic for his usual lab work. Liz mentioned to the medical staff that he'd had major surgery about 2½ weeks prior. Upon hearing this, Will piped up, "Mom, it wasn't major surgery. A face transplant is major surgery." His perspective on what he had been through was always refreshing.

Will remained quite fatigued after the surgery, but did the best he could in school. Will's report card arrived in the first week of March. He was always a good student and had done his very best, despite missing much more class than most kids. This time, however, for the first time, I noticed several Cs. His teacher, Mrs. Pankratz, told us he was putting forth a great effort. Considering how learning is like constructing a house, however, and with all the time that Will had missed school when they were laying the foundation and adding layers to each level, grade by grade, he was missing many of the essential building blocks onto which other concepts were built. In other words, cancer was now taking its toll on Will's schoolwork. It was just another casualty in this war. So then I started to worry: if Will beats this horrible disease, will he have enough left in his brain to get into college and earn a degree that will assure him a wage on which he could support himself and his family? But then the other side of me wondered: And if he loses this battle, then how is it I'm supposed to tell him to do his homework and study hard when God will welcome him into heaven with open arms whether he has good math skills or not?

–One Step Forward, Two Steps Back

Unfortunately, we did not get to relish the victory following Will's surgery for very long. Liz and Will returned to St. Jude's on March 8-10 and, to our horror, we learned that the tumor that had been removed only one month before was already growing back in the upper area of the right ventricle. The St. Jude's drug regimen was continuing to hold the two smaller nodules in check, but given that it had failed to hold back the larger one, we would have to change his treatment regimen yet again in the desperate hope of finding something that would work. Perhaps the tissue sample of the recently removed tumor would provide clues on what drugs might work best.

Liz, Will and I met with Dr. Wetmore on March 18 to discuss the dwindling options. We were now down to two: a leukemia drug called Ara-C, not generally used on brain tumor patients, and/or topotecan. Either drug could be administered intrathecally through the Ommaya reservoir, directly into Will's head. Neither drug, however, would offer a cure; they would serve only to slow the growth of the tumors in order to give Will some more precious time. The meeting with Cynthia was harder than usual. For the first time we were told that the cancer growth is accelerating; the prognosis is grim. Why can't this child of ours catch a break? He has done everything anyone has asked him all along the way. We asked Will to leave the room so we could talk to the doctor about things that no parent wants to ever discuss: What will our son's last few months on Earth be like? What symptoms will he experience before he loses this six-year struggle? In our hearts, we'd known for more than a year that this day would arrive; when it actually happened, that knowledge didn't make the news any easier to take. We wiped away the tears and rejoined Will in the waiting area. He was immersed, as usual, in his beloved video games; he didn't ask any questions. He trusted us to know where to lead him, but it felt like we'd lost our way. Did he know where this was headed?

Anxiety ruled as another weekend dragged on. We held a belated 12th birthday party for Will on March 19. Seven 12-year-old boys descended on our house. They played NERF gun tag and shot some pool; they worked on their impressions of the teachers who made their lives "interesting;" they chattered on excitedly about the promises in store for the upcoming summer; they crowded around Will to sing "Happy Birthday" and get a good look at his new presents; they piled noisily into the car to take in the *Diary of a Wimpy Kid* movie before they all returned to their homes and families. Simple, normal things really, but so special given the challenges looming down the road for Will. Bittersweet is the only way to describe it.

I took Will to the last match in his pool league. He played a girl named McKenna and lost three of his four matches by one ball, and lost two of the three matches by the cardinal sin of hitting in the 8 ball to a different pocket than the one he called before his shot. Is it a metaphor for his life lately? He shrugged it off. All I can think of is that there will be no "next season" to apply all the lessons learned from this first year.

March 22, 2010, was my 46th birthday. In the past, Will had made me wonderful homemade birthday cards. Doing this as a pre-teen, however, lost its luster, so I got a piece of construction paper with a monochromatic drawing in pen ... but it did say "LOVE WILL" at the bottom, so that was something. He was also in rare form with his quips. Liz was wearing a new outfit in orange and black, and Will found it amusing, for some reason. "Nice outfit, Mom. It matches your personality." Not sure what mood goes with orange (Will's favorite color), but there were certainly undertones of black floating around. Will didn't explain; we could only guess.

Will received the first dose of a leukemia drug called Ara-C from Donna Betcher, his nurse practitioner, and Dr. Wetmore. Will had a very special, close relationship with Donna. They loved to tease each other back and forth while she deftly cared for him; she allowed him to call her an "old biddy," because she knew it was said with affection. She and Dr. Wetmore prepared his Ommaya reservoir, inserted a needle into Will's head to withdraw a small amount of cerebrospinal fluid, and delivered the medication before flushing the reservoir with the cerebrospinal fluid to successfully complete the procedure. Will didn't move an inch or flinch throughout. In order to curtail potential swelling, Will then also had to endure five days of prednisone, which makes every patient extremely irritable. Would all this kill those tumor cells? It would be several more weeks of sitting on pins and needles until we would know.

Will told me that his hair was starting to fall out again. The loss of his hair was really bothering him this time, perhaps because he was older and more conscious about his appearance. If only there was something we could do to make it stay...

My sister, Kathy, brother-in-law, Tom, and 5-year-old nephew Ben arrived for Easter weekend. Ben is a little fireball and his motor was always going full steam ahead. It was interesting and fun to watch his enthusiasm for so many things he is learning about; everything was new and exciting. It cut through some of the cynicism pervading the atmosphere around here.

Will had to complete a vocabulary paper for school. He asked me about the word, "hospice." I could not answer the question initially; it hit too close to home, but I don't think he sensed the huge lump welling up in my throat. Eventually, he did some searching through his materials and concluded it was "a place where old people go to die." It became my fervent hope that my young son would not get to know this word any better than that.

On April 9, we got an e-mail from Will's 6th grade teacher. She had noticed a recent marked change in Will's memory. Twice he was in the middle of something – once answering a question and once telling a brief story – and each time he could not recall the beginning of what he had been talking about and gave up. This was not like Will. What was the cause? Was it this new leukemia drug? Had the accumulation of drugs to his brain for so many years started to take their toll? Was the cancer itself starting to steal his personality? More deep breaths.

God, give us strength for the journey that still lies ahead.

On April 10, the world's most passionate fisherman, Dr. Steve Adamson, invited me and Will and his friend Brendan Sagers out on his boat to work the area below the dam in Alma, Wisconsin. He guaranteed we would come home with some big lunkers. The water was still high from the spring runoff, icy cold and roiling. We tried several areas below the dam, but the fish had other plans that day. We enjoyed the cool sunshine and the camaraderie of men and boys, freed from the cares of the world for a few hours. A large bald eagle in a slowly greening tree along the river's edge watched our fruitless efforts. At the end of the day, we drove up to Buena Vista Park on the very top of the bluff and there, laid out before us in a feast for the eyes, was the tapestry of green and blue known as the Mississippi River. We could see forever up and down the valley. A couple of snapshots to capture the moment, a stop at the Nelson Creamery to devour some tasty ice cream cones, and another day of fishing behind us. This day will be tucked away in our memories, to be hauled out again and treasured when the pain comes in the future.

On April 11, we attended a bowling event for Brighter Tomorrows families sponsored by the Rochester Optimist Club. We witnessed a group of strongly bonded kids, both survivors and siblings, who had a great time bowling, laughing and enjoying life. After bowling, the kids, including Will and Katherine, went out and saw a new movie called *Letters to God*. The movie is based on a true story about a boy who battles medulloblastoma, just like Will. It chronicles the boy's triumphs and challenges in his short lifetime, before ultimately losing his battle to cancer. I know it deeply touched all the kids who went that night as they saw their own lives up there on the screen in many ways. Will found it was "depressing" but he was glad he went to see it. He said he would go see it again with Liz and me; Katherine wasn't so sure, but did tell one of the other girls that, in all, it had been "one of the best days of her life."

Will decided that he wanted to try out for the boys' baseball majors team. He was pretty sure he wouldn't make the majors, but he wanted to give it a shot "for the experience." We rearranged his chemo treatment to accommodate the three-day tryout schedule. There was one encouraging bit of news as we geared up: when we dug out his baseball pants and cleats from last year, he was bursting out of them with growth. On the first night of tryouts, Will was surrounded by kids who were head and shoulders above his small frame. Will was assigned Number 14. The kids paired off for drills, hitting, fielding, pitching and catching fly balls. Hitting went pretty well as Will connected with about half of the pitches, although the bunts were a no-go. Infield fielding was okay; he kept most of the balls in front of him, though most of the throws to the coach at first base fell short of their target. He landed three pitches in the strike zone. I cringed inwardly when it was his turn to catch, fearing a hard pitch might strike him in the head, but he managed to grab or deflect them all. Going after the fly balls was painful to watch; the spirit was oh-so willing, but the body, battered by cancer and chemo, was weak. Despite his best efforts, he couldn't catch a single ball. At one point, his baseball cap flew off, exposing his scalp and his thinning hair. Some of the boys stared, but mercifully none of them said anything cruel. I had to remind myself that he was giving it his all in the tryouts because he wanted to – not to torture himself or me ... but in the end, I still felt tortured. In the perfect world that I envision, there would be entire baseball teams made up of kids battling cancer so that kids like Will would not be forced to try to measure up in a world of kids whose biggest challenge is getting the homework done in time for school the next day, but we don't live in a perfect world. As expected, Will was not selected for the majors team. He took that disappointing news stoically, and remarked, "Well, I still get to play on the minors team with my friends from school." That's my buddy, always looking on the bright side. It would have been tempting to add that latest disappointment to the ever-growing list of "things that will never happen," but if Will won't do it, neither will I.

A few days later, Will and I were out playing catch when he complained, for the first time, about a pain in the back of his head when he bent over. A day earlier, Mrs. Pankratz had e-mailed Liz and me concerned that Will was going all-out playing soccer on the school playground, bouncing soccer balls off his head as goalie. At the time, I didn't know what to make of Will's aggressive play, especially involving such a fragile part of his body. Was it anger at his illness? A failure to care whether or not he got hurt? Or just the pent-up energy of a Minnesota kid who had been stuck inside due to winter weather for most of the past five months? Tonight, then, I wondered if a blow to his head from playing goalie was causing this current pain. The soccer ball had hit near the forehead, yet this pain was in the back of his head. Of course, the worst scenario played through my mind: I could only worry that the tumors were already growing so rapidly that the headaches we had expected to be months or more away were already upon us. We got him to bed and kissed him goodnight. Alone in my thoughts, I wondered if this was just the beginning of more symptoms to appear in the coming days. Our scheduled Twins games and much-anticipated trip to Disneyland were still weeks away. My heart ached hoping it wasn't time yet for Will to lose the ability to enjoy these last cherished events. Will then experienced intermittent vomiting and a low-grade fever, in addition to the pain that continued in the back of his head near the base of his neck.

Later that week we met with Dr. Wetmore following an MRI. The good news: it wasn't the tumors causing Will's symptoms, but something more benign like a virus. The bad news: the tumors were continuing to grow since the previous scan in early March. Consequently, it was unclear whether the Ara-C was really helping. Will had only had two treatments thus far, so perhaps the tumors would have been even larger if he hadn't been taking this drug. We decided to give him another week's rest and hope that the flu-like symptoms would go away. The hope was that after he regained some weight and strength, we would start a different chemo regimen – topotecan delivered intrathecally through his Ommaya reservoir directly into his head. Perhaps giving the chemo intrathecally would mean greater potency and effectiveness by not having to cross the blood-brain barrier. I looked over to see Will lying quietly on the exam table as we listened to Dr. Wetmore discuss the options. He looked so very weary. His quiver of arrows to sling at the cancer was growing empty. Scylla and Charybdis came to mind, those two sea monsters from Greek mythology: if you made it past one without being eaten, the other one would get you. Why do all the choices now feel like this?

– _May_

The beginning of May brought a Boys' Night Out for Will and me. Katherine was at a volleyball tournament and Liz was sharing some time with former co-workers. We started our evening by going to Mass at St. Francis Church. Like many kids his age, Will's initial response was to grumble at my suggestion of starting our night out by going to church. At the same time, however, I got the clear sense that he knew something good came from going to Mass. On the drive there, Will and I had one of those rare moments of time alone and the right opportunity to talk on a deeper level. I told my son that I knew the struggles he was facing and I told him that I continue to pray for him every single day. I caught a glimpse of his face in the rear view mirror. Beneath the usual mask of "Nothing is bothering me" was the clear appearance of appreciation. At the recitation of the Our Father during Mass, I reached for his hand; he embraced mine willingly. It felt so small, so soft and cool. In my mind, I was transported back to those hard days after his surgery and rehab when he held my hand for support as we ambled the humming corridors at Saint Marys Hospital, the very beginning of our difficult journey. The closing song in church was "You Are Mine" by composer David Haas. The song, which first registered with me and Liz in the hard months after Will's initial diagnosis, is about God being there for us in our darkest days and embracing our pain. Without fail, the song opens the spigot of tears that cannot be held back.

I will come to you in the silence
I will lift you from all your fear
You will hear My voice
I claim you as My choice
Be still, and know I am near

I am hope for all who are hopeless
I am eyes for all who long to see
In the shadows of the night,
I will be your light
Come and rest in Me

Chorus:
Do not be afraid, I am with you
I have called you each by name
Come and follow Me

I will bring you home
I love you and you are mine

I am strength for all the despairing
Healing for the ones who dwell in shame
All the blind will see, the lame will all run free
And all will know My name

Chorus:
Do not be afraid, I am with you
I have called you each by name
Come and follow Me
I will bring you home
I love you and you are mine

I am the Word that leads all to freedom
I am the peace the world cannot give
I will call your name, embracing all your pain
Stand up, now, walk, and live

Chorus:
Do not be afraid, I am with you
I have called you each by name
Come and follow Me
I will bring you home
I love you and you are mine

Will did not seem to notice my tears, or he had come to understand that his father was just a lot more emotional at times than he used to be; he gracefully let it pass without comment. We then continued our night at Will's favorite place, the Mongolian Grill Hu Hot. Will prepared the bowls of goodies that the chefs in funny black hats and sharp utensils cooked on the large round steaming grill. The way to a little man's heart is through his stomach. As Will's dinner disappeared, the conversation flowed and I basked in the moment. We had so many exciting events to talk about, primarily the next day's first Twins game at the new Target Field in Minneapolis and our upcoming vacation in California, making sure to lay out the plans for what he wanted to do when he got there. He even took note of some of the well-fed folks in the line (they seem to find the "all you can eat" places like bees to honey). It's pretty normal conversation for a parent and a 12-year-old boy. But for this father and his son, sharing one-on-one time, hearing all of his hopes for the near future – realizing that those are all he may ever have – I took in every word that he said and held on to them tight.

May 9 was Mother's Day and I know a mother who's so very glad to have her children. After several cold wet days, the day dawned sunny and bright with a light wind. We trekked north to Minneapolis and the light rail stop at Fort Snelling to head downtown with a crush of other kids and their mothers for baseball at an outdoor park. The Minnesota Twins came to the state in 1961 and played outdoors at Metropolitan Stadium for 20 years. They then moved to an indoor stadium, the Metrodome ... also called the Homer Dome, the Sweat Box, the Thunderdome ... where they played for the next 28 years. The Metrodome made it possible to play ball on days when the Minnesota weather may have otherwise cancelled a game or, at the very least, made it miserable. But the problems with the Metrodome were too numerous to count; it was never anyone's favorite venue for the Twins. Their new home, Target Field, is a wonder! Everything wrong with the Metrodome had been considered and fixed right. For the first time, a facility had been built just for the Twins. The exterior surfaces are authentic Minnesota limestone, not concrete. The playing surface is beautiful, green grass – not spongy manufactured turf. The sightlines are great.

On Mother's Day, we were greeted at the gate by a rep from the Twins organization, and whisked inside for our first game at Target Field. We were nearly breathless with excitement and anticipation. As we entered the concourse, we saw the huge new scoreboard, the deck with the hot rocks overlooking left field, the gleaming new stands, the perfectly manicured field and it was practically overwhelming; Will was like a little kid in a very big candy store. Liz and Katherine went off to check out more of the stadium and buy some food for our lunch. Will and I settled into our seats; we smelled the grass, felt the warm sun on our faces and proceeded to watch the Twins womp the Baltimore Orioles 6-0! I couldn't stop talking about all the amazing, wonderful things that I was seeing; Will kept replying to each comment, "that's great, Dad." Later in the game, as the action slowed a bit, I told him I'd tap him on the knee every time he said, "that's great," to which he replied that every time I did that he'd slug me on the left arm. By the end of the game, Will had a big grin on his face and I'd temporarily lost all of the feeling in my left arm from being "tapped" so many times, but it made him smile, and that was worth it to me. Will was given a baseball with the façade of the new Target Field on it that would go straight to his keepsake shelf. This day would go in the record books as a good one.

On May 12, Will started on a new chemo drug, VP-16. His usual physician, Dr. Wetmore, was in Vietnam on a mission trip. Will met, instead, with Dr. Arendt. I was not present at the appointment, but that may have been just as well. Dr. Arendt told Will, point-blank, that none of the treatment options would cure him. She gave him three treatment options to choose from – four actually, as "no treatment at all" was also an option. Will accepted this news stoically. He decided that the oral chemo called VP-16 would be his choice; he would be on the agent for three weeks, with one week off before repeating the cycle. VP-16 has the consistency of oil, as well as a very strong taste; it was to be mixed into juice. That night, Will worked very hard to get it down before bedtime.

May 13 was Will's class field trip to the State Capitol in St. Paul and the Mill City Museum in Minneapolis. All St. Francis sixth graders look forward to this full-day event. Liz dropped him off at school to join his class on the bus at 7:00 a.m. At 8:15, I was getting ready to leave the house with Katherine when the phone rang. It was Mrs. Pankratz. They were half way to the Twin Cities and Will was throwing up all over the back of the bus. She didn't know what to do, and I wasn't sure what to do either. So I asked her to call me back in five minutes while we both thought it over and to see how Will was feeling. I decided I would drive up to get him after I gathered some clean clothes for him and dropped Katherine at school. Mrs. Pankratz called again. She said that Will was feeling better and that he wanted to continue on the field trip. Realizing that he would need to get cleaned up, but that the bus and the rest of the class would need to stay on schedule for their destinations, a parent chaperone said that she would stay with Will at a truck stop in Cannon Falls until I could get there. I drove as fast as the speed limit would allow to get to him. When I arrived, he was pale, but had a small smile on his face that said, "I'm ready to go." He dashed into the bathroom, got cleaned up, switched his clothes ... and off we went to Minneapolis to join the class at the museum. There was no way he wanted to miss such a special outing with his classmates. Only God knows the willpower it took him to get through the day. He slept the whole drive home, then slept until bedtime and through the night. Later that evening, I checked Will's CaringBridge site. We noticed that Will's 1st grade buddy had posted a quote: "Don't tell God how big your storm is. Tell your storm how big your God is." Faith can move mountains, and it will need to be mighty to get us through the hard times like these.

Dr. Cynthia Wetmore was going to be moving to Memphis in June to take a new position at St. Jude Medical Center. On May 18, we had our last visit with her at Mayo. This was a very emotional moment for our family; we had built quite a strong relationship with her during all the time we had shared together at Mayo. Thankfully, our relationship would continue to grow, despite the separation. At our visit, as a good-bye and thank you gift, Will presented her with a personalized, autographed copy of Mayo's new book, *Doctor Jack, the Helping Dog* featuring his good friend, Jack, the therapy dog. Will signed his picture in the back of the book and wrote her a personal note. He even drew pointers so Dr. Wetmore could remember who he was and who Jack was, which was quite endearing. She especially loved the book because it was from Will.

Will's second baseball game of the season occurred on May 19. It was a beautiful spring evening, cool and calm, a great night for baseball. The game went along as most 6th grade games do until the offense overpowered the defense and the runs piled up on both sides. At the end of regulation play, Will got a crucial hit, got on base and later scored the tying run. After a marathon three extra innings, Will's Tigers came out on top, 15-14, in a real defensive struggle. ☺

On May 23, Will participated in the Junior "Kid's Cup" golf tournament once again with best friend Joey Viggiano. Will shot a 50 on 9 holes, finishing 2nd in the 6th grade age group. He golfed very well, especially considering he was receiving chemotherapy once again. He received a nice medal and other gifts for placing second. He also was the top fundraiser, raising over $1,500 for the cause, another great accomplishment. We were also honored that our friend Whitney Harlos designed Will's logo, "Will the Warrior Canan" and it was included by the sponsors on the "Kid's Cup" t-shirts.

May 30 – A very special day. Our good friends, Chris and Marne Gade, made arrangements for us to attend a Minnesota Twins game against the Texas Rangers with their family at the new Target Field. At around 3:00 in the afternoon, a long, black stretch limousine slowly pulled into our driveway and the Gade family emerged from the back seat into the sunshine with big smiles on their faces. Into the cavernous car interior we climbed. It seated about nine people, and included a stocked bar and snacks. Our excitement continued to build as we rolled through the countryside of southern Minnesota headed for downtown Minneapolis. We emerged from the stretch limo outside Target Field and had a brief group photo opportunity before joining the crowds at the gates. Inside, more surprises awaited our families. We headed to the elevator down into the shadowed interior of the stadium to the hallowed Champion's Club. We flashed our special ID cards to the watchful guards in the paneled corridor outside the Club and slipped inside to a softly lighted restaurant. The buffet tables were laden with all types of gourmet foods, meats, fish, pastas and fruits. Will and the kids, of course, gravitated toward hot dogs and nachos. The servers hovered nearby waiting to take drink orders. We finished our sumptuous meal and strolled over a few feet to the large picture window, which gave us a private view of some of the Twins players glistening with sweat as they took batting practice in one of the covered cages. Then, after grabbing some fresh hot popcorn, peanuts, ice cream cones and fruit bars to munch on during the game, we opened a door and took all of about 50 steps to our leather-like upholstered rocking seats, three rows up directly behind home plate. It's baseball heaven. Will could just about reach out and tap catcher Joe Mauer on the shoulder as he crouched behind home plate. We snapped many photos to capture the moment. A brief rain shower in the 7th inning could have dampened the enthusiasm, but the Twins reps magically appeared to provide us with complimentary ponchos. The game flew by; the seats were so comfortable and the sights so amazing that no one wanted to leave. In the end, the Twins prevailed over the Rangers 6-3. The limo pulled up to our home after midnight. Another extraordinarily special and unforgettable day for Will and our family. We give special thanks to the Gades and to the President of the Minnesota Twins, Dave St. Peter, who made it all possible.

On June 17, a touching experience occurred after Will's baseball game that needs to be shared. Paul Halverson is the president of Rochester Youth Baseball. He had recently learned about Will trying out for the majors team and intentionally delaying the start of his chemo so he could feel better for the tryouts. He was very inspired by Will's story and contacted us. He shared with us that he receives many calls and e-mails from parents, mostly those who are upset with their kid's coaches, the condition of the field their child plays on, etc. Will's story touched him deeply and reinforced what baseball for kids is supposed to be all about. Paul and four of the players on his son's team of 11-year-olds came to the field in hopes of watching the end of Will's game. They all wanted to meet Will and presented him with one of their unique striped jerseys, complete with his name on the back and the number 7 (also Joe Mauer's number). Will was named the honorary captain of the team, and will wear this new jersey when he sits in the dugout with the players at an upcoming tournament. We're so grateful to Paul for honoring Will in this manner.

June 19, 2010 – We departed for Camp Firefly in Pine Mountain, Georgia, a leap of faith promised by former "Growing Pains" sitcom star Kirk Cameron and his wife Chelsea. Other than being told to pack a swimsuit and being given our travel instructions, we boarded the plane for Atlanta not knowing much else except that we would be joining Kirk and Chelsea, their family and six other families who were also in the fight of their lives against childhood cancers. We were met at the airport by Becca Spaeth, Chelsea's niece; we climbed on a bus for the trip south to Pine Mountain. Our little band was headed up by group leader "Smokin Jo." Outside the bus windows, a steaming, unfamiliar landscape glided by: one-story wooden houses and businesses, magnolia trees bursting in bloom, green carpets of kudzu creeping across the terrain in many places. *"Toto, I don't think we are in Minnesota anymore."* Camp Firefly is located in several villas grouped around a small pool at Calloway Gardens, an enormous 12,000-acre resort in the southern Georgia woods brimming with trees, lakes and wildlife. As we drove into the resort, Kirk and Chelsea Cameron and their entire family of six kids, along with Camp Firefly staff and volunteers, were waving and smiling, eager to meet us all. We were given the keys to a beautiful four-bedroom villa with large picture windows opening up to the woods that surrounded the resort, as well as a brand new Lexus SUV for the week; a generous donation by Lexus Corporation, which took about two seconds to get used to.

The families at camp came from Minnesota, South Dakota and North Carolina: James and Marcie, whose son Matt is battling osteogenic sarcoma in his right leg; Bob and Heather, whose son Robbie is battling a tumor in his head below his right eye; Rodney and Dare, whose daughter Emmy is battling a neuroblastoma brain tumor, to name a few. As the week unfolded, many wonderful experiences awaited. On Sunday, we were treated to a Hawaiian luau with hula dancing. We all worked on perfecting our hula dances and I got to wear a lovely grass skirt, to the delight of my family. On Monday, we got to participate in the circus under the striped big top pavilion run by Florida State University students on their summer break. The biggest thrill was a chance to try a swing on the high trapeze. I watched Will strap the big harness around his waist and start the slow climb up the ladder to the ledge where the trapeze swung. It was quite warm in the pavilion and I could see the sweat beading on his body as he hauled himself up the gently twisting rope ladder until two earnest students helped him up onto the ledge. Having just made that same climb myself, I knew that his heart must have been pounding like mine was when he reached way out to grab the trapeze and swung out over the abyss, broken, it seemed, only by a safety net far below. But Will did it. He overcame his fears and swung like it was second nature for a few seconds before gliding to a rope-assisted landing in the net below.

It was quite a week; we ate like kings and slept in late. It was everything a vacation should be, made all the more precious because of the struggles of the children and the awareness that some of them would not ultimately survive the fight. Thus, more memories were carefully stored away for those hard days ahead. Kirk and Chelsea and the staff were very kind, listening to the stories from the parents and kids of obstacles overcome and pain yet to come. They have invited us to come and stay with them if we are able to take our vacation to Disneyland in California later this year; I can only pray that Will's cancer will not advance further so that he will get that chance.

The very full week flashed by quickly. We were treated to two clogging dance troupes, a wonderful multicourse meal at the resort restaurant, golfing for the dads – though Will also got to play golf with Kirk and Matt. The moms got their own special day and were pampered royally at a salon with haircuts, highlights, brow waxes, and makeovers. They were also given jewelry, made especially for the moms by a friend of Chelsea's. The ladies' day was capped off by a genuine tea party, complete with hats, gloves, and feather boas.

On the second to the last evening, the parents were taken out for a wonderful candlelight dinner while the kids enjoyed their own special night. They started their evening with a trip to the Wild Animal Park, where giraffes and other animals came directly up to the bus, sticking their heads in for rough tongue kisses and food from the kids! As the parents finished their elegant meal, the kids burst into the dining room to surprise us, bearing beautiful gift baskets decorated with flowers, and containing personalized cards and homemade artwork. There was not a dry eye in the room when we all saw our smiling kids streaming in carrying those precious baskets.

The last night at camp, we gathered at the ski pavilion for a buffet dinner. Once dinner was cleared away, three musicians came in and gave us each a drum that we played together and created beautiful music. As evening fell, all the families then gathered in a circle, holding hands, and reflected on the best memories of the week. Camp Firefly drew to a close as we gathered together to sing the camp song, "That's What Friends Are For."

Will shows his determination on the flying trapeze at Camp Firefly near Pine Mountain, Georgia – June 2010

– Summer

Upon our return from Georgia, Will continued to entertain us. For the most part, our son remained an ocean of calm even while waging his war against cancer. He was not averse, however, from noting that his sister was wired a little differently. He told Katherine with a straight face, "Well, here you go with another mood swing." Then she'd go to another, opposite emotion and he'd say, "See? Another mood swing." We could all learn a lesson or two from Will about poise.

We also learned quite a few life lessons from our friend Sue Hruska. Earlier in the week, Sue lost her almost five-year battle with a glioblastoma brain tumor. We had hoped and prayed that she was going to be one of the very few who could beat the odds and survive this terrible disease. At Sue's funeral, we were reminded how Sue carried on each day of her life: live simply, care deeply, love endlessly, and leave the rest to God. She was one of the most positive, faithful people we've ever met, always optimistic about what the future held for her and for her family. People wanted to be around her and her smile; her infectious attitude about life will be sorely missed.

July 14 – we headed north through the rolling fields of Southern Minnesota, across Old Man River and on into the hardwood forests around Lake Wissota for the annual summer gathering at my sister Kathy's house. We'd make it a short trip this year because of Will's baseball tournament on the weekend, but we packed in a lot in just a couple of days. Because Will's blood counts were too low, he wasn't allowed to swim in the lake. But that didn't mean he couldn't enjoy a long day out on the water on Thursday soaking in the spray and the sun on the Jet Ski, and getting pulled with his cousins behind the ski boat on the tube. Will wasn't his usual self though and we soon found out why. He spiked a fever of 102 on Thursday evening; this is in the danger zone when blood counts are low. After a frantic call to Mayo Clinic, we headed off to the ER at a Mayo-affiliated hospital in Eau Claire, Wisconsin. Katherine tearfully opted to stay behind with my extended family. The ER staff took a blood sample to check Will's counts; to our relief, they were higher than expected. They gave him some IV fluids and an intravenous dose of antibiotics to knock out any harmful bacteria, and sent us packing at 2:30 a.m. back to Tom and Kathy's house. Will seemed much better the next day and was able to go out driving the Jet Ski with me. As we danced across the waves with the wind teasing our eyes, I soaked it all in, but couldn't help wondering if this would be the last time we'd get to enjoy this simple pleasure. Will handled it well at up to 40 mph before we headed back to the dock for some final shared family time over a meal and the trip back to Rochester.

July 18 – Will could barely contain himself as we rolled back into town on Friday night. He slipped into his orange and gray Tigers uniform and we headed out to the baseball field for Game 1 of the tournament. The expectations for his team were low; they struggled all season to reach a final record of 6-7. But they pulled out a win in Game 1, so back we went on Saturday. They lost Game 2 but, to our surprise, they won Game 3. Will's team was down 4-1. In the last inning, his team ended up scoring seven runs and then got three outs on the opposing team to win the game 8-4! Will had two solid plays on defense and a couple of walks that scored a run. Then he scored the winning run of the game on a bases-loaded walk to send his team to the championship game on Sunday afternoon.

The day was warm in the sun as we gathered in our places behind the dugout for the game. Will had been chosen team captain for the last game and was on the field for the coin toss. One of the coaches was gone, so I filled in as third base coach. Unfortunately, this day, the bats were mostly silent. There was one tough inning that the boys could not overcome, although Will finally managed to connect on one hit. Still, their sheer joy at their accomplishment of reaching second place in the tournament was palpable; they had beaten several stronger teams and could hold their heads high. We were so very proud of all of them: for the team as a whole, for being so kind to Will in his struggles to compete and never losing faith that he could make a contribution to the team, and for Will who had never before gotten to play on a team that reached such lofty heights in the final standings. His second place trophy received a favored place on the dresser in his room. We could only pray that there would be more baseball to cheer for next season.

July 23 – Liz and Will returned to St. Jude's in hot, sticky Memphis for another MRI scan to measure the progress in the cancer wars. We were elated to learn that the MRI showed that his tumors were stable! Will was pleased, but said to my sister-in-law Karin, who had accompanied them to Memphis, that "it would be great news if they were all gone." I so wish we could give him that news, but not losing more ground is progress after this much time in the fight. Will was to continue on VP-16 and return to St. Jude in three months for another scan and to visit Dr. Wetmore. My mother-in-law, Pat Levy, had a premonition about this trip to Memphis, telling us, "I knew we'd receive a miracle today." The gift of additional time with Will is indeed a miracle to all of us. Once again, it's worth commenting on St. Jude Medical Center;

it is a very special and unique place. You feel so welcome and part of a big, extended family the minute you walk in the doors. Liz was near the cafeteria and saw Will's nurses, Lizzie and Dori, who greeted her warmly with a "hey" and tight hugs. As Liz and Will were walking back from his MRI, they heard strains of music drifting through the air. In the area near the cafeteria, a group of young teens had decided to crank up a boom box and a bunch of kids, siblings and patients of all ages, were doing the "Cha Cha Slide" together. Liz thought to herself, "Where else but at St. Jude could this spontaneous act happen and feel so appropriate?" With warm good-byes to the staff, Liz and Will headed back home and we prepared for Will's next adventure.

On July 25, rested from his trip to Memphis, I drove Will 2½ hours to Camp Courage near Maple Lake, Minnesota, northwest of the Twin Cities. Camp Courage is designed for campers with a physical disability or visual impairment, not just kids fighting cancer. Will would get a few days to enjoy outdoor activities ranging from swimming and horseback riding to boating on the wide blue lake and crafts. Will gave me a big hug after I got him settled into his room and said good-bye. Midweek, we got a letter from Will at camp that read like this:

Hi everyone. It's Tuesday today and I am just writing this note because I'm just giving you guys an update on pretty much everything. Well first of all you probably want to know how the food is, it's great, but not as good as yours, Mom. Yesterday, we played the girls in kickball, and we kicked their butts. Today we went on a scavenger hunt, but unfortunately we lost by a hair. And, tonight they planned something special for the campers. And who knows what will come for the rest of the week. I love camp, and I love you all.

Love,
Will

P.S. I am not sure if you can write back, but if you can, do it!

By the end of camp, he'd made a tie-dye shirt and also a pillowcase listing his hopes and dreams for the future. Here's his list (including his exact spelling):

One day go fishing in the Caribean
To become a proffesional baseball player

One day be cancer free
While I am a child or teenager get a laptop
Become really good at pool/billiards
When I grow up have a son just like me, but without cancer
One day be in a movie.

Oh, to be with the genie from "Aladdin" and have him grant me three wishes so that I could make some of these dreams come true.

Several weeks previous to this, we had learned that Will was to be awarded the first-ever Rochester Youth Baseball Association (RYBA) "Player of the Year Award" for his sportsmanship and dedication to youth baseball; the ceremony would take place during the Rochester Honkers game at Mayo Field. I was on a camping trip in northern Wisconsin with friends, but was able to make it back just in time for the presentation before the game on August 1. Will was called onto the field and tossed a strike to start the game. Then he walked right past the huge "Player of the Year" trophy and started to walk off the field before they called him back and awarded him the trophy. Almost as tall as Will, and complete with spinning baseballs, the trophy was very cool. It's hard to put into words what youth baseball has meant to Will and to us. We're fortunate that they have given him the opportunity to pursue his passion.

On August 7, we began our trip east to Camp Sunshine in Casco, Maine. We flew to Boston and spent the night with Liz's brother, David, and his family before borrowing their car to head north to Maine. We jockeyed for position with all of the other motorists on the tree-lined highway corridor as we crossed first into New Hampshire and then across the tall arching bridge over the Piscataqua River into Maine. Our excitement grew as we left I-95 and headed through the rolling hills west of Portland toward Lake Sebago, onto the winding camp road until the "Camp Sunshine" sign came into view and we caught sight of the three yellow doors on the main building that symbolize Camp Sunshine.

The camp staff was waiting with open arms to help us unpack our car and move us into our room for the week, which epitomized the warm and welcoming environment. It had been five long years since we had been at Camp Sunshine. Some things had changed: the main lodge had a new second floor to provide more space for parent and teen activities and there was a new Frisbee golf course, among other things, but for the most part, it was much the same. We spent part of the day on Monday in our first session with the other parents. You could feel the shared sense of purpose, as well as sorrow, upon entering the room. Every person in that room, filled with about 40 people, had their own cancer journey and personal hell involving their battles with their child's brain tumor; they felt your pain in a way few people on earth could. When I first encountered this group of parents back in 2005, we were in such a different place in our journey. Will had not yet had any relapses. I had every reason to believe that he would be in the 80% of children diagnosed with medulloblastoma who would be cured. So I believed that, while they were all very kind, we would not be needing their help and support because we were going to be putting this tumor behind us and moving on with our lives. Now, five years, three relapses, and countless hours of surgeries and treatments later, the future did not seem quite so certain. Letting all of these empathetic people into our lives was now comforting, and so we listened as they told their stories. And painful stories they were. One family whose child had endured 38 different surgeries. In another family, three of their four children had developmental disabilities, including a child with a brain tumor, on top of which the father had just been diagnosed with colon cancer. Another family faced the imminent loss of their house because both parents had recently become unemployed and were grappling with large medical bills. You can feel sorry for yourself for just so long when you realize that your sad story is not the saddest story in the room by a long shot.

Upon our return from Camp Sunshine, Will started his third round of VP-16. It had taken about 4-5 weeks for his white blood cell count to recover enough to re-start chemo. We hated this long lapse because we felt like we weren't attacking those tumors daily, as we felt we must; but we knew this was out of our control. Will's bone marrow was "tired" from all the previous treatments, so it took a while to rebuild the blood counts. Thankfully, he had continued to feel well and did not have worrisome symptoms.

Will (at left in red shirt and blue cap) and other campers at Camp Sunshine near Casco, Maine – Summer 2010

Will, Katherine, Mom and Dad at Camp Sunshine near Casco, Maine – August 2010

Chapter 7 – Will Starts Junior High and Becomes a Teenager

Character cannot be developed in ease and quiet. Only through experience of trial and suffering can the soul be strengthened, ambition inspired, and success achieved.
– *Helen Keller*

August 31 – The first day of school for Will. He's made it to 7th grade – junior high at St. Francis. Physically set apart from the kids in the primary grades, the junior high gets a separate wing of the large school building, the kids get their own lockers, and there are more teachers with specialization for each subject. It's a new level of difficulty and, for the first time at St. Francis, I'm a little apprehensive as we drop him off for the new school year. Will did not feel he was ready for the beginning of classes, and he was worried about the workload and pace of 7th grade. We met with the teaching team the week before school to share Will's story and to discuss the help he would need to make it through the year. He had a "504" plan in place to accommodate his needs: preferential seating – close to the teacher to address the effects that cancer had on his hearing and vision – and fewer homework problems than the other students in order accommodate the loss in processing speed, as well as the fatigue, caused by the tumor and the treatments. Will always enjoyed school, but his enjoyment decreased proportionately each year as the cancer stole a little more from his brain. Now he referred to himself as "stupid." He seemed to know that he had lost a bit, like the aging process taking place about 70 years too soon, and it was just another thing about this whole damned mess that we could not control. The one saving grace here was that the kids and the teachers liked Will; I think they all learned from him – learned about grace under pressure and compassion for suffering – real life lessons that you don't always learn from textbooks. It gave Will a sense about why he was there and it helped ease the hurt just a little.

On September 10, Liz and I had the honor of attending "Axel Hour," celebrating the one-year anniversary of Axel's departure from Earth to Heaven. It was a gathering of wonderful people, all who had been touched by Axel's presence in their lives. We all gathered around on this warm, sunny day and toasted Axel at 12:13 p.m., the moment when he left us. It was an emotional day, but there was a lot of laughter and recalling fond memories of Axel; a wonderful tribute to the impact he had while he was here.

September 27 – Will signed up for fall baseball this year. It's a little different from the summer as they bring together kids from all skill levels to form teams. Will was happy to see his friend Ben Gustafson on his team. Ben is a leukemia survivor and one of the stars of the team; it was certainly heartwarming and encouraging to see that some kids get to beat cancer and shine when they step out of its shadows. Fall was in its full splendor as the kids gathered on the field at Soldier's Field Park: the maples were wearing their orange coats and there was a slight nip in the air. In the 5th inning, Will finally got his request granted: Coach Greg said that he could pitch. And what an inning it was. Will yielded a single to the first batter, but got the second batter to ground out to the second baseman. A quick flick to first base turned the double play and two runners were out in a flash. Then the frosting on the cake: Will struck out the third batter. Inning over. The small crowd gathered there rippled with applause. We fretted whether to let him pitch at all, worried that he would get a line drive hit back to the mound at his head and he would not get his mitt up in time to protect himself, but he proved us wrong, as he often had before. He came back to the dugout with a big smile plastered on his face. The warm glow from this event lasted for hours.

On October 6, we rode up to the Twin Cities with friends Chris and Marne Gade to watch Game 1 of the playoffs between the Twins and Yankees, the first playoff game ever played at Target Field. During the national anthem, they rolled a huge American flag onto the field and honored war veterans. The moment was so emotional, taking it all in and feeling so grateful to be there with our entire family, including our biggest Twins fan, Will. We enjoyed every moment of the game even though our Twins came up short.

October 9 brought the return of the annual Brains Together for a Cure (BTFAC) walk. Liz and Katherine helped set up the night before and Liz worked during the event on Saturday. The weather was warm and we had a strong turnout for the event. Liz, Katherine, Will, and I, and Will's buddy Joey Viggiano, all walked the 3+ mile course. It's always a very emotionally draining day for us. While it was so gratifying to see all of the brain tumor supporters, each year it seemed that another brain tumor friend was no longer there for the event. This year, that person was Sue Hruska. However, her husband Ed and their son participated in the event. They also presented a check for an amazing $11,111 in contributions in Sue's memory to BTFAC. All of the money raised at the event goes toward innovative brain tumor research at Mayo and we're thankful for everyone who has supported the cause.

October 14, Memphis – It's 6 a.m. Saturday morning and Liz and Will have just departed, bleary eyed, headed for the airport and it is quiet here in our room at Grizzlies House. My later flight gives me a chance to reflect on what's happened. A quick visit to St. Jude's Medical Center and we are given more sad, but not totally unexpected, results for Will. For the most part, the tumors have continued growing, particularly the one in the upper left ventricle. Dr. Wetmore recommended a new drug regimen, something called SAHA with retinoic acid/Accutane. Yet another new drug regimen is about to begin for Will once again.

There are certain images from this trip that will forever linger in my mind: getting Will to cast a faint smile next to the "Z is for Zofran" picture long enough to snap a photo; Dr. Wetmore enjoying her new freedoms here at St. Jude, exemplified by her orange cowboy boots, which would never have passed the "Dress and Decorum Committee" at Mayo Clinic; Will and I playing catch outside in the shadow of Grizzlies House with the St. Jude Children's Medical Center sign framed in the sunshine over his shoulder. The most poignant memory, however, was me telling Will, "I'm sorry about your test results" and his response, "Dad, I'm not worried about it."

Thoughts flooded my mind. Will knows he is dying and he is accepting of all that will mean. So why can't I come to grips with that knowledge as well? Will is the one in our family most like me, for better or for worse. We've shared playing pool, chess, coin collecting, and hundreds of hours of playing catch in the front yard. He is my energy conserver, turning off lights when they are not needed. He asks questions about geography and history, subjects close to my heart, which I am happy to try to answer. He knows just which of my buttons to push to piss me off. He "gets" me. How will I ever be able to go on when he is gone? I struggle to get a handle on the range of emotions this journey has sent us on: sorrow, pain, rage, euphoria. It's like being in a long train tunnel, under a mountain, far from the end of the line. Will and Liz and Katherine and I are running away from it, but the speeding train in the distance is approaching, bearing down on us, and the oncoming roar drowns out our screams; we know there will be no escape. Or it's like those old war movies where the bombs are raining down from the planes onto the warships, the ammo has run out and so we are reduced to throwing crescent wrenches to bring the planes down – an act of defiance but, at the same time, of utter futility. I didn't know whether to be enraged at what Will had lost so far, or be glad that he is actually doing better than many other brain tumor patients six and a half years out from diagnosis. The cancer is destroying him bit by bit, the cataracts caused by the blasts of radiation are stealing his sight and his ability to process information, the chemo has stripped him of his ability to hear high frequencies, the surgeries have affected his hand-eye coordination. How much more can be taken away before he has lost his humanity all together? God has a plan here, to teach us all through Will, about suffering and compassion and service to others. I see His hand in it at unexpected moments. *Don't let him suffer Lord. Give us strength to complete the journey and let Will show us the way and help us to make lasting memories in whatever time he has left to console us when You have called him home to be with You.*

– *Autumn*

Once back in Rochester, Will seemed to be tolerating the new medications well. Because Accutane dries the skin and mucus membranes very quickly, we needed to be vigilant with frequent Aquaphor applications; a nosebleed, thankfully, was not a harbinger of something bad, but most likely a side effect of the drug.

On October 22, my dear Aunt Loretta, the wife of my Dad's brother Pat, left us after a courageous, lengthy battle with breast cancer. She's a wonderful wife, mother and grandmother, so kind and generous with her love toward others. It was difficult as my Dad and I joined with Loretta's extended family in Annapolis, Maryland for her funeral and to lay her to rest. Her youngest son, Scott, gave a moving eulogy about his Mom as we said good-bye. Cancer claimed another life in my family and Will was fighting to hold onto his. How much longer could he keep the upper hand before it claimed him too?

Halloween was fun for us. Will dressed up as a young woman, thanks to Katherine! It was totally spontaneous so Katherine gave him some of her clothes, complete with a padded bra stuffed with socks and a green polka dot headband! He was a pretty convincing "girl" when the costume was complete. We joined the Viggiano kids and trick or treated around the neighborhood and enjoyed coming back and watching them count and swap candy on the floor of the great room when the evening was drawing to a close.

November. A new month: a month of transitions from warmth to cold, from light to darkness, from life to hibernation. The first week began with Will serving the 10:00 a.m. Mass at church. At first reluctant to go, but always dutiful in the end, he headed back to the sacristy to dress. I watched him from time to time throughout Mass. At one point, I caught a memorable glimpse of him. Framed in a semicircle over the shoulder of another parishioner, I could see the faint sunlight gleaming off his cassock as it reflected the glow from the stained glass windows, his eyes were turned up toward Father Reker on the sanctuary, a look of peace on his face as the notes from the choir hovered in the air around him. What thoughts was he having just then? What was he telling God? What was God telling him? And my heart became heavy as I wondered, "Is this going to be the last time I see him serving at the altar with his classmates?"

November 10 – A change in the weather is coming. Daylight savings time has ended and the dark of evening comes early now. I left work early to pick up Will from school and we headed home. Will and I went outside to play catch for a few minutes. The fleeting clouds in the west crowded in, tinged with encroaching darkness, and carried on the leading edge of the blustery wind as a storm drew closer. Another metaphor? The wind made the game a little more difficult as we dropped more balls and had to concentrate more closely. The forecast is for the arrival of a winter storm in the next day or so, which in all likelihood means the end of playing catch outside for this year – a day that always brings me sadness. Is Will going to be able to play catch outside again in the cold sunshine when spring finally comes again next year? Finally, the uncooperative weather became too much and we called it a day. I couldn't say anything about the significance of the event to Will as we head inside. What's the point in telling him about these thoughts coursing through my head?

On November 16, we celebrated a big accomplishment as Will scored a 100% on a Math quiz and was the only one in his class to receive a perfect score! With all of the collateral effects of Will's many treatments, math had become a real challenge as the junior high work became more difficult. Yeah Will!

November 23 – It's the last night for Sports Night, my weekly Tuesday visit with a dozen developmentally disabled guys run by the Park and Rec Department. I've finally persuaded Will to join us, to save him from another cold windy night stuck in the house playing too many video games. We entered the gym at the local middle school. Despite being the shortest one in the room, Will seemed to fit in right away. I chatted with some of the guys about their week as we shot baskets for a while. The music of Neil Diamond's "Sweet Caroline" filled the air as we did warm up drills. Next was a football relay – including football trivia questions for the winners, and a kick off the tee for an extra point – then a game of kickball. All these activities were right up Will's alley, and he jumped right in to participate in everything. We closed the evening with a game of keeping a beach ball hovering in the air as long as possible. I noticed him talking with some of the higher functioning guys, and observing the others. He's not been around many developmentally disabled kids in his life so I watched his reaction.

On our way to the car, I asked him if he had fun. For a moment he let his guard down and answered, "yes I did" – somewhat to my surprise. The drive home gave us a chance for a great talk. I told him that he while calls himself "stupid" because of what the cancer and the treatments have done to his thought process, the kids he met tonight have gone through their own struggles with things that he will never have to endure. He asked me if any of them are married or have children; I tell him no, none of them are married or have any children. I think there were flashes of real insight for Will tonight that there is always someone who has more challenges than you do, but yet a realization that these guys are, for the most part, happy and accepting of their lot in life. Your life is what you make of it. I hope that is the message he got.

For the second night in a row before bed, Will hauled out our old favorite Dr. Seuss book. I thought that perhaps the book had lost its magic for him as we had not read it in such a long time, but we skipped through *Gertrude McFuzz*, the bird with the "smallest plain tail ever was." Then on to Will's personal favorite, *The Big Brag*, about a rabbit and a bear that are standing on a hilltop in the forest arguing about who is the best and a worm that pops out at the end of the story and shows them that they are both fools for arguing about such a stupid thing. Will never told me why he liked that one so much. Maybe it's the message to forget posturing about who's up in life and who's down and just get busy living the best life you can; I don't know. All I do know is that when you don't expect "a blast from the past," it's just that much sweeter when it comes.

November 28 – Another good day in the journey. My Mom and Dad came over for a visit, which started with Mass at St. Francis. I got a chance to lector today, doing one of the readings from the pulpit. It gave me a great sense of calm to look out over the congregation and see my family, including my parents, assembled there for the first Sunday in Advent to reflect on where we've been and where we're going before Christmas and the commemoration of the birth of Jesus. It is not often that I get such a blessed opportunity, and it is one to be savored. I pray I've done justice to the readings. On the way home from church, I discussed with Will the turkey tetrazzini I had made with the Thanksgiving leftovers. He told me that I have a chance to become "Bobby Crocker – an even bigger star than Betty Crocker," which really made me chuckle. If he only knew just how limited my cooking skills truly were. My Mom had brought some old photos of our family, and Will sat with us a bit as we shared the pictures and discussed our ancestors. Unlike in the past, he now took a real interest in the photos; he listened carefully as Grandma explained who these persons are and how Will is related to them. We decided that I look a lot like Grandpa McLaughlin in his proud graduation photo, and that Will looks a lot like me in those photos from the old days at Holy Name of Jesus Grade School in Kimberly. With the photos sorted, Will and Dad and I headed off to a local sports bar to catch the last half of the Green Bay Packers game since they are blacked out when the Minnesota Vikings play at the same time. To be with two guys I love so much, sharing our passion for the Packers, in an unfamiliar place is special. Unfortunately, the Packers defense was not up to task of subduing the Atlanta Falcons … "but there is always next week." Once home, Will and Dad took up residence down in the basement at the pool table. Dad has not played pool with any regularity for over 50 years, but Will has drawn the old skills out of their dusty dungeon and the two of them go at it with gusto. I come down to watch briefly, but Will tells me I'm not welcome (it's a moment for he and Grandpa to share, which is OK with me) and there are whoops and guffaws rising up the stairs from the basement into the kitchen that suggest the intensity of the match. Dad wins two, but Will pulls out the last game in a squeaker after some errors by Grandpa. The day ends with Will hauling out Dr. Seuss again. We cuddle up together on our bed as he makes his way in his halting adolescent rough voice through *How the Grinch Stole Christmas* and *Yertle the Turtle*. In former days, I often had to beg to let me read to him before bedtime; now he comes to me with Dr. Seuss twice in one week? What small kindness have I done to deserve this honor?

On December 1, Liz and Will had an appointment with one of the Mayo neuropsychologists, who will work with him to develop other strategies for memorizing and studying for tests. She will also develop recommendations for the teachers to use in support of Will's learning. Several days before a test, she will observe him studying and offer suggestions. Finally, Will is going to get some occupational therapy to help him with typing skills. The visit was very helpful. Our ultimate goal was to provide the most supportive learning environment for Will to succeed. We continued to be amazed with his determination to work hard in school. He was also starting to truly participate in his care and was not afraid to ask questions of the doctors and nurses, another sign of his growing maturity.

On December 5, we piled into the van for our annual trek down to Whiting's Nursery to get our Christmas tree. The kids enjoy the Whiting's Yellow Lab dog and warming up with cider and cookies afterward to shake off the cold collected during the tree selection process. As we searched for the perfect tree, Liz asked Will which one he liked. He quickly responded, "I don't care. I only come for the cider and cookies!" We all laughed at that, including the sales person. Will's always ready with a quip at unexpected moments. The perfect tree turned out to be a beautiful 8-foot Fraser Fir that smelled wonderful once we got it set up inside our house.

On December 16, Liz and Will had a follow-up appointment with Occupational Therapy to learn more about adaptive technologies that might be helpful. The appointment was in the Rehabilitation Unit at Saint Marys Hospital, where Will had spent a year of inpatient and outpatient time in 2004-05 regaining strength and use of his left arm and leg. Although they had not been back there for over five years, all of the memories of his time there came flooding back when they walked through the door. A number of staff immediately recognized Will and called him by name; several came over to talk to him as they waited for the appointment. We will always remember and appreciate the caring and wonderful staff in Rehab who helped Will so much. Will got to experiment with different programs, such as Dragon (voice recognition software) and Word Queue 2, that could help him with typing and writing. He took a typing test and scored 10 words/minute. With practice, he may be able to increase his speed, but the occupational therapist did say he had very good form and knew where the letters were located on the keyboard. The therapist was also very helpful in educating Will and Liz about other online resources, as well as a community resource center, where you can check out and try different adaptive technologies. It's information we wish we had learned much earlier in Will's journey.

December 18-19 – I started the day at the morning graduation ceremony at my *alma mater*, the University of Wisconsin–Eau Claire. I've served five years as a representative on the Alumni Board, giving them feedback from alums about the university. Though I've enjoyed my time on the Board, my term is winding down. I'm there to "pin" the new graduates for the Alumni Association, which in these enlightened times has morphed from an actual pin into a license plate surround embossed with "Alumni, University of Wisconsin–Eau Claire." I had forgotten the significance of my own graduation day from so long ago. The smiling faces of the graduates in their caps and gowns and the beaming faces of the parents who recognize the struggles that brought their son or daughter to that day refreshed my memory. I watched the graduates float down the ramp from the platform, squeeze the hands of the Chancellor and professors as they were met with a big "congratulations," and then watched most of them move back to their seats on autopilot as they began to grasp what they'd just experienced. As I listened to the commencement speeches, I was struck most by the student speaker, a young woman from Wisconsin. She used the analogy that the experience of the students is much like the "Game of Life," the board game we all played as kids. Start the game, decide whether to go to college or choose a career. Pick out a car, get married, have children, buy a house, spin the wheel to see if you will move forward or back, keep going until you retire and the player with the most money at the end wins. She urged them to make their choices wisely. After I returned to Rochester that afternoon, I encouraged Will to play a game with me; somehow, it's poetic that we decided to play the "Game of Life." In our game, Will gets the whole deal: he gets to choose a career, get married, have children (he gets three girls, so good luck for him ever getting into the bathroom at his house in his virtual world), buy a house. He makes it to retirement and has amassed enough money to win at the "Game of Life." Is he going to get the same kinds of chances in the real world? In the game, everyone gets to retire eventually, even if they don't have enough money to win. In the real world, can I give him some of my Life tiles in an effort to buy him some more "Life"? Make life imitate art? Wish I could.

On the way home from Sunday Mass, Will asked about the meaning of the phrase "begotten, not made" from one of the prayers. That's a real head-scratcher. His memory and concentration may not be what it used to be, but what a thought-provoking question. "Begotten" means to share your nature with someone else, according to wiser minds than mine. So when it says that Jesus was "begotten, not made" I told him that I guess it means that God did not just make Jesus, He saw to it that Jesus shared His very nature. I imagine that many parents hope they share this attribute with their children. I see some of me in Will – his budding interest in civics and coins, his dedication to hard work and loyalty – and maybe some of the things I'm not so proud of, like having a quick temper at times. I hope that Will was really "begotten" and not just made when someone is thinking about what his life has become.

He also asked about who made God. Another tough one, which mere mortals may only guess at. I tell him I don't know, but I wonder if someday he is going to get the chance to ask God himself. He will be so much wiser than I. Later that Sunday, Liz and I went to the Christmas concert of the Rochester Bella Voce young women's choir. The church was glistening in the late afternoon as light waned and evening approached. We were taken on a magical journey as the lips of the young women opened; we grabbed hold as the notes began to soar in the darkening sanctuary. The voices spiraled up and down and around in such perfect pirouettes of harmony that it brought some of those in attendance to tears. Will wasn't present, but I wished he was there to share in the moment. We need beauty such as this to light a candle and curse the long days of approaching winter darkness.

December 24 – Christmas Eve, another snowy day in the winter wonderland known as Minnesota. The day started with yet another round of clearing snow out of the driveway; there's so much now it's getting hard to figure out just where to throw it. My big task for the early part of the day is to help another soul embarking on a cancer journey, Mariah Ackerman. She had just learned that she has cancer, although exactly what type and how extensive remained to be seen. Mariah worked as the backup to my legal assistant at work. Everyone at my office has missed her and most have chipped in some money for restaurant meals to help feed her family. I know from our experience with Will just how helpful it is, after a long day at the hospital, to come home to a warm meal that someone else has lovingly prepared. Some 35 coworkers of Mariah have contributed cash to this "dinner fund," but I rethink how to present it on my drive to the nearby small town of Kasson. I pulled over to count just how much money we had raised: $364.00. It's obvious that my original plan to get her a gift certificate for one restaurant is not too wise, so I tore around in the late morning and early afternoon of Christmas Eve trying to spend the bounty wisely – gift certificates for a little Chinese food here, some home-style American there, topped off with some grocery and gas cards. Finally, the money is spent, the gift cards are gathered together, and I pulled up at her modest home. Her young son, Logan, came to the door to meet me and let me in. It's hard to know what to say in situations like this, except that we've been down this road and we know how hard it is, so the gifts I bear do all the talking. My envelope contains the concern of 35 coworkers who want desperately to help somehow. Mariah's eyes filled with tears and she wrapped me in a big hug as I handed over the envelope. What other gift could be better on Christmas Eve than something from the heart? I drove back home in silence wondering what the future holds in store for Mariah and her family.

Back at our house, the kids were bored – so it's time to haul out some of the old home movies. I chose one from late 1997 and early 1998, a good era when Katherine is approaching 2-years-old and Liz is pregnant with Will. It's odd for a few moments to be transported back in time. Katherine is back in the matched outfits from Gymboree, a bit unsteady on her feet, as she had just learned to walk not long before. Her hair is much blonder, her voice a little squeaky as she searches for a word. In the movie, we are visiting Cheyenne Mountain Zoo where we feed the giraffes; they extend their long scaly tongues to wrest the giraffe biscuits from our daughter's tiny grasp. Katherine makes the interesting observation that "you and Mom seemed happier then" and it's obvious that she's right. Liz smiles often as the movie chronicles her pregnancy and Will's birth in February 2008. I captured Will's birth in the delivery room, a little too graphic. Katherine turned away from the blood and the gore; Will, on the other hand, sat mesmerized watching the screen, scarcely believing that this little, bluish, slimy thing coming from Mom is him, getting his start on life. The film shows Will as he takes his first breath and cries softly as he's wrapped in a receiving blanket and handed to Mom to hold. You can't help but look back at that time and wonder if there is another "thread of life" we could have followed from that point, a life line that would have meant a "normal" childhood untouched by cancer. I'm sure Will wonders the same thing.

After a dinner of fondue, we gather at church for Christmas Eve Mass. The church is aglow in candles and boughs of pine and red bows. Will looked sharp in his red striped zippered sweater and khaki pants. The story of the birth of Christ is read from the Gospel of Luke, the one that always takes me back to Linus stepping into the spotlight on the stage in *Charlie Brown Christmas* and telling the other kids the real story about Christmas before it got run by some "big eastern syndicate." The priest speaks about Secret Santas, and how the coming of God and the gifts he brings are like the best Secret Santa ever. The choir plays all the old Christmas favorites; Christmas Eve is one of those nights when the congregation seems to sing with gusto. I looked down the pew a couple of times and both of the kids were singing, a rare event, so maybe they were caught up in the moment as well. So ordinary and yet so special, and over much too quickly. Home to check the Santa tracker (it was a little more magical when the kids did not know who was chowing down on the milk and cookies every year). According to NORAD, Santa seemed to be caught in a holding pattern somewhere over Newfoundland so if he was going to get to our house – and everywhere else on Earth – tonight, he'd better step on it. Before tucking Will into bed, I wished I could wrap up a cure and hide it under the tree...

– The New Year

January 14, 2011 – We ventured back to Memphis for another set of MRIs to see where we stood. After the MRI was done, but before we got the results, we had the opportunity to tour Sun Studios in downtown Memphis. We got the VIP treatment, thanks to Katie, a niece of a Camp Sunshine family, and her husband, Chris, a co-owner of Sun Studios. In the main recording studio, Will got to strum a guitar once used by Elvis Presley and sing into a microphone once used by the King of

Will, Joey and Gracie Viggiano dressed for trick or Treating – Halloween 2010

The Canan family picking out the Christmas tree at Whiting's Nursery, Rochester – December 2010

CHRISTMAS 2010

Rock and Roll, which was a thrill. Katie and Chris were the paragon of kind southern hospitality and we were very grateful for it.

The next day we met with Dr. Wetmore to review the scan and see if the drug SAHA was working. I had high hopes because Will seemed to be feeling so well, but I could tell from her welcome hugs that things were not good. The tumors had nearly tripled in size since October and the spreading dark mass in the middle of the left ventricle looked vaguely like a black hole on the MRI, pulling in healthy light-colored cells from the area around it. Liz and I took the news hard; we had hoped and prayed for a different result. We discussed some options for treatment, intrathecal topotecan through his Ommaya reservoir being a last ditch attempt at palliative care to try to slow the tumor. Dr. Wetmore gave us a few minutes alone to digest the news. Before leaving though, she told us, "Will, if anyone deserves a miracle, it is you."

Will asked point-blank if he was going to die and I told him yes, if we could not get the tumor growth to stop. He cried briefly, which was uncharacteristic for him, and then was silent. Liz told him that we all have to die someday and I told him how proud I was of him for how he carried himself through this fight. The words seemed to register as he pursed his lips, but he said nothing. I had always pictured that when this moment finally came I would have my thoughts well rehearsed and that Father Tom Loomis would be by our side to explain how God had different plans for Will and that he was going to get to heaven before we were. But words seemed totally inadequate at this moment. How we carry on from a hard day like today, God only knows. We snapped back to reality as we needed to dash to the airport to return home. Then one final bit of irony. Just inside the front door of the Memphis airport is a large, gleaming sign. It is a photo of nine smiling, partially bald, children from St. Jude's with the caption, "No child should ever die in the dawn of life," which is a quote from founder Danny Thomas. I glanced over at Will as he walked beside me and he winced as he walked by the sign. *God, my child is still in the dawn of his life! Why can't you send a miracle to the folks at St. Jude so he doesn't have to die, too?*

As I sat on the plane that day for the very long trip back home, I got thinking about how you parent a child who is dying. All of the normal frames of reference no longer apply. It's a little like that Tug McGraw song, "Live Like You Were Dying." Does Will need to go to bed on time? So what if he doesn't? It won't kill him. Does he need to wear a hat and mittens in the bitter Minnesota winter to keep from catching cold? Why? He's already dying, so it can't really hurt him. Does he need to do his schoolwork? He's not going to get to finish school, so it doesn't really matter, does it? That YMCA membership I offered to get him to build up his strength? The rest of his body could be Olympic body builder strong, but if we can't stop that tumor from growing, it makes no difference to build him up. Doing chores around the house? Well, if those responsibilities were meant to train him for the future, why make him take on jobs when his time on Earth will be so brief? The only thing that would seem to still matter would be to make some lasting memories with us and prepare him to meet God in heaven, since that is where he is surely headed. I could only pray: *When the time comes God, please don't let him suffer, take him quickly with a sign to us so that we know he is safely in your hands. Forgive his sins, few though they may be in comparison to mine with so many more years to err. Ease his sadness and let him know that he will always remain in the thoughts and prayers of his dear family. Let him find a way to continue to inspire us and others in the years ahead with his quiet strength in the face of years of adversity. And keep him in your loving care until we can join him in your time.*

Upon our return home, it was a struggle to continue on as before. Katherine took the news hard. She found solace with her friends and through Facebook. Despite the bad news, Will forged ahead. If no one told you, others would never know that inside his head he's fighting this terrible disease. It was important to us to remind his friends and classmates not to be afraid of Will, but to continue to embrace him and continue to be his friend, invite him over to play, or go to a movie. Will just wanted to maintain his normal routine. At the same time, he couldn't seem to help himself from the cynical observation, "I like the smell of BS in the morning." I don't know exactly what BS smells like, but there has been plenty of BS throughout this entire ordeal.

January 19, 2011 – The torrent of alternative treatments came pouring in this day as we met with Dr. Khan, a kind oncologist at Mayo who was ready to step in and help us all find our way. We talked about the long journey and how we are lucky that Will has not suffered severe deficits in ways that many other brain tumor patients have; yet, with teary eyes, we have to linger for a moment on the fact that we are going to run out of time before we are ready. We talk about hospice care and the advantages of being able to have meds delivered at home; it's clear that hospice isn't what it used to be. Dr. Khan suggests oral administration of the topotecan as a gentler alternative than administration through Will's Ommaya reservoir and promises to follow up on other possible modalities. We have now arrived in uncharted territory. It really feels like some kind of 19th century carnival midway show: "Step right up, sir, come! Take my bottles of medicinal elixirs! They'll fix you right up and have you feeling better in no time. And don't pay any attention to my competitor over there promising you a cure! He doesn't know what he is talking about!" You want to be able to walk up to the chemo carnival barker and look him in the eye and say, "Where's your proof that your mixture is going to work better than that Acme Medical Guy's stuff?" And of course, because we are beyond established medical protocols, the barker has nothing firm to offer. "Well I had one kid who looked a little better for a little while…" You look farther down the line of hucksters and the testimonials are, for the most part, just as thin. You might have better luck picking a winning lottery ticket … but at least we have Dr. Wetmore telling us what numbers to pick ... right?

January 21 – We headed up to St. Paul for the Rascal Flatts concert. The country band is a personal favorite of Will's; even Katherine, the rap lover in the family, likes them. The anticipation was building as we descended from the street level down to the darkened floor of the Xcel Energy Center through the hum of the crowd waiting for the opening act. As the result of a random drawing, we had the opportunity for a little pre-concert backstage meeting with the band. We were ushered, along with several other people, into the press conference room where we got to meet each of the guys in the band and had our pictures taken with them. They were very nice, greeted us with handshakes and hugs and commented specifically on the concert T-shirts that Katherine had made for herself and for Will. Then it was off to our seats in the nosebleed section in the back for the concert. As the opening act was finishing up, luck would have it that one of the ushers dropped by with three seats right down on the floor of the arena only about 100 feet from the stage. The band was great! I'm not a longtime Rascal Flatts fan, but they played all of their old favorites including, "God Bless the Broken Road." The fans gently waved glowsticks during the song for an ABC-TV special. They even did excellent covers of some Eagles, Journey and Boston songs, among others, for rock dinosaurs like me. Will smiled several times during the evening and seemed to be having a very good time; if only for awhile, the clouds of despair lifted from around him. The band did not play "(Skin) Sarabeth." This is a song about the girl with cancer who loses her hair and fears she will not go to the prom, but her date shaves his head so they can go to the dance together, bald. It would have been awesome if they had also played that song, but it was a satisfying evening that lifted all of our spirits, which we needed so desperately.

On January 23, we gathered at Dr. Jack's house with Marcia and Gary to watch the NFC Championship game between the Green Bay Packers and the Chicago Bears. Despite playing poorly on offense, the Packers did find a way to win. My thoughts turned to wondering if we can somehow make a trip to the Super Bowl in Dallas with Will a reality so that we can watch our beloved Packers play the Pittsburgh Steelers for the world championship.

January 26, 2011 – The e-mails between Memphis and Rochester fly fast and furious this week as we debate every option for Will's care.

Dr. Boop, a surgeon at Le Bonheur Hospital in Memphis who provides pediatric brain tumor surgery for St. Jude's patients, has weighed in at Dr. Wetmore's request. He has decided that the formerly impossible was now possible, namely that he did think it was possible to operate on Will to remove most of his tumors and give him a fighting chance to survive. He did it knowing in part how well Will is feeling and has performed neurologically, and on the condition that Dr. Wetmore has something in her arsenal to follow up with after the surgery. Based on what happened last time, everyone is eminently aware that the tumors are likely to come roaring back after they have been removed. Dr. Boop surely wields amazing power: One moment, Will, surely doomed to a slow and painful death in the near future, is redeemed and given, if not a cure, a brand new lease on life and the hope of at least another year or two to pray for another treatment option to become available to continue the fight. In large part, Will made the "cut" because of how he has fought so far. If he had been just a little sicker or a little more impaired in his functioning, Dr. Boop could have opted to not perform the operation, which would surely doom him to an earlier death. It's really the ability to play God here on Earth if only for a short time.

Mayo seemed to be in catch-up mode once they heard about the game plan being offered by St. Jude's. We met with Dr. Wetjen, the young Mayo surgeon who operated on Will in February 2010, who now also thinks it is possible to operate. The screen with the menacing MRI image of the large tumor in Will's left ventricle loomed over the doctor's left shoulder as he spoke with us. He discussed the potential advantages and disadvantages of entering the brain in one location versus two different incision sites. There are the usual risks and complications of surgery, and one incision would obviously be less invasive, but Dr. Wetjen felt that if he used the two-incision approach he could follow existing pathways into the brain, which would likely have fewer side effects. We'd follow up with intrathecal topotecan … and then wait and see, as we always have, whether the tumor is smart enough to cloak itself in a different guise and attack again. In the end, Dr. Wetmore's strong sense that the complexity of this operation and the greater experience of Dr. Boop weighed out over the local support that Dr. Wetjen and his staff could offer. The surgery is set in Memphis for February 10 with a pre-surgery consult the day before.

I also receive my own good news. I'd been troubled for several weeks by a new bump in my mouth; of course, I assumed it was cancer. Dr.

Tom Salinas in the Mayo Dental Department assures me that it is, in fact, nothing to worry about. I can breathe again and maybe even sleep again for a couple of weeks as we have been given another opportunity for Will to fight on.

On January 29, what seemed only a distant dream of going to the Super Bowl became a reality. It started when Will mentioned his dream to his friend Ryan Pardi. Ryan then told his Mom, Elaine, that Will wanted to go to the Super Bowl. "Well, then," she said, "no matter what, we have to make that happen." Over a span of a mere six days, Elaine started making phone calls and sending e-mails; soon an entire community of friends, family, colleagues, and complete strangers had come together with unbelievable and unwavering generosity to provide for Will and me to attend the Super Bowl on February 6, 2011! For two of the world's biggest Packer fans, it is the best father/son experience one could ever imagine. Will was thrilled when he found out! Our realization to what had been accomplished began when Will received a new Aaron Rogers (#12) jersey to wear, a gift from friend Kathy Holets and her family. During homeroom at school, the St. Francis students are encouraged to share any important news in their lives. In homeroom on January 31, Will was the first student to raise his hand, because he simply couldn't contain his joy any longer. "My mom told me not to brag or anything," Will told his classmates, "but I can't keep it a secret anymore. I'm going to the Super Bowl!" Will's classmates then threw a "pre-Super Bowl" party, complete with green and gold Green Bay Packer cupcakes (thanks to Liz's capable administrative assistant Scarlet). Mike Kesler, the head football coach at Lourdes High School, helped to acquire the tickets for the big game and handed them over to Will at the celebration. A local TV station, KAAL, and the newspaper covered the event. The good news got even better when we learned that they had secured two extra tickets and so our good friends and rabid Packer fans, Gary and Marcia Fritzmeier, would be able to join us for the festivities in Dallas. The special people who made this dream possible for Will included Elaine Pardi, Chris and Marne Gade, Greg Anthony, Mark Hayward, Barb Plenge, among others. Mere words are wholly inadequate to express the deep gratitude on behalf of our family to all who made this happen. Miracles really do happen, sometimes when you least expect them.

–My Super Bowl Diary

February 4, 2011 – It's quiet here at the hotel in Dallas. Will is breathing softly in his sleep. The city lights on the horizon are winking out as dawn breaks on the North Texas plains. Yesterday was a long day that started at 5 a.m. to catch an early flight from Minneapolis. The roads in Dallas were snow covered and icy on our arrival, with nary a snow plow in sight, which made me appreciate the efficient job our Public Works crews do in Minnesota. Gary and Marcia arrived after a difficult 18-hour journey from Rochester; it brightened Will's face to see good friends so far from home. You could feel the city's excitement build as the hotel and restaurants grew crowded with Packer fans. Today we have tickets to the "NFL Experience" at the Dallas Convention Center where we hope to get autographs from an NFL player or two and revel in the Super Bowl pre-game circus. Greg Anthony, a friend of ours, knows Lee Weyers, the Packers treasurer, who is down here for the game and is seeing if he can make something special happen for Will. Two simple objects caught my attention this morning as I prepared for our big day. The first was the battered envelope peeking out of my coat pocket. Labeled, "Will's Money," it contains the precious dollars plucked from the little safe in his bedroom closet that he has brought to purchase Packer memorabilia for the many people, young and old, who made this trip possible. The other is Will's pill container. Will was a boy when this journey started, too young to have to worry about needing one of those tools you associate with the elderly; but now, nearly seven years on, his pill container is well worn, the letters for the days wearing away – a small symbol of the struggle, yet a sign of continued life when it is opened every day. I hope the day brings unexpected gifts. More thoughts tomorrow.

February 5, 2011 – We had a good day today, Saturday. The sun came out and melted the ice off the roads and it felt like spring was in the air. We met up with Gary and Marcia and Randy Ziegler, a retired Mayo photographer now resident Texan, who would chronicle the day. On our arrival at the Dallas Convention Center, we met Larry Weyers, a member of the Packer Board of Directors, who gave us a personal tour through the NFL Experience, a multimedia carnival for fans. Will enjoyed the Wii football game and shocked Larry with his accuracy for hitting his receivers darting down the field. Having watched Will carve me up as a batter from the virtual pitcher's mound back home, his video expertise did not surprise me at all. We wandered through the sports memorabilia, and Randy snapped photos at Clay Matthews' locker. A life-size Packer mannequin, just waiting for insertion of your head, made for an excellent photo op. We marveled at the plaques showing all the Super Bowl winners and at the glistening silver team rings from Super Bowls past. The day ended with a visit to the Mesquite Barbecue with Randy and his wife Mary, and Gary and Marcia. The food was delicious, the service was attentive, and the owner, who had learned about Will's battle, added dessert and T-shirts on the house, topped off by pictures with a bison head. A very good day.

February 6, 2011 – Super Bowl Sunday dawned cool and mostly clear. We started the day with some time alone. We talked about the Scripture readings for the day and prayed for safe travels; we certainly gave thanks for our many blessings. We got our green and gold gear on and made a short video before our trek to the stadium. Will seemed to get great amusement out of telling the vapid but persistent lady inside our GPS to "cork it" when she started getting a little too insistent that we were once again going astray. Gary and Marcia had seats on the opposite side of the stadium and so made their way to the game separately. We found our remote parking lot and, after a short bus ride and a good hike in the cool sunshine, we arrived outside the stadium perimeter. An audible buzz arose as we approached: people yelling and cheering, bands rehearsing, sirens blaring, horns honking. Will and I sat outside and watched the crowd while we ate our lunches. There were people of every size, shape and color, wearing outfits, face paint and wigs of green, gold and black. We entered through the security screening and into the Super Bowl sideshow. It was a sight to behold watching raw capitalism as vendors with "rare" goods plied their wares to customers whose wallets were extraordinarily flush with cash. Programs, soda pop, barley pops, cotton candy, popcorn – all at prices heretofore unseen. A beer and a burger cost a mere 10 bucks apiece. Karl Marx would have seen this as evidence of the exploitation of the proletariat by the bourgeoisie, but no one seemed to mind. Other evidence that the beers were moving could be seen in the lines for the bathroom and the mounds of paper debris on the floor from the overflowing trash containers.

Once inside the stadium, we stopped for a moment at a landing overlooking the field on the four-story climb up to our seats. The view of the field was amazing; an edifice tall enough to accommodate the Statue of Liberty with late afternoon natural light flooding through the large windows and a Jumbotron extending from one 20 yard line to the other. We got to our seats, and again took in the view. We were two rows from the top of the stadium and the figures on the field were small, but no detail was missed thanks to the large TV display. The excitement in the air was palpable as the fans filtered in. We were in the heart of Steeler country, but the fans around us were gracious. I got a chill, and I know Will did too, as the announcer introduced the Packers. Christina Aguilera sang the National Anthem with beautiful soaring notes, followed by an Air Force F-16 flyover. The cheers rose in a deafening crescendo as the Packers kicked off and the camera flashes were a galaxy of stars come to Earth as Mason Crosby kicked the ball and the game was underway. The Packers led throughout the first half with some brilliant throws by Aaron Rodgers and some artful catches by the Green Bay receivers. At halftime, we checked in with Liz and Grandma and Grandpa Canan back home before taking in the Black Eyed Peas in the halftime show. The set up of the show was as choreographed as the performers. Fergie wowed everyone with her vocals. A light show, better than any I have ever seen, including performer costumes pulsating with electric lights of different hues, concluded the halftime show.

The second half of the game was nerve-wracking, with Steelers making repeated runs to take the lead and the Packer defense beating them back. When the Steelers final drive failed at 4th and 5 with 39 seconds to go, I knew the Packers were going to be World Champions once again. I looked over at Will and the image is seared in my mind of the grin on his face from ear to ear, a smile not often seen since 2004. We counted down the final seconds and the crowd erupted at the final gun. Will and I moved down closer to the field and reveled in the presentation of the Lombardi trophy to the Packers GM and the MVP award to Aaron Rodgers. The Packers fans hooted and high-fived as we made our way out to our cars. Our shuttle bus stood us up, so we made the rest of the way to our car via a bicycle rickshaw. An interesting end to a most amazing day. We owe many thanks to the countless people who made this day a reality.

–Surgery

Will and Liz, along with Liz's parents, flew to St. Jude's on February 8 to prepare for Will's surgery. Katherine and I arrived in Memphis on February 9 in a Tennessee winter wonderland. The natives were paralyzed by a winter "storm," which brought some ice and a couple of inches of snow. Ah, the South. I wished I'd packed a snowplow and crew in my carry-on bag. After crawling into the city from the airport in a transport van, we arrived at Le Bonheur Children's Hospital where Will and Liz awaited us. I bedded down for the night with Will at the hospital while Katherine and Liz headed to Target House and my in-laws headed to a local hotel. It was a restless night for Will and me in a strange place with strange beds, the murmuring voices from nearby TV sets, and the intermittent clang of alarms from infusion pumps and monitors. First thing in the morning, the surgical team arrived to take us down to surgery. The knot in my stomach grew as we approached the surgical area. We met Dr. Boop, who has a quiet calm way about him. His staff has obvious respect for him as they hover nearby getting ready. Will is pretty chatty; he has a question for the anesthesiologist about who invented the breathing tube they stick down his throat during surgery. He also has to know where she got that Spanish accent that seems oddly placed with the "y'alls" issuing from the mouths of the other staff, and we learn she is from Cuba with parents from Spain. Will gets to pick out a prize before heading off to surgery, and he chooses a Whoopi Cushion. ☺ Soon it is time to say a quick prayer that Will's surgery is successful and our good-byes; I give Will's hand a squeeze before they wheel him away. Why does this feel a bit like Russian roulette and each surgery is a pull of the trigger and a whispered prayer that this is not the time when there will be a bullet in the chamber? Liz and I head upstairs to Will's room to wait. I pretend to read the paper as the minutes slog by, but the words are a blur on the page. The first report at one hour into surgery is good; everything is proceeding as planned. Before we know it, four hours have gone by and Dr. Boop is at our door. He tells us that the surgery went smoothly; they got everything they could see of the two tumors they went in to remove. There were no complications and Will did not need any transfusions. There were undoubtedly a few layers of tumors cells left, not easily removed with a scalpel, and Will's scalp bears yet another huge incision. All in all, this is an outcome over which any parents seven years into the battle should rejoice. Words of gratitude seem wholly inadequate to the man who has just given your precious son months or even years more time with us here on Earth, but we convey our deepest thanks as best we can. Dr. Boop, our local miracle worker, sweeps out bearing a faint smile for a job well done.

Will is returned to the PICU to recover. The nurses who cared for him in the PICU said they've never seen a child with a craniotomy do so well. Will is mostly conscious very quickly and cranky as he works out the cobwebs of anesthesia. He asks me if "girls can be gay?" I tell him yes, but where do these questions come from? Does it have anything to do with the fact that someone has been inside his head moving his brain around and cutting away parts of it? His blood pressure spikes a bit, but medication gets it back under control. Around 6 p.m., a startling moment occurred shortly after receiving a morphine shot for the pain. Will became very flushed and threw up his Jello and pudding without warning, including some projectile vomiting on me, the ice chip delivery guy. But with some fast work, and new gown and linens from our capable nurse Katie, Will is cleaned up, in fresh bedding and feeling better almost right away. Sleep steals upon him quickly. I'm grateful that he's comfortable enough to finally get some rest, and I hope it will arrive for me as well. Unfortunately, since they have filled him full of IV fluids and with the nurses doing neuro checks every two hours, the night is not as restful as we had hoped, but it's a start.

By February 11, Will has continued to improve. He has been eating and drinking without nausea. The nurses have removed all of his monitors and IVs, so Will has been up and walking. Physical Therapy assessed his balance, vision, and strength, and found all of these about the same as they were prior to the surgery.

Will then had a post-surgery MRI to determine how much of the tumors had been removed. When the attendant brought him back from the MRI, Will almost took a head-first dive out of the wheelchair. The wheelchair brake wasn't on and when Will stepped on the footrest, the wheelchair tipped forward lurching him out of the chair. Thankfully, I was just able to catch him in time and ease him back into the chair. It took several minutes after this for our hearts to start beating normally again.

Dr. Boop had been anxiously waiting for the MRI results. We walked down with Will to a viewing room to see the scans. Will sat right next to Dr. Boop, who pulled up the "before and after" images. The largest tumor in the left ventricle was gone – no longer visible at all on the MRI. There was a tiny spot remaining in the upper right ventricle, but we hoped this could be addressed with radiation and/or chemo. When Will saw the scan, he turned to Dr. Boop and said, "I'm amazed." There was a pause before Dr. Boop could respond, "Will, I'm amazed at how well you are doing." It was all amazing, indeed.

I needed to return to Rochester with Katherine. Liz would stay on a few more days in Memphis with Will and her parents. Katherine needed to get back to school, especially in light of the upcoming big Turnabout dance. Before we left, Katherine sat on Will's hospital bed next to him and Will held her hand; he didn't want her to leave. It was moving for all of us to witness this before we said our good-byes and started back home. Will recuperated in Memphis for a few more days. Will became nauseated and vomited, and he felt some pressure in his head. We learned from Dr. Boop that this was likely due to blood that accumulated into the ventricles during surgery, and was now breaking down and circulating. With the help of a multi-day dose of steroids and Zantac, Will finally overcame these challenges and started feeling much better. Before departing for Rochester once more, Liz happened to ride the elevator with a young mother and her four-year-old son. He'd had extensive brain surgery and appeared to have a growth on the right side of his face. He was a precious little boy. Liz visited with them and learned they lived in Memphis. The little boy told her, "We're going to my Grandma's because we had a shooting where we live, but my Momma wasn't involved." Out of the mouths of babes... As difficult as Will's journey had become, there would always be things we would take for granted that others did not, and for those things, we would always be grateful.

February 19, 2011 – Will celebrated his 13th birthday at home. He's now officially a teenager with all of the adolescent angst that comes with it, in addition to his cancer battle. A big thank you to the Green Bay Packers organization for sending a package to Will that included a signed card from quarterback Aaron Rodgers (#12), an autographed football, and other great items. We had the Viggiano family over for barbecue and birthday cake. I cued up the video camera to capture Liz sliding a wonderful white frosting birthday cake with a big Packer "G" on it in front of Will as we chimed in on "Happy Birthday." Will has a wistful look in his eyes that you can't miss. Is he wondering if this is his last birthday party, like the rest of us are? I ask him to make a wish before he blows out the candles, but there is no wish. Are we at the point where wishes are beyond being granted or has it already been granted by this surgery giving him more time to enjoy another year of sunshine and baseball with us? I'm not sure.

February 21 was President's Day. The kids, Liz and I were off for the holiday and we were in the midst of a large snowstorm, which meant we were all together in the house. Katherine was napping. All of a sudden, Liz couldn't find Will anywhere in the house. She started to panic, but then I checked Katherine's bedroom; we found Katherine, asleep on her bed, and Will sound asleep in the bean bag chair near her. These days, it seems he just wants to be close by her and that she feels the same way.

On February 22, the day started for me with sad news at work. One of my former legal assistants, Mariah Ackerman, would not be returning to work as she had hoped. When I had brought her the gift cards from our colleagues on Christmas Eve, she was unsure of the primary site of her cancer; she had since learned that she had advanced colon cancer. When I saw her at a recent hospital visit, the telltale signs of the battle showed in her eyes.

On February 23, the community was shocked with the news that Mike Podulke, a long-time member and current chair of the Olmsted County Board had passed away unexpectedly. Why does this life suddenly feel like "Wheel of Fortune"? Step up and play and spin the wheel, hope your spin does not result in a "bust," from which you never get to return. What did Mariah and Mike do to deserve such a fate – two kind, compassionate people dedicated to serving others? Is it better to avoid that long, slow decline and pass away secure in your life's work without always keeping one eye on that looming disaster coming down the road?

On February 23, we met with Dr. Nadia Laack, Will's radiation oncologist at Mayo. When we were at St. Jude's a week ago, Dr. Tom Merchant presented us with a "go for broke" – or what I referred to as the "cure him or kill him" – option. He recommended giving Will a dose of radiation over a span of a few weeks in excess of all the radiation he has received over the course of his illness. The possible side effects were legion: brain necrosis, white matter disease, serious impairment of his already affected memory and concentration skills. Will's recovery from this latest surgery has been slow. He has been at school for partial days and coming home to nap in the afternoon. I'm unable to imagine what a massive dose of radiation would do to that effort to regain some of his old self. During this visit at Mayo, Dr. Laack suggested a more focused dose of radiation around the tumor growth areas in the ventricles. It's not going to cure him, but it should give him some more quality days of life with fewer side effects. It's to be followed up by intrathecal topotecan after a few weeks of rest in between. Liz and I are in agreement that this makes as much sense as anything at this late stage in the game, but neither of us has the heart to break the news to Will that he is about to embark on another course of treatment with all of the side effects that come trotting along with it. When is enough enough? Are we there? It was just barely a month ago that we had told Will he was dying and to prepare for the end. The surgery gave him a new opportunity for a longer life to share with us. But shouldn't he have a say at this point whether he wants mostly good, but fewer, days before that damn tumor comes roaring back … or whether we offer more time, but at a greater cost in his stamina and peace of mind? Whoever said it was fair that a young man of 13, who has fought this evil for more than half his years, should be in such a position to have to make such a choice?

February 26 was Liz's birthday. After a meal out at a restaurant, we rented a movie to watch at home, *The Last Song*, starring Miley Cyrus. The story ended with the father dying of cancer. This hit so close to home that it was difficult to watch. When it was over, Will said, "I didn't like that ending. I thought the Dad would get better and they'd live happily ever after." We all had to fight back the tears when he said this. Will deserved the same type of ending for his story.

On March 1, Will met with the medical team at Mayo; the surgical incision was healing well. Will had a special MRI for radiation treatment planning purposes. We decided that Will would undergo five weeks (Monday–Friday) of re-radiation to the anterior parts of the upper left and right ventricles only. He would start on March 9 and have the treatments twice per day, because research suggested that smaller doses, at least six hours apart, may be safer and cause less damage. This is an option we had hoped we would never have to pursue, but it may be the only one to keep the tumor growth slowed or stopped. The radiation will cause fatigue; we will closely assess how Will is feeling and tolerating the treatment as it progresses.

March 6, 2011 – We finally have tucked Will in for the night. Outside the window, a white veil is silently drifting down, coating the sidewalk in the winter that will not end. We went out for dinner tonight at Applebee's with friends Laurie and Anna Sutherland. Will ordered an enormous plate of food – sliders and chicken wings, – which was a little unusual, but then again he seemed to be eating more lately because of the steroids he has been taking. Right after we ate, I ran Katherine and Anna to a movie. When I got back to the restaurant, Will was quiet and flushed. He started feeling nauseated and before we could run to the bathroom, he vomited repeatedly in between a couple of rows of patrons trying to enjoy their dinners. It's one of those moments where you feel caught in the prison searchlight as it freezes you in your tracks: Will losing his meal, me watching him with one eye and the horrified diners with the other eye, and yet being unable to move, unsure if dragging him the rest of the way to the bathroom while he is still throwing up is better or worse. I finally get him to the bathroom and after a few more efforts, he is done and I get him and the stall mostly cleaned up. I feel so sorry for Will that he had to endure this in a public place. Tomorrow is the start of a new round of radiation and so maybe it's just a case of nerves, thinking about what is to come.

Back home, I learned that Will got his report card from school last Friday: B and Cs mostly, with an F from one teacher who shall remain nameless. Liz and I are both angered by this. There was no warning this was coming. To be honest, what's the point of giving this child, who is waging the fight of a lifetime just to survive, much less work and come back to school the next day, a failing grade? Will it cause you a guilty conscience to give him a "D" rather than an "F"? I tell him that it's okay and that Mom and I both know he is doing his best despite all the hardships. I've started reading *Profiles in Courage*, the Pulitzer Prize winner by President John F. Kennedy. In the foreword, his brother Bobby tells a little known part of the story. John Kennedy endured years of serious medical hardships throughout his youth, as well as the severe spinal injury from his PT-109 command, his campaigning on crutches, and a fever of 106 while travelling in Asia, from which he nearly did not survive. Yet, he overcame enormous odds to become a well-loved and respected president. I shared this with Will. I hope it will inspire him in some small way to know that persevering despite overwhelming obstacles is possible. He has certainly done it himself just to get to this point.

We discuss the school play, *When in Rome,* with Will. Will has a small role and has missed nearly all the practices due to the surgery and recuperation period at home. We tell Will that maybe it would be best to see if they can find him a spot in the stage crew so that he can still participate but would not have lines to learn and daily practices to attend; he agrees. But Stacy Ellingson, the director, bless her heart, says that she knows of Will's struggles and she will find a way to keep Will in a small part in the cast, no matter what happens. The play becomes something to look forward to come April.

In the quiet of evening stillness, Liz shares her concerns about the radiation course we have chosen. Is it the right one? We know how Will suffered the last time – the skin irritation, the nausea and loss of appetite, the effect on his cognitive functioning. But this is less toxic than the "go for broke" radiation offered by St. Jude's and, with rounds of different chemo agents showing dwindling effectiveness, what choice do we have? I tell her that we don't have to finish it if the effects on his weakened body are too great. He will tell us and I am sure we will see the signs when the cost has been come too great to bear. God is in the driver's seat and we are riding in the back seat with an unintelligible map balanced on our laps showing the way. *Give Will strength, and us as well, to endure the hardships of this next trial.*

On March 7, Liz and Will had an appointment with Dr. Nick Wetjen, the Mayo pediatric neurosurgeon to "clean up" Will's incision and remove the glue and flakes before radiation begins again. This did not bother Will in the least. As Dr. Wetjen was working on him, Will said innocently, "Boy, you're good at this." Dr. Wetjen laughed, "I should be! I do this for a living." A little humor to cut through the tension building as we awaited the start of radiation.

On March 11, Will finished his third day of radiation. Amazingly, he went to school for full days the entire week. He did it all with a positive attitude, and continued fortitude. One of the Mayo medical staff had heard that Scott Hamilton, former professional skater and brain tumor survivor, was "lit from within" in terms of his strength, positive attitude and bravery in the face of adversity. The medical staff immediately thought of Will and that he is too, "lit from within." It describes him well.

March 12, 2011 – Liz, Katherine and I dressed for church today to attend the funeral of fellow parishioner, Will Dickes. Young Will was only 12 when he was diagnosed with leukemia in 2008. He waged his personal war bravely but succumbed earlier in the week at age 15. Will was born an orphan in Korea and was adopted by Steve and Loretta Dickes, surely saved from one hard life in Asia only to encounter another one. He made a substantial impact on his classmates though.

Our Will could not join us. Understandably, the funerals of the other fighters were too filled with the anguish of grief for their loss, as well as his own uncertain future. The church was full of young men and women when we arrived; we met Sherrie Decker and others from Brighter Tomorrows. A funeral is an interesting thing. Your place of worship is filled with people who are there to honor someone they loved or respected; they don't know the etiquette or perhaps even accept the theology that goes along with being a regular member of a congregation. But for an hour, they pretend that they do; the clash in practices between believers and non-believers and believers of different faiths is subtle, but distinct. Father Reker did a nice job making everyone feel welcome, but the whole event, while beautiful, was a bit surreal. There, up at the front of our church, was our priest, talking to the congregation about the loss of a boy named Will to cancer. Every time he referred to "Will," and with each reference to appreciate Will's life and accept the fact that he had moved on to heaven, I couldn't help but feel this was some kind of a dress rehearsal for what lay ahead for our son. "Did you like that song by the choir?" "How about the homily"? "Wasn't the signing of the helium balloons by the kids and releasing them at the cemetery into the cold wind before committing Will to his final resting place in the frozen ground a nice idea?" I could only admonish myself to get my mind off what may come and focus back on what is right now.

Our Will has decided now that he no longer has much time for Dad and games in the evening. I guess I knew this day would come, but it doesn't make it any easier that I lost out to "Super Mario." It's hard to keep asking to be let in, and continue to be turned down, and I'm at a loss right now on how to turn this around. He started radiation on March 9, and has completed six treatments in only three days. So far, so good, but we remember that the side effects don't really begin to mount until a few weeks have gone by. Will is closing up more and it's hard to get him to talk about anything; when he does, it's in a negative way. Is he shutting down so that no one gets too close so that the end, when it comes, will be less painful for him and everyone else? Is there really nothing left to talk about that I can say that's relevant?

Liz also recently came across this telling statement in a brain tumor newsletter. Written by the sibling of a brain tumor patient, it describes the impact of the illness on her own life:

I've recently been thinking a lot about what it means to be the sibling of a brain tumor survivor, how it's changed my life, and set me apart from those around me. ...And, while I have come a long way, I still sit here in college and feel ultimately different from my friends, who have little to no awareness of their own mortality and that of people our age, when I have an acute awareness of it. ...When my brother had his first tumor, I couldn't think of anything BUT the fact that it could happen to him again, it could happen to me, and it could happen to anyone our age – no one was safe anymore in my eyes. My parents never knew how hard it was for me growing up because I strived to hide it from them, until I couldn't anymore. What sibling wants their parent to have to deal with their fear and anxiety on top of a sick child? Secretly at night from the time I was 11 until I was probably 16 or even 17, I would touch my finger to my nose "just to check." And every time anyone said they had a headache or were dizzy, I would shrug it off like everyone else and so "oh you must be coming down with something," but in reality my head would swirl with the same terrible thoughts.....

I didn't feel like my brother's baby sister often; when we went to camp together, I watched him like a hawk. I acted like an older sister, and at times like a mother, and of course he didn't like it. But that's the thing, siblings don't really know what to think, how to act, and what's normal. And it's scary. There is so much out there for patients and for their parents, but siblings go all but forgotten in most cases. We're the healthy ones–sure, but we're also the guilt-ridden ones, the ones who have to hold it together, the ones who have to bite their tongue – sibling rivalry?– the most bizarre thing in the world in the family of a tumor survivor.

I realize now that my childhood was different. Despite how blessed I am to have a family who made sure I never went without attention, they couldn't stop the thoughts running through my mind, and they couldn't have known, or dealt with that. ... And yet, the thing is – it doesn't matter how well off your sibling is. Once it happens, it happens. Of course I couldn't be prouder ... but I also couldn't be more afraid of whether or not he will finally get the uninterrupted chance to pursue his dreams. Sometimes, being a sibling, is like waiting for the other shoe to drop.

... despite the fact that I believe it's something I will always carry with me, I am living my own life away from home, getting good grades, making friends, in a positive relationship with a wonderful and understanding boy. I am still scared, and I always will be a little, but I

actually think it's had a positive effect on who I am today, and who my family is......

I'm sure Katherine could identify with all of the sentiments this eloquent young woman expressed.

March 15, 2011 – Yesterday marked seven years in this epic battle for Will's survival. It's an anniversary no one wanted to celebrate, as Will started Week 2 of his radiation treatments. But today was better. I took Will with me for the last session of Sports Night, the weekly gathering of the young adults in Rochester who are developmentally disabled. The smiles started coming back to Will's face almost from the moment we walked into the gymnasium at John Adams Junior High. John had to tell Will "nice shirt" as he does to everyone he meets. Andy peered at Will through his thick glasses and slowly the connection was made that this was someone he knew and he patted Will warmly on the back. After a quick warm up, we passed out the sticks for floor hockey, divided into teams and in a flash we were underway. Shouts rose from the floor as the puck shot back and forth and squeals of glee rang out as the puck slammed home into the goal. Will played for the Red-Yellow Team against the Blue Team (stick color). It became evident quickly that this was something Will was good at. It was a defining moment in some ways. When he played kid's games with kids who had not battled cancer for years, his limitations were apparent as he struggled to throw and kick and run as they did. But here, playing with developmentally and physically disabled young men and women, it was his abilities that were apparent. Down syndrome is a paradox: it robs these delightful young people of their fine motor skills, as well as the ability to receive and process information and translate it quickly and efficiently into a body in motion, and at the same time it often leaves them without the brooding and weighty cares that seem to come with adult life. Will's moves in floor hockey seemed nearly effortless in comparison as he moved up and down the court, deftly handling the puck, slapping a shot across court to one of his teammates, grinning as he reached out to stop a careening puck headed for the goal. It seemed he recognized this as well and the acceptance that this group gave him when he showed them he could play and excel. It made me see Will for his athletic abilities and not the limitations cancer had extended to his body. We all need to have our eyes opened to a new way of looking at things every now and then.

Will's radiation treatments continued. When Liz and Will drove to the treatment sessions, Will loved to plug in his iPod Shuffle and blast his music. Ironically, the songs he listened to the most were "Don't Stop Believing" done by the cast of *Glee,* and "Eye of the Tiger." Both of these songs are about never giving up, maintaining hope, and overcoming adversity. While Will hadn't said this directly, playing this music as they went to and from treatment gave both of them strength to carry on.

March 29 – Ten more days to go until Will completes radiation. The highlight of the day was that Will's iPad 2 finally arrived! Liz and Will went to Best Buy to pick it up, and he outfitted it with an orange Smart Cover. Will took a wad of cash out of the tiny safe he kept in his bedroom and paid for it with his own money. I helped him set it up and download some apps. It's quite a technological marvel. We know he will enjoy the ability to have video games, photos, music and more available at his fingertips and it will make the upcoming days more bearable.

Will's final radiation treatment was scheduled to occur on April 12, 2011. By April 2, his spunk, energy and sense of humor remained intact; however, he was, understandably, "sick and tired" of going to Desk R in the Charlton Building at Mayo for radiation. Liz and Will met incredibly kind, concerned and courageous people during their time there. There's a couple from Perham, Minnesota, Larry and Romelle, who "adopted" Will; they brought him deliveries of delicious licorice, made fresh from their nephew's business in Perham. Larry observed Will opening the licorice and not taking some for himself, but first offering it to others in the waiting area, the Radiation Oncology staff and patients. Larry was so touched by his unselfishness and generosity, but again, that is how Will has always been. On one occasion, an older woman came over to Will and asked, "Are you William? I've been watching you all week and I just want to tell you how brave I think you are." She then went back to where her husband was sitting, in a wheelchair, and pushed him over to Liz and Will. The man was visibly pale and his hair was gone. She said, "My husband's name is William too." He held out his hand and Will shook it, smiled that beautiful, kind smile of his and said, "Hello" before they were called back for treatment. Others who were present during their daily visits to Desk R took notice of Will and took the time to comment: "Will is such a gentleman." "He has so much integrity, even at his young age."

Courage and kindness are always present in the waiting area outside the treatment rooms and Will led the pack.

April 12 – Two events framed the past week, one happy, one sad. The week began with the news that Mark Sveen, one of my favorite clients from my former law practice, had passed away at the age of 46. Mark was a rare individual, a gifted athlete in high school who was offered college scholarships; he was so talented as a builder and carpenter that the CEO of Hormel Foods sought him out to build his home. Mark always came into my office with a smile on his face and brightened our day, even though troubles seemed to follow him wherever he went. I helped Mark with matters involving his family and his construction business; no client seemed more thankful for the help I gave than Mark did. My former legal assistant, Mary Kubista, and I attended the visitation before his funeral. We were surprised to learn that he had taken his own life, leaving behind two former wives, three children and nine brothers and sisters – none of whom had answers about how a man they loved dearly could decide that he had nothing left to give in his life and that the future held only the promise of pain. There was nothing we could say to his grieving family that would help them understand why he did this, except to reassure them what a fine human being he was while he was with us here on the Earth.

The date also was a milestone. Will completed his five weeks of radiation, two times a day, five days a week. Liz and I spread the word that he would be finishing up and would be ringing the bell at Desk R at Mayo to join that small but courageous group of cancer fighters who took what those x-ray machines could dish out. By the time we showed up for Will's afternoon appointment, some 30 people had appeared, including Marcia and Gary and Jack, Sherrie Decker, friends from work and Brighter Tomorrows, even fellow cancer patients, to celebrate this accomplishment. Will emerged from the treatment room with a big smile on his face, his red Twins cap pulled down low on his forehead to cover his hair, which was beginning to fall out once again. He clanged the bell hard a couple of times with the Desk R staff grinning behind him, then made his way down the assembled cast to hand out high fives and collect some hugs, including a big one from me. "Whatever," Will uttered when he finished slapping upraised hands, implying "no big deal, doesn't everybody have the guts to do five weeks of radiation?" Well, no, they don't, as a matter of fact. Will moved even some of the adult radiation patients with his quiet determination, a group that has seen some of the worst that cancer can send your way. A couple of quick snapshots next to the bell, then just as quickly, the moment was over and the group dispersed and life moved on. I was struck by the contrast between Mark and Will for just a moment: Mark, a guy blessed with many talents who would seem to have everything to live for who decided that pressing on with life wasn't worthwhile, and Will, a young guy who has been dealt a tough hand in his short life deciding that there were still sweet times to be had in his life, despite the hardships, and so opting not to let life end, but to press on to see what lay around the corner. I'm blessed to be along for the ride.

April 27 – Two weeks have already passed since Will rang the bell. There was some comfort during those five weeks, knowing that we were actively doing something to try and kill those cancer cells in his head. While we were glad that Will's body got a well-deserved rest, there was also a constant uneasiness about what those cells might be doing during the resting period. We remained anxious until we knew what the next scan would show. Will tired more easily in the two weeks after radiation. He lost more hair in the front and down the left side of his head; the skin in the radiated area was brown and peeling. Liz did her best to keep it lubricated and protected from infection while healing. During those five grueling weeks of radiation, Will attended school and, we found out, made the 7th grade "B" Honor Roll. To say that our hearts wanted to burst from all the emotions swirling inside would be an understatement.

April 30 – The weekend began with Will's first school dance at St. Francis, the last one of the school year. I had promised some time ago to chaperone; I wanted to be there for this coming-of-age event. I had taken Katherine to an out-of-town track meet , and I was getting back into Rochester a bit late. I dashed home to find Will in his T-shirt and red Puma sweatshirt, jeans and old shoes. I paused for a moment to dust off those memories of my own 1970s junior high dances: doesn't he still need to shower and put on a nice shirt so the girls will welcome him ... or are those rules out the window now? Will's hair had fallen out in front from the radiation; what was left just covered the incision scar from his surgery. I told him he looked great, and off we went. We arrived at St. Francis – the gym was darkened, punctuated by flashing lights and throbbing music. Will spotted some classmates and off he went before so much as a quick bit of advice about the ground rules could leave my lips. I was teamed with four moms, policing the goings on around the dance floor, and making sure that that the soda and potato chips and Oreos kept coming. I'd forgotten how much these dances reminded me of animal mating rituals: the packs of boys circling, showing off, looking for a member of the opposite sex as a partner; the packs of girls coming out in twos for the mandatory forays into the girls' restroom to make sure that everything looked just so, and whispers about who is with who. My mind raced back to that long ago moment in the chapel at Saint Marys Hospital soon after Will's diagnosis when he had lost much of the use of his left arm and leg and I wondered if, when he got older, he could find a girl who could look past his shortcomings and appreciate him for what lies deeper within. One of the moms tells me that I should go take a peak in the gym as the strains of Christina Aguilera's "You are Beautiful" emanated from the speakers on the stage. I slipped into the semi-darkness and there to my mild surprise is Will dancing arm in arm with classmate Lizzy Bauer. Lizzy, who has a brother with serious health concerns of his own, knows pain and has compassion; she said "Yes" to a dance with Will. He is smiling and she is too, even though the arm's length dance is awkward, as they step across the teen-age threshold to the new experience of a moment with a member of the opposite sex. I hear the words, "You are beautiful no matter what they say. Words can't bring you down. You are beautiful in every single way... Yes, words can't bring you down. Don't you bring me down today..." The tears come for me: it's too perfect, the right girl from the class, the right song at the right moment about overlooking the faults that others have labeled you with in life and rising above them, and then just as quickly, the moment has passed. Will danced with five different girls from the 7th grade class, enjoyed strutting with the boys and cracking jokes and, before I know it, it's over and the lights are coming back on and the kids are streaming out the gym door with looks of regret that the evening has ended. I've promised to mop up the gym after the dance. I complained to Dan Smith, the DJ, that all the good junior high dances from my era weren't complete without hearing Led Zeppelin's "Stairway to Heaven" and as my mop starts to sweep across the polished wood floor, I hear those one-of-a-kind notes from Jimmy Page's guitar coming down the gym to greet me. As I swept, I was transported back to Gerritts Junior High in Kimberly for a minute, the darkened gym lit by the spotlight with a four-color filter, the DJ at the long table with two turntables and long rows of LP records behind him, the warm sweaty bodies as we clung tight to our dance partners and felt the rush of emotions (and hormones) while Robert Plant did his magic for 8 minutes and 2 seconds. That era feels so very long ago; it had a simplicity to it. I want so much to share it with Will, but once she has bought her "Stairway to Heaven," we are back out into the cool night to call it a day.

May 1 is the day we promised to visit Hannah Brandvold's photography show at Luther College in Decorah, Iowa. Hannah is a senior at Luther, a 21-year-old cancer survivor who has walked this road herself. She wanted to feature the kids of Brighter Tomorrows as part of her senior project. She has a quiet, easy way with the kids that puts them at ease. The overarching theme of the show is "Kids as Superheroes," so many of them are photographed wearing capes. Will's photo is in profile, his arms outstretched and his cape extended behind him. He's grinning in the photo and having fun being a superhero. She's done a wonderful job. We are grateful for her efforts and hope that she will be able to persuade Mayo to find a space to share her fine photos with the public. I mention as we depart that "we are all members of that club no one wants to be a member of" and Hannah gives us that brief moment of pain and understanding in her eyes that shows she knows this is no ordinary group of kids. She's done well.

Back in Rochester, Will and Katherine persuaded us to take in a movie, *Soul Surfer,* based on the true story of Bethany Hamilton, the accomplished teenage surfer from Hawaii who lost most of her left arm in a shark attack. An excellent story, it's compressed given the movie time constraints, but gives hints of the pain she endured, both physical and mental, on her way back to competitive surfing. Bethany overcame the limitations her body now put on her; she overcame the fear of getting back on the surfboard to compete in the ocean swells once again. She's supported by a loving family and a strong faith in God, and ultimately is moved from her despair by a mission trip to Thailand following the Asian tsunami in 2004. She found that putting the needs of others suffering with difficulties ahead of her own concerns lifted her from the darkness. After the movie Will asked Liz, "Do you think I've gone through as much as Bethany has?" Liz told him, "Will, you've gone through more." He then said, "What about Katherine, as the sibling?" Liz responded, "Yes, she's gone through a lot too." That's Will, always thinking about others. There are many parallels between the movie and Will's life: the pain he overcame in his multiple surgeries and his determination to make those parts of his body that had failed him after surgery begin working again to play baseball. Like Bethany, he also has the support of a family that loves him and a belief that God has worked His way already in his life. The belief that Will's journey has, in many ways, actually been more difficult than Bethany's makes the fact that he is still with us to share her story that much more remarkable.

Another baseball season got underway for Will and his friends on May 10, and we were so very thankful that he could play. Will and Liz went to Sports Authority and he got some new baseball cleats, new tennis shoes to replace his worn and ragged old ones, new baseball pants and a snazzy new bat. Liz had fun shopping with and for Will. When they checked out, the cashier leaned over and said to Will, "You're lucky your Mom spent so much on you." Will just smiled. Liz told her, "He is so worth it." She will never know the full value of the truth in that statement.

On May 20-22, Will and I spent some of the weekend at my sister Kathy's home on Lake Wissota near Chippewa Falls, Wisconsin. Will was the king of the fishermen for the weekend and caught a 22-inch Muskellunge! We returned to Rochester early on Sunday so that Will could play in the Junior Kid's Cup golf tournament. While Will and the other competitors only got in five holes due to weather, Will finished 2nd in his age group! He was also the top fundraiser, raising $1155. He received a medal and a cool, orange Nike gym bag that he really liked. The week ended on an up note when Will's blood cell counts were checked and were good. When Liz told Will his counts were good he said, "Mom, did you expect something different?" For Will, the future always looked bright.

June 3 – We learned that Emmy Spicer, a very special young girl, part of the Spicer family whom we grew to know and love during our week at Camp Firefly, lost her battle to neuroblastoma brain tumor. Emmy was a beautiful child – short hair, radiant smile and the most piercing blue eyes you can imagine. During our week together in Georgia last year, Emmy immediately took a liking to Katherine and the feeling was mutual. From early on, they began holding hands and Emmy wanted to ride with Katherine, sit by Katherine, and just be with Katherine. We have wonderful images in our minds of Emmy and Katherine together, smiling and so happy, free of the cancer world and all of the unfair burdens it places on children and families. The entire Spicer family will remain in our prayers as they mourn the loss of beautiful Emmy.

On June 10, Will returned to Mayo for another MRI of his brain and spine. The scan results were mixed. The good news was that Dr. Laack, his radiation oncologist, was very pleased at how responsive the tumors were to radiation. There was barely anything visible in the areas where the tumors were removed in February. She was also pleased at how well Will had tolerated this last round of radiation.

The bad news was that the tumor in the cerebellum, near the location of his original tumor back in 2004, grew a little bit. We knew there was a lesion there going into the surgery back in February; however, it wasn't possible or safe for Dr. Boop to go after that tumor. It could be radiated, but Dr. Laack said that would be a last resort measure because the risk was higher for significant damage to vital functions of the brain and/or death. There's now also a small tumor in the lower left ventricle, in an area that had not been radiated recently. There's a chance that this area can be treated with Gamma Knife. And more chemo would have to be given in hopes of slowing or decreasing the growth of the spot on the cerebellum. The news that he would have to endure this again broke our hearts. But Will told Dr. Laack, "If there are still options, then I want to try something else."

June 13, 2011 – A week ago, Will started vomiting. It generally happened in the evenings, particularly after he had eaten food that was a little bit spicy. One night, it was after eating ribs, another night it came after a taco casserole. On June 11, 2011 we had the good fortune to be invited to attend a Twins game at Target Field with other families from the Rochester Ronald McDonald House. We owe a huge thank you to Jo Merrill who helped make this outing possible. Her husband Bruce passed away from a brain tumor about two years ago. He was an avid Twins fan and worked for a bank, which has sponsored this baseball outing for families in Bruce's honor for the past year. It was our first game of the year and a nice sunny day. We sat at the very top of the stands in right field. At times, it was cold and we were glad to have our coats. The Twins' bats were hot and started out the first inning with five runs scored. Soon the sun came out from behind the clouds and it beat down on us. There was little wind as we were shielded. Suddenly, Will began vomiting and threw up all over a nice young man from the Ronald McDonald House who had been seated in front of him. We scurried to wipe it up and to get help from housekeeping. The leader from Ronald McDonald House bought a new T-shirt for Will and the young man so they would have something clean to wear for the rest of the trip. Even the Twins victory couldn't lighten the ominous feeling that Will's episode had brought.

Donna and the team at Mayo didn't find anything obvious that should be causing the vomiting. Does this mean the tumor in the cerebellum has finally moved into the brain stem area? Is this the beginning of the end? How many times have I asked that question before? I've been plagued over the past several weeks with pain and weakness in my left arm, a symptom perhaps of all of the stress of the past years finally taking a toll. Is this all in my head or am I losing control over my body too? I guess I realized a long time ago that we never really have been in control of any of this.

I'm so proud of Katherine! She passed her written driver's test and got her learner's permit, a great milestone. I took her out driving for the first time the night before we sent her off to Camp Olson for a couple of weeks. She did great. The sun was setting as she crawled along a quiet residential street near our house, crept up to a stop sign, slowly turned around in the parking lot of a nearby golf course. She will be a confident driver not too far down the road with a full-fledged driver's license. I want to be here and I want Will to be here to witness that day as she continues to grow and spread her wings as a young adult. But Will is getting weaker and we seem powerless to stop that progression.

June 19 was Father's Day. Will made me a nice card with "time coupons" inside it redeemable for time with my son. What a thoughtful and creative gift! There is nothing in the world that I would rather have from Will right now than the gift of his time with me. Thank you Will for giving this to me! After several days of off-and-on vomiting and a change in his anti-nausea medication, Will's stomach finally seems to be more settled. Will, Liz, his buddy Joey Viggiano and I went to Rochesterfest, our summer community celebration, for dinner. Will and Joey split a rack of ribs and ate every last bite. They also had fresh squeezed lemonade and Italian ice cream for dessert. It was so good to see Will eating and able to enjoy food once again.

June 28, 2011 – We rose early today with the sun to take Will to Saint Marys Hospital for his Gamma Knife procedure. Liz and I were both apprehensive as we made our way through the quiet Rochester streets to the hospital. Dr. Wetmore, Dr. Laack, Will's radiologist, and Dr.

Pollock, who was to complete the procedure, all weighed in with their opinions. Originally, we intended only to irradiate the smaller tumor in the posterior horn, a relatively quiet area of the brain and relatively safe. It became apparent, though, that the larger tumor in the posterior fossa, near Will's brain stem, could not wait for a future treatment as it was likely pressing on the area of the brain that controls nausea and was the cause of Will's recent nausea attacks. Dr. Pollock also told us that the cancer had started spreading into the fourth ventricle, where it would eventually enter the spinal column, leading to a much faster spread. We decided, after much soul searching, that Will would have both areas treated. Will also wanted to have these areas treated. We had encouraged our teenager to participate in the decisions about his care. For the first time, too, he was admitted to the adult area of the hospital. We did laugh briefly when they brought Will a pair of hospital pants that were about twice his width; he could have made a sail for a boat with those.

Lost in our thoughts, we rolled slowly down to the procedure room. We kissed him on the forehead before they whisked him away, yet again, to do battle. He was under for roughly four hours, receiving over an hour of radiation to the spots that needed it. When he came back to the hospital room, he seemed to shake off the effects of the anesthesia pretty quickly, aided by a special visit from "Dr. Jack" and Marcia and Gary who cheered Will up. When Jack arrived after a long day of visiting patients, he was only interested in two things: trying to get a lick of Will's orange Push-Up, and nestling next to Will under his covers to sleep. When we brought Will home, he perked up and was even joking around with us, despite the massive dose of steroids he had received earlier in the day. I hope and pray that his recovery is uneventful; I am off to Montana tomorrow for some desperately needed time to try to heal myself. The pain in my arms continues. Now they think that a bone spur in my spine might be causing my pain; another MRI after my trip will see for sure. I'm just thankful that Dr. Pollock bought Will some more time today and that there will be more baseball games to attend with Will in our future.

July 17, 2011 – Finally, some time to reflect on the past couple of weeks. Will's Gamma Knife procedure went smoothly; there were none of the serious side effects, such as impacts on his breathing or eye movements that could have resulted from damage to the brain stem during the procedure. My trip to Montana went well. The highlights included riding on the Hiawatha Bike Trail, a renovated Milwaukee Road rail bed up in the mountains on the Montana-Idaho border. The first tunnel was 1.2 miles long, inky black as you caromed in, the tiny bouncing lights on the bike handlebars swallowed up by the darkness that blotted out the tunnel entrances and the sound of rushing spring water coursing down the rock walls. The views of the Bitterroot Mountains were spectacular. The chipmunks were fearless, coming up to within an inch of your shoes to beg their next meal from bikers. The other highlight was hiking in Glacier National Park with my friend from law school, Brian Bekker. We saw a moose grazing in the still waters beside one of the glacier-fed streams and a curious mule deer who ventured out onto the trail to see what I had to offer. It was good to "recharge the batteries." There have been too few moments in our lives lately that have awed and inspired us and a trip like that reminds you what lies undiscovered in that big world out there.

Then I was off to Camp Sunshine in Maine to meet up with my family and gather with other families who are also fighting brain tumors. Rick and Leslie Brown and their son Lenn, who is 15-years-old and is also fighting a medulloblastoma tumor, were there; we enjoyed the opportunity to get to know them much better this year. We share so many of the same heartaches and challenges as our families try to lead a normal life during this battle.

It was so amazing to watch Will and Katherine during this week. They feel safe, so welcome, here at camp. They have no inhibitions to try things beyond their normal comfort zone; they know that they will be supported and cheered by their camp families. Will decided at the last minute to do stand up comedy at the camp talent show and tell jokes in front of a room full of people. He told two jokes beautifully. The laughter and cheers from the audience was warm and heartfelt. He also got up on stage with all of the teens during karaoke at the parents' dinner and sang "Don't Stop Believing" (Will's request) and "Poker Face" (Katherine's request). Katherine and Will were locked arm in arm along with all the other teens fighting cancer and their siblings. It was a powerful moment.

Katherine also loves Camp Sunshine and the chance to reconnect with and meet new siblings whose brothers and sisters have a brain tumor. The teens are all together throughout the week; we really only see them at meal times and when they finally come to bed late at night. It's safe here at camp to stay out late talking, discussing their experiences. Katherine was also asked by Nancy Cincotta, the camp Psychosocial Director and an amazing person, to sit on the panel of siblings that spoke to the parent group about their lives. Katherine did a wonderful job. Liz and I also learned a lot from her insights and from the other siblings as well.

Will agreed to participate in a session for cancer survivors to talk with their peers about their journeys. Nancy did not share much about it with the parents, but said it was a good session. Will wanted to go and we are very glad he did.

Finally, we always are deeply moved by the wish boat ceremony. It's so powerful every year when the kids craft those little wooden boats adding their own personal touches and then light their candles and float them out on the pond as the sun sets. The energy emitted by all of those fervent, collective wishes can move mountains and touches everyone present. Then we go back and have the Celebration Show with a slide presentation set to music with hundreds of photos taken at camp during the week. It always concludes with all of the camp volunteers on stage singing "That's What Friends are For." You can't leave the room without being deeply moved every time you participate.

Back home, there was an evening that Liz and Will were watching the TV news. As it had been countless times, the topic of the federal budget deficit was headline. The broadcasters projected the possibility that soon the U.S. might not be able to pay their bills. Typical of Will and his generous nature, he said to Liz, "I have money in my safe that I could contribute. Wouldn't that help, Mom?" He was, of course, entirely serious. If generous people like Will ran for office, our country would surely be a better place.

On July 18, Will had a long day at the Clinic that started with a 9:00 a.m. Dermatology appointment and didn't end until about 3:30 p.m. Will had what looked like "cradle cap" on his scalp since late January and it continued to worsen. The dermatologist sent Will over to the hospital to have his hair washed numerous times with special solutions and shampoos to soften the scaly "plaque" build up on his scalp, and then nurse Teri would comb his hair gently, removing pieces of plaque. She was very gentle and skilled at removing many layers of dead skin that had built up. The plaque had literally smothered Will's hair follicles so that new hair wasn't able to grow and also tightened Will's scalp. The doctor said that patients with neurologic issues, such as brain tumors, often have oil glands under the scalp that secrete either too much or too little oil. Will's glands had done both, which led to the build up. Teri got a lot off of Will's scalp, but eventually stopped because she didn't want to cause any more trauma to the head that had already been through so much. As always, Will was a trouper and never complained. In the end, Will said it felt good to have his scalp massaged and to get that "gunk" removed. Just to highlight how thick the plaque was before Teri removed it, you couldn't see the incision scar from the February surgery; afterward, the line was evident. Because the condition would be chronic, a prescribed regimen of three different shampoos on a rotating schedule would be an on-going necessity. Frankly, the ability to have a condition we could manage and actually treat was a blessed opportunity. There were so many other things beyond our control.

On July 21, Will had an appointment with Donna to check his lab work and assess him before his scheduled trip to Camp Mak-A-Dream in Gold Creek, Montana on July 31st. His counts were good and Donna thought he looked well. We also got reacquainted with Dr. Amulya Rao, the new pediatric neuro-oncologist at Mayo who replaced Dr. Wetmore. We had met her two or three years previously when she did her fellowship at Mayo under Dr. Wetmore. Then she spent an additional year at D.C. Children's Hospital working closely with Dr. Roger Packer. She has a very kind and gentle manner and is very thorough. Will liked her immediately and so did Liz and I.

On the weekend of July 29-31, we had a fun weekend at Uncle Tom and Aunt Kathy's on Lake Wissota. All of my family was able to be there, except for my sister Maureen and her family who live in Virginia. There was precious time for inner tubing, boating, water skiing, and s'mores around the firepit in the back yard overlooking the lake. Will decided not to tube but late Saturday night told Uncle Tom he regretted not doing it. We did not know it at the time, but it would be our last family get-together at the lake.

From Chippewa Falls, we headed west for the airport in Minneapolis to put Will on the plane to Montana and arrived just in time. All three of us got to accompany him to the gate to say our good-byes as this would be the first time he would fly unaccompanied. Of course, Liz cried some but Will smiled and said, "Mom, don't cry." We all got big hugs from Will before he headed down the jetway with a Delta agent to the plane.

Will sent us a text from his new cell phone that afternoon: "Hi Mom. I'm in Missoula." He was also allowed to call us briefly later in the afternoon to say that he'd made it to camp. He told us that the camp was surrounded by mountains, the cabins were nice and that he'd met at least one of his roommates, Kyle from Connecticut, whom he had actually met last year at Camp Sunshine. He seemed happy to be there and that helped put our minds somewhat at ease, even though he was apart from his family so far from home.

We got an update in the middle of the week on the camp's Facebook page as to what the kids had been up to. They had helped run a carnival for the local Boys & Girls Club and for a local youth shelter. They had fun running food and game stations for the other kids who attended and also participating in the games themselves. The game Will ran was called "Pyramid of Destruction." They also enjoyed using the camp climbing wall, and participating in an evening Tie Dye Party and Fireside Chat. We all felt Will's absence acutely during this week, even though he had been gone to camp before; we could hardly wait for his return home. Finally, Saturday August 6 arrived and we were tearfully reunited with Will at the gate in Minneapolis. He was exhausted from his week at camp and slept for 21 hours when we got him back home. Will also shared that he loved hiking the Butte trail to the top, going to "Splash Montana" – a water park in Missoula – and to the "Art Barn." It was so good to have him back safe and sound.

August 22, 2011 – It's hard to believe that more than a month has elapsed since I last felt moved to write. I learned three days ago that my former legal assistant Mariah Ackerman's colon cancer has metastasized and she is entering hospice care at the tender age of 33 – the final stage of her cancer journey. Her young son Logan, age 5, was heard to tell a coworker of mine that he is "angry at God" about what is happening to his mom. It's a long line he enters when he starts feeling that way.

Will's strength is not what it used to be suddenly and neither is mine. We head out to the front yard to play catch and it's harder than ever to snag those errant balls that weren't thrown just right. Katherine agrees to join us – a rare event – and the duo becomes a triangle; I give my mitt to Katherine in exchange for a pair of work gloves and off we go. The ball hums through the fading summer light to the ring of hammers and distant rock music and the banter of the roofers re-shingling the house down the street; fireflies hover over the arcing ball, outlined against the darkening leaves of the maple tree. Katherine and Will tease each other, and I watch and take in every moment of it. Will this be the last time? The ache in my left arm grows tonight as Will's MRI and meeting with Dr. Rao approaches tomorrow. The therapist tells me that all the testing shows that there is nothing they can find as a physical source for all my pain; it is my submerged emotional depths struggling to break out, manifesting itself as physical pain in my neck, shoulder, arms and hands. Whatever the source, the pain is no less immediate and gripping. I'm emotionally crippled, and they will help me find an outlet to help me bleed out the torrent causing my pain. What about Will? How does he find a way to calm his mind on nights before a test that may determine if his life swings in the balance? Or has he done this enough times that he does not worry about the results anymore and relies on the surety that it is all in God's hands and that anguish about it all serves no one? How much longer can we wage the battle, worried that our minds may fail us before our bodies do? The promise of a new school year, 8th grade, the end of middle school, is only a week away. How does Will do homework from the teachers when the lessons of life are being poured out before our eyes? Lingering over books seems a trivial exercise in comparison. *Give us all some inner peace tonight Lord, and steel us for whatever blows may be meted out tomorrow.*

Chapter 8 – Reflections on the Journey

I wanted a perfect ending. Now I've learned, the hard way, that some poems don't rhyme, and some stories don't have a clear beginning, middle, and end. Life is about not knowing, having to change, taking the moment and making the best of it, without knowing what's going to happen next.
– Gilda Radner

Before we learn what Will's latest MRI results will mean, this is a good opportunity to reflect briefly on how far we have come and a chance to anguish about where we go from here. I HATE THIS DAMN DISEASE!!!!! It has stolen so much from Will. For over seven years, we pumped poisons of various kinds into Will's small body to kill this monster, but the monster no doubt has more than nine lives. Will was a happy, healthy, strong child before we started the cancer journey. This fight left him – and us – physically and mentally exhausted. There is no girding your loins for this battle. It is akin to an enormous storm out on the distant horizon; you know that you cannot escape it and the maelstrom approaches, ever so slowly, as you act like a deer caught in the headlights unable to flee. I had asked Will to pray that his treatments would be successful and that God would give him strength to handle them well. I privately wondered if it had shaken his faith, when he saw what he had to endure that his friends and classmates did not. I believe that God heard me when I prayed for Will to be cured of his illness, but God has His own ways and His own time for making His will known. We cannot know what that may be, as much as we would like to.

Cancer has stolen so much from our family. Cancer is kind of a "family business" for the Canans with a family tree whose branches groan under the bitter fruit that this disease has spawned. It claimed some in the family: my maternal grandmother, who died in the 1940s from breast cancer; I have often wondered if she could have survived this illness today, given the medical advances since that time. It has crippled some of the rest of us: striking my Dad's prostate in 2001; claiming much of my brother Steve's right arm, which was amputated to save him from a growing sarcoma, in 1988; I lost my thyroid gland to the disease in 2003. Before being utterly victorious, cancer slowly robbed Will of some of his hand-eye coordination, his stamina, and some of the upper frequency range of his hearing. The boys of the family appear to be mostly taking "one for the Canan team" for reasons that are unclear; we are all part of yet another club to which no one wants to be a member. The girls stand by and bind our wounds as we exit the medical battlefields, with the exception of my dear Aunt Loretta (a Canan by marriage) who recently lost her battle with breast cancer and had lost a sister to breast cancer and a brother to thyroid cancer just within the past year.

Cancer has stolen so much from other families near and dear to us. We have lost other small warriors along the way in this battle, most recently Tim Bays and Jackson Schneider and Axel Johnson and Emmy Spicer and Robby Caskey and Will Dickes and soon to include Shannon O'Hara. Sadly, the list goes on and on: children who deserved the same chance to live and thrive that their peers have.

Cancer has robbed us of some of the peace of mind that comes with living a "normal life." Liz and I lost the ability to plan far ahead because of the twists and turns that this illness demanded; it required flexibility to handle each round of battle. We tried to carry the heavy burden of this disease on our backs every day as we earned a living and devoted ourselves to tasks other than worrying about Will and his illness. We endured the agitated sleeping patterns that accompany the suppressed agonies of what the present and the future would hold for our son. The natural byproduct of the sleepless nights made it difficult to get through the next day; the realization that the cycle would simply keep repeating itself was daunting. Poor nutrition dictates feeling ill yourself; worse eating habits take hold as an attempt to find something – anything – to make you feel better, if only for a while. For me, excessive exercise became my outlet and futile effort to fight the stress caused by this illness. Liz and I agonized as we watched Will struggle to keep up with his friends on the baseball field as he endured chemotherapy; his body was waging war inside, but his teammates did not have those burdens.

Cancer is a firestorm; it reaches out and chars you, altering every fiber of your being.

And now it seems that life has become a series of battles being waged while we sit on the sidelines waiting and watching. There is the titanic battle going on inside Will's head right now as we hope and pray that the latest treatment is winning the war against the tumor cells coursing throughout his brain. There is the struggle between Will the child, who took joy in looking to his parents to help him meet his challenges, and Will the teen, who finds refuge in the television and video games; Will the teen does not want to play games with his parents to fill his free time any more, and with growing frequency does not want us to talk to him or even touch him. There are the battles that Liz and I wage trying to balance work and home life and making sure that Will's illness does not marginalize Katherine and her important needs. At times I stand on the sidelines watching the firefights and keeping an eye out for stray bullets from the skirmishes, and other times I have my body armor on in the thick of it with my weapons primed and holding on for dear life. Some days I serve in both roles, lick my wounds, and help pick up the fallen soldiers on the battlefield when the fight has waned, but it seems that more than seven years of the fight has left us all with a bit of post-traumatic stress disorder.

Don't get me wrong. There have been some good things that have come out of this horrible illness. We have met and been helped by so many kind and caring people along the way, including other parents through the Brighter Tomorrows organization facing similar challenges, Jack and Sherrie Decker and their daughter Shanna in particular. Will has gotten to meet people (including professional baseball players) and go places as a special guest (Disney World, Sea World, Alaska, Yankee Stadium, Target Field, the Super Bowl) that he never would have gotten to do as a child without a serious illness. If his life is compressed, it will have been a very meaningful one. This struggle has made me appreciate the fact that every single day matters, and to really mean that and not just treat it as another trite motto. So I play catch and shoot baskets, play one more board game, beg for one more Mario Kart session on the Wii with Will as often as he will let me, just to have that time with him. It has made me glad that Liz is here to help Katherine and me go through this, as I am here to help them – even though, at times, they will not let me in to help.

But where do we go from here? How long does Will have? Does he have one more year or 50 years to live? How do I discuss this issue with him when he does not think about the fact that he may die in the not too distant future? How do I explain to him that I have tried not to fail him as a parent because this was one thing I could not "fix" for him as my child? How do I discuss all of my potentially lost hopes and dreams of watching him grow up, get his driver's license, maybe become an Eagle Scout, have a girlfriend, graduate from high school and college, find a career that suits him, marry a nice girl and settle down with a family of his own so that I have his children to dote on in my old age? How do I explain to him the urgency of making each day count since he may not have too many left? How do you measure whether each day did "count"? What do I tell his sister, who may be left without a sibling, who will be missing the shared life experiences that only a brother or sister lived with day in and day out can bring? How do I stop the pain that I felt when I lost my brother, when I fear that I may lose my other brother who is a cancer survivor – especially since that brother has, until not long ago, introduced carcinogenic tobacco smoke into his body every day? Or my father who is battling prostate cancer; I worry that the cycle is about to repeat itself and there is nothing I can do to stop it? I hope that if and when Will's time with us here on the Earth ever comes to an end, I can say I was there serving Will and Liz and Katherine when they really needed me and that they all know that and appreciate it.

And what is it about that place that he is headed for – heaven? That place where everyone wants to go, but no one has been there and come back to tell us all what it is really all about. Okay, I'm a parent … So heaven is just like another school field trip, but it just lasts a lot longer and takes more time to prepare, right? So how do we get ready? You find yourself wanting to pack his backpack with his school books and papers, and of course his iPad and lots of games, and a hearty lunch in case he gets held up on the way there because you want him to be busy and not hungry while he's waiting to get in at the line queued up at the pearly gates. And what responsible parent sends a child of 13 on such a journey alone? You want to be there to walk beside him and hold his hand along the path, or at least walk behind and be there to help him if he falters along the way. I have no doubt God will be there to welcome him with open arms when his journey has reached its end. And how does heaven operate, for those of us earthlings who are used to nametags and organization and transportation to get us through our days intact? Who is going to get Will through orientation and make sure that he takes his special medications and spends time outside in the sunshine running and playing instead of hunched over his iPad mastering another cyberspace opponent? Who will make sure that he gets to bed on time and makes friends with other cancer kids his age who have lost their fights before him and are old hands in heaven and can show him "the ropes"? It's all foolish of course because we of this Earth have no concept that Will will have left his body behind and his soul will receive all of the sustenance it needs in heaven, but we can't shake that nagging feeling that sending Will off to heaven unaccompanied is somehow just one more way we have failed him here on Earth.

I have had this recurring dream. It is a late summer evening, the shadows grow as the sun slips beneath the horizon up the street from our house and the darkness, both physical and symbolic, approaches. Will and I are playing catch again as we always do. I mix it up to keep it interesting, throw him fastballs and grounders and "high-pops." It is a challenge for him to keep up as the cancer has robbed him of some of his dexterity but he wants me to keep those throws coming fast as he wouldn't have it any other way. The balls arc through the air and catch the fading light of the sun, punctuated by Will's chuckles at my often inept fielding of his grounders. We pretend that we are in the bottom of the 9th inning at the World Series, we can hear the dull roar of the crowd and I am Joe Mauer catching Will's Joe Nathan fastballs screaming over the plate as he mows down the batters, then he moves back to shortstop to take care of those pesky pop flies I throw him. The night is coming faster now and so I send one more ball his way and wait for him to haul it in and put another day of catch "in the can," but I slowly become aware that he has slipped away. He isn't there to catch it anymore because God's team in heaven needed another shortstop and Will has finally been called up by God to join his "majors" team in heaven. Somehow I know that Thoreau is there to greet him when he arrives, his tail wagging patiently (fixed after his unfortunate encounter with a UPS truck years ago) and help him shag those stray balls that get away – though I suppose in heaven, balls never get past the shortstop. Will turns back toward me, smiles and waves, and the pearly gates close. I glimpse Will and Thoreau head off to his first game in heaven as shortstop on God's team; he'll have a hot dog (with ketchup, but no mustard) and an Orange Crush (his favorite) and wait for the rest of us to arrive in our folding chairs on the sidelines to watch him perform once again. And I wait here on Earth for that return throw that never comes and wonder what will become of Liz and Katherine and me.

I close by saying that I pray each day for Will, that God will cure him, that God will give me and my family the strength to handle whatever comes, without losing our health or our sanity or our faith in the process. I pray that if God says that it is time to take Will home, that he will be ready to greet Him with a glad heart and that we will be accepting of the fact that we have to let him go. I pray that the other children who have preceded him to heaven, who lost their fight with cancer, will be there to welcome him with open arms to his new home where there will be no more tears, no more pain and no more sadness, but only the joy of eternal life and the assurance that he will be reunited with the rest of us someday, not far away.

Will, Katherine, Mom and Dad – "Miracles of Mitch" weekend at the Mall of America, Bloomington, Minnesota
– September 2011

Chapter 9 – Will's Cancer Spreads to His Spine

I think a hero is an ordinary individual who finds strength to persevere and endure in spite of overwhelming obstacles.–
-Christopher Reeve

August 24, 2011 – Will had an MRI of his head and spine done yesterday, and a follow-up MRI of his entire spine today. It showed that the tumors have spread now from his brain to several locations along the length of his spinal column. This takes the progression of the disease to a whole new level. It's akin to the radiation fallout after a nuclear explosion, the seeds of destruction being carried forward and sowed in new fertile ground where they can take root. Watching Dr. Rao show us the spread of the lesions on the MRI was like that dream where Liz and Will and Katherine and I get hit by a speeding train; Will falls under the wheels headed for certain destruction and we fall on the tracks to be run over, but survive the ordeal badly maimed for life. Will is stunned by the news and tells Dr. Rao, "This is more than I can process right now so can we talk more about it tomorrow?" The only bit of good news is that, mercifully, the new lesions are not yet large enough to cause symptoms for Will.

Dr. Rao is a little different from Dr. Wetmore, a little more interested in what Will wants to do (though in her defense, he is older now and more able to participate meaningfully in these discussions); she is kind in listening to his questions and offering her opinions. He tells her he wants to pursue treatment, but wants the side effects minimized so he can "go to school, play outside at recess, be able to run and walk." This breaks our hearts to hear our son asking for – and hoping to be able to do – the basic activities in a child's life that we all take for granted. Liz and I were not able to hold back the tears. It was even harder to look over at Donna, his favorite, experienced nurse practitioner with whom Will has a close bond, and see the sadness, anguish and tears welling up in her eyes. Every day, we gain a better appreciation of the many, many lives that Will has touched along his journey.

There is a metronomic chemo option, a cocktail of drugs offered up at different times over a weekly schedule, which has shown promise in helping some other kids who have experienced relapsed medulloblastomas. As we weigh the options, we know that Will's inner reserve of physical and emotional strength is depleted a little more with each round of drugs that is thrown at the cancer fortress, only to be dashed into pieces; it's difficult to muster up your medicine soldiers for another charge to carry the day. Side effects from the tumors entering the spinal cord are coming: there will be numbness, weakness, tingling, shooting pains as they slowly start to strangle Will's nervous system. Is the anticipation worse than the disease? His quality of life has been very good up until now; he hit those tennis balls out in the front yard well tonight, but I have already started worrying when he said his knee was hurting him some. *Don't let him suffer, Lord. Please let me take some of his cares out of his cancer "backpack" and put them in mine so he can continue on his way with a lighter burden.* In the end, we decide the best option is a combination of a number of drugs including the chemotherapy agents VP-16 and Cytoxan; statins; an NSAID (pain reliever); thalidomide; and Avastin, a drug that works to cut off the blood supply to tumors. All of the drugs will be taken orally, except the Avastin, which will be infused through his port-a-Cath every two weeks in the Pediatric Infusion Treatment Center. His blood counts will need to be monitored very carefully as his immune system is already compromised due to all of the past treatments. We leave the exam room with very heavy hearts knowing what this will mean for Will, but it is the best we can do given the circumstances.

On this very same day, we learned that 6-year-old John Shapiro had gone to his final reward in heaven; we thankfully had the honor of getting to know him over the past couple of summers at Camp Sunshine. John was the most outgoing, friendly and kind child you could ever meet. He was, appropriately, given the title of honorary "Mayor of Camp Sunshine." We remember John in funny, tender ways – he was always anxious to help the kitchen staff serve breakfast, serving popcorn to people at the camp talent show, and wearing a chef's hat that was nearly bigger than he was as part of a funny skit with camp kitchen staff in the Celebration Show. John was happiest when at Camp Sunshine. We remember him leaving camp with his family – and we watched many of the staff coming to say goodbye with big hugs – knowing that this would probably be the last time they could say goodbye to John in person. We will miss his smile and the joy that he brought to the people around him.

August 27, 2011 – Once word got out that Will's cancer had advanced, the e-mails and posts on his Facebook page began pouring in, and the kind people from our school and church were lining up to provide us with meals. What a profound blessing to have so many people concerned about Will offering their support and their prayers. It seems that as people know that the length of Will's remaining life may be limited, everyone wants a piece of his time. It's hard to be able to share him with others gracefully. "Meet the Teacher" for the new school year was hard, knowing that Will is not likely to be with us for "Meet the Teacher" next year. Many parents of classmates hovered nearby with sorrow in their eyes. They can find no words adequate to convey their compassion and concern; they look at their own kids and feel a pang of guilt, knowing that they will not have to endure what lies ahead for us.

After the "Meet the Teacher" at school, we were off to a birthday party for our old neighbor, Ron Kearnes, with his wife Debbie and their family and employees at Azotic Coating in Rochester. It was one of those perfect late summer evenings when we arrived: the cooling shade settled in from the shadow of the company's building as we grabbed our food and joined the party. Will made a new friend – a little girl named Cassidy – who was about 2, had curly golden locks and was a ball of energy. I caught a glimpse of them at one point as I looked down the parking lot: the sun was setting behind them putting them in backlit profile. Will was sitting on the curb, talking to her softly, and holding a piece of birthday cake that he was feeding her. Cassidy was chewing and doing a little dance to the music from the band, which had just launched into the lilting strains of Harry Chapin's "The Cat's in the Cradle" about the missed opportunities in his child's life watching him grow up because he was too busy doing other things. I reflected for just a moment: I had always tried so hard not to be that father in Harry's song; I was never too busy to play catch with Will; I'm sure I have failed him in other ways, but his illness has made me focus on him and I'm grateful for that.

Then later that week, I attended the funeral of Mariah Ackerman, my former legal assistant, who lost her battle with colon cancer at the age of only 33. Mariah was always there to lend a hand at work when we needed help. She came to the office with a smile on her face every day. We miss her presence greatly. It was hard to hear her mother talk about the loss of her daughter to cancer. The family asked me to read from a book she liked called *I Hope You Dance*, by Mark D. Sanders. It reads in part "hope takes never ceasing to be amazed, wearing your soul on your sleeve, holding your breath, waiting to hear 'I love you too,' believing that tomorrow could be better than today, that you'll get a second chance." We want all these things for Will – that his remaining time with us will be filled with simple pleasures and experiences we'll treasure, that we can pluck out and gaze upon when we feel lost and empty down the road, to remind us how Will moved people in our lives.

On September 2, Will and Liz ended up spending several hours in the ER. Will developed hives from his head to his knees and large, irregular shaped areas of very red skin on his torso. He also itched terribly. He said his swallowing was not difficult, but he had to swallow several times to get water and pills to go down. The ER Staff examined him, gave him Benadryl and then watched him closely for another hour or so. The Benadryl definitely helped. They also prescribed steroids for five days as a precaution to the swallowing issue, in case there was any airway/throat involvement. We also learned how to use an EpiPen, and were instructed to keep one at school and with him at all times.

September 2-4, 2011 – We had a good weekend at the Mall of America, courtesy of a foundation called "Miracles of Mitch." We all enjoyed the log ride at MOA, but Will got so wet that I spent nearly a half hour in the bathroom with him trying to dry his clothes under the hand dryer. Will enjoyed the Apple and Microsoft stores; he played an NFL video game with a clerk at Microsoft on a 103-inch TV and ended up tying him to send the game into overtime before we had to go. He and Katherine enjoyed the Rock Bottom roller coaster before we ended with a quick stop at the merry-go-round for a picture. After the full, long weekend, he said to me as I tucked him in and kissed him good night, "tomorrow is gonna be hard." Of course, I thought, yet another round of treatment with your life on the line. "No," he said, "it's hard because tomorrow is school and then I'll have to work for the rest of my life." No, he wasn't thinking of his own mortality, like the rest of us were; he was being typical, humorous Will, weighing in on the dreariness of a future filled with paychecks and pensions. I pray he gets that chance to see how hard a life of work can be.

On September 6, Liz and Will were at appointments pretty much all day and Will received his first Avastin infusion. He also took the first round of his new daily oral medications, which made him very sleepy and hard to rouse in the morning for school. Notwithstanding the start of yet another treatment regimen, Will was in an upbeat, silly mood. Among the great questions he had for Dr. Rao was whether a person can vomit when they are upside down. We all hope that Will is not going to find out the answer to this question himself anytime soon.

On September 7, Will had his first symptoms attributable to the spinal tumors – significant pain in his back and tingling in his left foot – another unwelcome milestone. Liz gave him Celebrex and Tylenol for the pain, which seemed to get it under control, but he stayed home from school to recuperate nonetheless. I got out my hand massager and worked on his back and his foot for a while, and it seemed to calm his pain a bit. He was in a mood for talking and asking a lot of questions tonight, so we sat downstairs in my office, with all of the pictures he had drawn for me over his life up on the wall, and talked. He told me about his favorite picture he had drawn with the orange stickmen and red clouds with the boat churning forward in the blue water, right next to the "Happy Christmas" card he did. He asked about my childhood, and how many houses I lived in as a kid and how old my brother Dave was when he died, and whether Uncle Steve had lost his right hand to cancer. He wanted to look at old pictures of Great-Grandma Conn when she was a girl out on the prairie in South Dakota and wearing "funny hats" as a nursing student in the 1920s, and Great-Grandpa McLaughlin wearing his ROTC uniform from his time at Marquette University during WWI. He wanted to see the family tree I had previously spent so much time mapping out and see which ancestors came from far off Ireland and Germany across the ocean, and he wanted to add in some info about Liz's parents. He asked where his children would go on it "if I haven't died by then." I tried hard not to tear up, and I showed him where those children of his he will never get to have would go. Priceless time. Then it was time for him to take a shower and the moment passed. I give thanks he shared it with me.

On the evening of September 9, at the invitation of dear friend Tom Ryan, the County Parks Director, we spent the night "camping" out at Oxbow Park near Byron – a night I knew would, in all likelihood, be the last campout I would have with Will. We ordered takeout pizza to start the evening, which fit perfectly into Tom Ryan's definition of "camping," but it was simple. Tom took us on a personal tour of the zoo just before dusk on that beautiful night. Tom brought out a small owl for Will to hold, which he was excited to do. We got to watch as they unloaded some new animals that would be joining the zoo. Then we built a roaring campfire, made s'mores, and stayed up telling stories and jokes until midnight. We spent the night in a house on the park property, away from the zoo, in a wooded peaceful area. Will and I really enjoyed this adventure, and Tom was a gracious host. Tom has walked the road of loss and grief before when his son, Brendan, died as a result of juvenile diabetes. We are forever grateful for Tom's friendship and kindness.

September 13, 2011 – Will tells me he has been practicing his smile for picture day. If he can crack a smile, then I think any of us can. Will is also aware that Lourdes High School Homecoming is next weekend and his sister does not yet have a date for the evening. Will sweetly told Katherine tonight at dinner, "Katherine, if you don't have anyone to go with you, I'll take you." She smiled and said, "thanks." We were all touched by his comment. There aren't many boys who would offer to take their older sister as their date to a school dance.

On September 15, the conversation with Will revolved around the opposite sex. It started when he asked Liz "if you don't have a girlfriend by high school, are you considered 'weird'?" She assured him that you aren't considered weird at all and that she certainly didn't have a steady boyfriend when she entered 9th grade. The conversation continued as I drove him to school. He said he intended to send a note to classmate Lizzy Bauer, asking her to be his date/girlfriend for school dances at St. Francis and to go on "dates" –unless she decided she wanted to go with somebody else or he was "too ugly." Lizzy is one of the sweetest, nicest, most polite girls we have ever met and so I told him it would be a good choice – and that he should not think he is "too ugly." He said if she would not do this, then he would ask Gracie Viggiano, the twin sister of his best friend, Joey Viggiano. Both great choices.

This is the first time that Will has ever indicated an interest in girls as a "girlfriend." *How much time do we have left Lord? Will they say yes because they really like him or because they feel sorry for him? Will they say no because of the scars and limitations he carries due to his illness? Will they say no because they worry about getting attached to him and then having to endure the pain and loss because he has passed away?* I'm breathless with anticipation to see how this goes today. I don't want him to be hurt, but I also want him to have a chance, like other kids, to experience this and know the happiness and exhilaration that love for someone his own age can bring to his life before he leaves us.

In the end, Will wrote Lizzy a note and slipped it into her locker. His note went something like this … "Dear Lizzy, would you like to be my girlfriend so we can go to dances together, see a movie and go out to dinner occasionally?" He told us he forgot to sign it, so he put another note in her locker that said, "Lizzy, it was from Will." Lizzy wasn't quite ready to be Will's girlfriend, but said that she would be willing to go to a movie with him sometime; we're glad he has this to look forward to.

September 19, 2011 – Will's class at school had a wonderful surprise in store for him yesterday. Four of his female classmates had heard about Will's latest round of challenging news and they wanted to do something special to show him how his class was behind him. The afternoon started when he arrived at school and was met in the parking lot by his classmates, all arrayed in identical orange T-shirts emblazoned with bright blue letters that said "Go Will's Team 11-12" on the front; on the back, it listed all of his classmates and the words "we're all behind you." They all clapped and cheered as Will leapt out of the van and started high-fiving his classmates. We wouldn't have missed this outpouring of love for the world; we all headed into the school. Then the class took to the gym floor, led by Mr. Arvold, and paired off by homeroom to start a game of "Townball." Will got the honorary position of chief pitcher (normally reserved for the illustrious Mr. Arvold) as the young men and women kicked, and sprinted and threw the ball across the gym. At the end of the game, we were treated to a performance by the "cheerleaders" – parents Mike Schweyen and John Cierzan, and teachers Brian Krenik (Will's Grade 3 teacher) and Dennis Schreiber (Will's Grade 8 teacher) – in drag, leading the crowd in cheers. They were outfitted in contrasting skirts, and some of the worst wigs ever seen at St. Francis of Assisi School. Then they insisted that Liz and I had to kiss in front of everyone, – reminiscent of "Kiss Cam," a feature at Minnesota Twins games – with Brian Krenik coming over and wanting in as well. Then a break for some homemade cupcakes, lovingly baked and frosted by the Class of 2016. The day came to a close after the kids gathered together for a game of whiffleball with Will again pitching his best. It was so good to witness this all: the kids gathering around Will and genuinely doing their best to lift his spirits and set aside his pain for a few hours; the parents congregated nearby, and Liz and I got the blessed chance to thank many of them one on one, talk a bit about the journey, ask how their families were doing this school year, and figuratively cry on a few shoulders. It was the absolute best example of what Catholic school is supposed to be all about – shared sacrifice, faith in action, hope for the future.

September 20, 2011 – Will is being pulled into the "vortex." We have a joke among one of my more charismatic co-workers that you can't get too close to Tammy or you risk getting pulled into the "vortex." Now that everyone has been reminded too painfully that Will's time with us is limited, suddenly everyone wants a piece of him, have him over to play video games, go out for a movie. His dance card is all filled up, leaving the "girls" here at home anxious for a little quality time with him before he creeps up to bed and pulls up the covers to his chin exhausted at the end of another day. It's hard to believe that his stock has changed so quickly. Everyone is waiting for him to say something memorable, including me, because every time with him might be the last time for this or that.

I find myself thinking again today about Will and heaven. When he isn't playing baseball on heaven's team, he should be signed up to man the celestial defenses against those who might try to breach the perimeter without permission. Anyone who has seen his skills at video games would know that God is going to get an extraordinarily talented defender who can recite all of the words from all of the scenes of all the *Star Wars* movies and can take out the bad guys with the very best of them. And surely he gets to take his iPad 2 with him, so he can check the baseball and football box scores and play his 43 game apps. I mean he'll probably be busy in heaven making friends with the other kids who have lost their cancer battles – but he's got all eternity to catch up, right?

Katherine was asked to Homecoming by classmate Michael Brandt, and the festivities took place on September 29. We stopped with Will at a local restaurant where Katherine and Michael and their other friends had gathered to eat dinner. Will wanted to go so we could get some pictures of he and Katherine together on her big night – and so that he could meet Michael. Michael passed Will's test, which is not easy to do because not just anyone is right for his sister!

October 8 -14, 2011 – The week starts as we gather with family and friends for the annual Brains Together for a Cure Walk in Rochester.

It's a warm, sunny day for a change. Mom and Dad have come over from La Crosse to support the cause and over 700 people have shown up to join them. The buzz is palpable as the participants drift around the crowded gym at the local community college, checking out the silent auction and the Wall of Remembrance, photos on a stark black background of those in the fight and those we have lost along the way. Will does the entire 5K walk, digging deep to find some hidden energy reserve. The participants reconvene indoors to listen to Denny Nigon, former head of Rochester Catholic Schools, as he tells his story of struggle to overcome Stage 4 throat cancer, inspiring all in attendance. We draw strength when the silent majority – the survivors – take shape in tangible form and stand up to be counted in the fight.

October 14 brought a brush with royalty. Dear friend Chris Gade, from the Communications Department at Mayo, needed two local pediatric patients to present a bouquet of flowers to the King and Queen of Norway when they arrived in Rochester for a short visit. Will got the call and we swung into action. He got a new dress shirt, pants, belt, tie and shoes, worked on learning to say "welcome" in Norwegian, and he was ready for the big event. As the time approached, a large crowd of people started to gather in the atrium of the Gonda Building at Mayo. Velvet barricades separated us from the growing number of spectators. Will was a little fidgety, but looked so handsome in his new outfit with his new friend Hannah, a 10-year-old leukemia patient, who was tapped to present the other bouquet. Friend Art Larson came up with a little Norwegian flag to set just the right tone. Suddenly, a Minnesota State Patrol car loomed into view, followed by several Suburbans. A door on one of the silver SUVs slowly swung open and, gracefully, the King and Queen emerged. They shook hands with the CEO and Administrator of Mayo out at the street and headed inside to where we waited. I could see the smile grow on Will's face as they cleared the revolving doors and caught sight of Will and Hannah. They grinned as they met our young ambassadors and leaned down to greet them. We could not hear their conversation from our vantage point nearby, but learned later they greeted them, and asked their names and ages. The Queen smiled gently as she received the two bouquets, shook their hands, then moved on to visit other dignitaries. Will was calm despite all the clamor around him; no real surprise, given what he has been through. He was a little upset that the photos of the event caught the back of his head where his thinning hair was becoming quite apparent, but happy that he got the chance to make them feel welcome, if only for a moment. We were so proud of him that day. He shone in his moment in the spotlight. *"Take that, cancer! I'm still here despite all your efforts to deny me that opportunity."*

–A Reprieve

By November 22, Will had completed the latest round of tests, as well as a full MRI of his brain and spine, and now it was time for the appointment with Dr. Rao to go over the results. The cold wind slapped my face as I headed down 2nd Street SW to the Clinic; my mind swirled with anticipation. *What will the tests show? Will he be stable, with no change since the last time? Or will the scans show that the tumors have grown even further and that the end for Will approaches more quickly?* Dr. Rao enters the exam room with a smile on her face. *Huh? A smile? We haven't seen one of those on Mayo 16 in a very long time.* A little chit chat to catch up and finally she can't hold it in any more – the scans show remarkable progress, the tumors have shrunk in size dramatically, in some cases more than 50%. Our disbelieving eyes shift to the MRIs. Yes, a spot there gone, another spot there gone, another spot much smaller than before. *What, how can that be? We've actually won a round with the beast? Will gets more time, yippeeeeee!* It's not a cure and this is still a fight we could lose down the road, but the smiles on the faces of the medical staff, Donna Betcher most notably, speak volumes about what this means to Will and to the many people who have been watching his progress. The news is quickly shared with family and friends who are equally amazed; even Dr. Wetmore, who as much as admitted that this fight was mostly over, was so pleased with Will's progress. It's tempting to put Will's MRI out on Facebook so all the world can see the results for themselves, but the HIPAA issues that would create in my lawyer's mind are nothing short of endless, so a description in words of our joy must suffice. Thanksgiving this year is sweet, shared with our friends the Viggianos, who know that Joey and Will's friendship will last a while longer. My Mom and Dad, and sister Kathy and brother-in-law Tom Biskupski, arrive later in the weekend to share in our triumph. They know our struggles all too well; they know what this milestone means. We have a reprieve, a chance to catch our breath, think beyond the next 30 days about what is possible – a family cruise in the Caribbean, high school for Will, a return to Camp Sunshine instead of planning a funeral and mourning what might have been for Will and for all of us. Let's make the most of it!

On the weekend of December 16-18, Will and the rest of us travelled to the Appleton, Wisconsin area over the weekend for my niece Kristin's graduation from college and an early Christmas get-together with the Canans. Will and Grandpa and Uncle Steve and I even snuck in a quick trip to the Packer Hall of Fame in Green Bay. Will enjoyed being with the Canan boys and checking out all of the Packer memorabilia, including Aaron Rodgers' uniform from the Super Bowl we had attended in Dallas just months before, sitting at Vince Lombardi's desk, and seeing the Packers four Super Bowl trophies. He especially appreciated reading about Vince who lost his own battle with cancer so many years ago, but was a true hero and inspiration to many, just like our Will.

On December 30, Will had his first tennis lesson at the indoor tennis center near our home. He worked on his forehand and backhand for 30 minutes with his instructor, Tim Butorac. Will really enjoyed it. We truly hope he's found another activity that he can do and enjoy. As Liz watched him hit balls, she couldn't help but wonder how much better he would be at tennis if he hadn't fought cancer for over seven years. It can make you angry at what cancer has done to Will's body and to his dreams if you dwell on it. But, we have the present. Will loves learning a new sport and we will relish that time for as long as we are able.

Will learning tennis at the Rochester Indoor Tennis Center, Rochester – December 2011

January 10, 2012 – A new year, a chance to undo the mistakes of last year and start fresh. The old year ended with Liz, Will and me at home, straining to stay up until midnight to watch the ball drop in front of thousands in Times Square ushering in the New Year. At midnight, we each get a heartfelt kiss and a tight hug from Will, tangible evidence of the promise that the new year offers. Today is a study in contrasts. I hurried home at lunch to wake up Will, get him dressed and fed, and off to school. The new chemo regimen still seems to be working on keeping the cancer at bay, but Will's poor body is exhausted after so many treatments and he can't seem to get up in time for school many of the days. We head out into the 55 degree sunshine (yes, no one can quite believe it – our grass is turning green in January) to deposit him at St. Francis with his classmates. Later, I join Liz at the swelling church at St. John's for the funeral of Shannon O'Hara, a 13-year-old girl from Rochester diagnosed nine months ago with a glioma brainstem tumor. Though I did not get to know Shannon before she passed away, she was, by all accounts, a spunky kid who loved life and touched many. The church was filled to capacity, many of the seats occupied by junior high and high school kids. Her teammates came in uniform from the Mayo High School golf team and from her girls' hockey team, the Rebels, her soccer and lacrosse teams. Her Uncle Mike and Father Mahon talked about the impact Shannon made on those around her, how she never did anything without giving her all. Father Mahon offered the kids a chance to sit on the steps near the altar as he preached his sermon, but there were so many that every space on the sanctuary and up the aisle was filled; they got a chance to touch Shannon's casket and whisper their goodbyes before returning, teary eyed, to their seats. The music included "You are Mine," that song that resonates so deeply for Liz and me about the promise God offers at the really difficult points along the journey. It was a moving hour of outpoured love. I left the funeral early to take my brain tumor survivor to his tennis lesson. I watched him as he took the court with the pro and started to hit forehands and backhands and hit volleys at the net. There had been something niggling at my thoughts lately, and today it finally became clear what had been on my mind. As last fall drew to a close, Will's spinal tumors grew and spread; they had started robbing Will of his mobility and his ability to stretch out as we played our nightly game of catch in the front yard. Yet as I watched him today, it was evident that he had been freed from the spinal bonds that had held him down; as the chemo regimen shrank his tumors, his freedom to move was returning. It was a new lease on life! There are few things more beautiful to watch than something that had once been taken away now, by the grace of God, given back at least for a while. It is ours to savor. Will has the opportunity to rejoin the world of the "regular kids" who never gave their ability to move a second thought. Will recognized it too and smiled as he came off the court. God took something precious from the O'Haras today and he gave us something precious back. There is no explanation why this should be; the O'Haras were just as deserving. I grieve their loss, but relish Will's resurgence nonetheless.

January 19 – This has been a challenging week for Will. He has been very fatigued, which is likely caused by the thalidomide he is taking, though Dr. Rao does not want to cut back on the dosage just yet. Will also started having some blood in his stools earlier in the week, and it's still continuing. Despite all this, he feels pretty well overall and wants to attend another tennis lesson. He tried out for the school play, and got the part of "Mr. Hood" in a musical version of Little Red Riding Hood, called *Do Wop Wed Widing Hood*. Will's also been hard at work on a science report. We had recently decided to take the kids on a short cruise on Royal Caribbean out of Florida to the Bahamas over the long President's Day weekend in February. Once Will found out about this, he changed the subject of his science paper. When we were discussing the possibility of the cruise, he immediately said, "I think we'll be cruising near or in the Bermuda Triangle." His science teacher suggested that this would be a great topic for Will's science report.

January 24, 2012 – Last night we had a steady storm of freezing rain. This morning we woke to sidewalks and streets glazed with a thin sheet of ice. Today while I was at work, I got a message from Liz that Will had been out walking Buddy, our 80 pound Lab, and had fallen and hit his head hard on the sidewalk. Liz had looked out our bedroom window to see him lying face down on the sidewalk with Buddy remaining by his side. She screamed to Katherine and they both ran outside. By this time, Will had gotten up and was staggering toward the house. *Oh, God, please not his head, the head we have taken such great pains to protect.*

After I raced home, I learned more. Buddy had been pulling on the leash and Will, knowing the dog's propensity to run off, was determined not to let that happen; in the process, Will had fallen not just once, but several times. At least one of those times, he fell face first on the sidewalk, hard enough that it knocked him out for several seconds. A huge goose egg was swelling on the left side of his forehead when I gently looked him over. Liz, Katherine and I also noted that he seemed to have difficulty responding correctly to questions; he was having vision problems and had a harder time than usual hearing what we said. In typical Will style, however, he sat down and did some math homework while we iced his bump and decided what we should do. Erring on the side of caution, we hurried off once more to Saint Marys Hospital, this time to let the ER docs have a look at him. The ER waiting room was crowded with all shades of humanity when we arrived, young and old, tall and small, coughing and moaning softly in pain, many it would seem from their own falls on the icy sidewalks. Because of Will's history and head trauma, they got him back fairly quickly, for which we were very grateful. A neurologic exam and CT scan showed that he had no signs of internal bleeding, but most likely he had sustained a concussion. We took him home and tucked him in bed at the close of a very long day. Will needs to rest physically, but more importantly he needs mental rest and not do a lot of thinking and homework for several days. There's no treatment for a concussion and each person recovers at his or her own pace. We're grateful it was not worse, but who knows what havoc an unexpected concussion might wreak on his poor brain, which has already been to hell and back. He seems somewhat better the next day. I note the tremor in his left hand is a little stronger than usual but, given time, he will bounce back from this, as he has from so many other things on this very long road.

January 31, 2012 – Ah, the end of the harshest month of the year. You know what that means if you live in Minnesota: the worst days of winter are usually behind us and easier days lie ahead. Does that apply to life in general? On February 3, one of Will's thyroid-related tests comes back a bit on the low side, but his endocrinologist wants to repeat it again in two months before putting him on thyroid replacement medicine. He's monitored closely for thyroid and pituitary issues because radiation can cause problems and the thalidomide he's taking can impact thyroid function as well. Will also had a new set of questions for Dr. Rao and the other medical staff up on Mayo 16. First, he asked Dr. Rao if she was a US citizen. She responded, "No, I'm a resident alien." She added, "Will, you always ask interesting questions."

Then Will decided to poll her and others on the floor about who they would vote for if the presidential election were that day. It's funny, but he didn't get any specific answers, only vague responses like, "I haven't made up my mind;" "I can't vote because I'm not a US citizen;" and the best one of all, "I wouldn't vote for any of them."

February 25, 2012 – It's been a whirlwind 10 days. On February 16, we departed for Cape Canaveral, Florida for a special birthday present for Will: a three-day cruise on Royal Caribbean's *Monarch of the Seas* to the Bahamas. As we drove up in the rental van to the cruise dock, I watched Will and Katherine's eyes bulge with amazement as they took in the 10-story building with a keel underneath and marveled that this enormous thing could actually move under its own power and take us out to sea. There was a big party up on the pool deck when we got underway; Will laid on a chaise lounge and we watched the Kennedy Space Center in the distance slide astern. The seagulls gathered around us, insistent on picking up some last morsels from this floating island until they gave up and headed back home. The cool sea air felt great as we turned southeast and headed for Nassau. There were about 2,300 passengers on this floating city, two pools, two hot tubs, a basketball court, climbing wall, and even ping-pong. We had two staterooms next to each other on the 7th deck with nice size windows overlooking the ocean. We had a wonderful dinner and the kids loved the service (waiters unfolding your napkin and placing it in your lap), the chance to try a variety of food (because if you didn't like it, they brought you something else), and of course, dessert. They also enjoyed virgin strawberry daiquiris, served in special Royal Caribbean cups with bottoms that had revolving lights. We sailed overnight to Nassau, in the Bahamas.

Day 2 brought us to Nassau, and then a transfer to a smaller boat where we headed off to a nearby island for the Blue Lagoon Dolphin Encounter. Will and Katherine were enthralled as we entered the water and stood on a slightly raised platform and Salvador, our chosen dolphin, approached. With the help of a trainer nearby, he was quick to plant a kiss on our cheeks, let us give him a hug, dance with him with extended flippers and even mimic a farting sound when the trainer made a bad joke. Will grinned from ear to ear until it was time to get out of the water. We then watched them feed the sea lions in an adjoining area before clambering back into our small boat for the trip back to Nassau.

The next day, our floating palace arrived off Coco Cay, Royal Caribbean's private island. Will was not feeling very well when he awoke and we decided that I would go over to the island and snorkel for a little while the rest of the gang remained on the ship to see if Will would improve. My snorkeling adventure was a glimpse into another world; large schools of pale blue fish with yellow stripes whirled around me as I made my way slowly underwater through the lagoon. Will was feeling better by the afternoon and I went back to the ship to get him while Liz and Katherine came over for some mother-daughter time on the island. When Will and I got back to the island, we had time for a wild Jet Ski ride around several of the adjoining islands. With Katherine on the back of my Jet Ski and Will on the back of Liz's, we were soon leaping waves and drenched in warm salty spray as we twisted and zoomed following our guide. Will and Liz found it a little too wild for their liking, but Katherine and I had an awesome ride. Back on the ship, we were treated to the last of our fabulous meals. Liz had ordered a delicious chocolate birthday cake for Will. The waiters all gathered around "Willy" and helped to sing "Happy Birthday," 14 precious years marked in time. An elephant made from a towel awaited Will back at our stateroom. The staff was wonderful and Will and the rest of us found the experience was over all too soon. Hopefully there will be another cruise in Will's future to share.

One day after our return, Katherine crept into our bedroom at 1 a.m. crying. "Wyatt is dead." Wyatt was Katherine's first and only boyfriend. They had dated for most of freshman year, and broke up as summer vacation 2011 began. Wyatt was a bit of an enigma to us, something of a class clown with a big smile, but he always seemed to be holding something back. It later turned out he had struggled for some time with depression and had taken his own life. It was a very hard week for Katherine as she was as close to him as any of his female classmates, but her friends were quick to console her.

The funeral was held on February 25 at St. John's Catholic Church. The funeral for a teen is so different from that of an adult. Because of the manner in which he had passed away, it was decided to cremate him, thus the kids did not have the benefit of a viewing where they could see for themselves he was gone and have some closure in paying their last respects. The images from that day linger in my head: little groups dressed in black hovered everywhere in the gathering space, Kleenex boxes clutched tightly, as they tried to resolve a seemingly happy life cut short. The church was crowded with students and parents and family for the funeral Mass. With no casket, there was no focal point, so we had to imagine him as he was. Words came from the pulpit about Wyatt and his smile and how, despite his struggles, God was welcoming him home. His family, huddled in the front row, was obviously devastated by Wyatt's decision. Katherine and her friends cried the entire funeral. And then, all at once, it was over. I wondered as the people slowly filed out if God lets you look down from wherever heaven or hell or purgatory might be and you get to watch your own funeral and see the devastation that your decision to commit suicide has created. Do you get to see all of the people gathered there who cared so much about you that you get the chance to wonder if you made a horrible mistake, which you would get to undo if you got the chance? Was it the just act of a tortured body and soul unable to take it any longer, or the selfish act of a young man who did not care what his actions did to those he loved? *Death, you come again – only this time to someone who did not know in advance the true value of life.* It's a reminder with Will's life that those days you move on the earth and reach others are a treasure, not to be squandered before God says your time to depart has come.

After much thought, and making sure that Katherine was okay, Liz and Will flew to Kansas City to spend the weekend with Liz's parents and attend the "border battle" basketball game on February 25 between Kansas and Missouri. Kansas was ranked #4 and Missouri was ranked #3 in the nation on game day. Their wonderful seats (two rows up from the court), a parking pass right outside Allen Field House, and the opportunity to have lunch in the Atrium Club with Grandma and Grandpa Levy were a gift from friends Tom and Judy Bowser, to whom we owe a very large thank you.

The place was packed with over 16,000 screaming fans, reaching a level of 119 decibels at the loudest point, comparable to a jet engine. KU played poorly the first half and trailed by 19 points at the half. Will said, "Mom, they're going to lose." Liz replied, "Will, the second half is a new ball game." While she didn't think KU could do it, they overcame the 19 point deficit and tied the game to move it into overtime. KU eventually won 87-86. The crowd, including Liz and Will, went absolutely nuts! It turned out to be the largest deficit where KU had come back to win in their storied history – one of the best games ever to be played in Allen Field House. Liz got chills down her spine just to be able to be there with Will sharing this experience.

On February 27, Will had another set of MRIs of his brain and spine. We met with Dr. Rao on February 28 to review them with her. The results were not what we had hoped. Basically, the brain and spinal tumors had grown back to roughly the size they were in August 2011. The one bit of good news was that Will had no new tumors. Will had missed about six weeks (three doses) of Avastin, partly due to healing from his concussion, and Dr. Rao believed that may have contributed to what we're seeing on the scans. Liz and I had been worried about the results from these tests more than usual. We had noticed that Will was having more short-term memory loss and the tremor in his left hand was also more pronounced. Dr. Rao said these symptoms are being caused by where the tumors are located. Where do we go from here? The plan we discussed, which Will wants to do, is to keep him on the same medications, but also give him two other drugs intrathecally, through the Ommaya Reservoir in his head. The spinal tumors at this point are inside the lining in the fluid and not into the spinal vertebrae. The hope is that chemo put in through the Ommaya can directly circulate throughout his cerebrospinal fluid and hopefully shrink some of the tumors. We'll do scans again in 6 weeks to evaluate if this new plan is working or not.

On March 6, Will received the first injection of the new chemo mixture into his Ommaya from Donna and Dr. Rao. It went smoothly and there was even some laughter in between the serious, focused moments, which was greatly appreciated. Will tolerated the first dose very well. He had to take three days of steroids, which is standard protocol when taking the drug intrathecally. Donna e-mailed to check on him. Will's response was, "Why is she doing that? I'm fine." He's also interested now in going out for the Lourdes High School 8th grade golf team, coached by Mr. Arvold, which will have to be worked in around play practice and endless medical appointments. Only Will our Warrior could have that sunny outlook at this stage.

On March 14, we marked the eighth year since Will's original diagnosis. Ironically, we were in the ER with Will, eight years to the day! Even before the scans several weeks ago, we'd been noticing a gradual decline in Will's short-term memory. His long-term recall is good, but it's like he has dementia even though he's only 14-years-old.

Yesterday, Will had an episode that really scared us. He lost his ability to think of words and to speak. He also had some blurred vision, dizziness and a slight headache. This "episode" seemed to last about 1-2 hours, but by the time we got him to the ER, he was back to his baseline "normal." A CT scan was normal and there was no evidence of bleeding in the brain. They opted to keep him overnight in the hospital and run further tests including a MRI, MRA and EEG. How did Will handle this? With the usual grace and calmness that he always has shown. He was very talkative and so polite to all who came into his room; he even ate a good dinner.

When the EEG test results came back, they didn't show any "spikes," which would be indicative of a seizure. It did show some "slowing" in the area of his brain where he had surgery and radiation last year, an area that is important for speech and expression. The MRI didn't show any further tumor progression compared to the one done on February 28; however, there hasn't been a lot of time in between scans. The MRA test, which was looking to see if there is narrowing of the blood vessels in Will's brain, did not show this, which is a good thing. Therefore, the doctors still truly don't know what happened to Will when he had this episode. What does this mean for the new treatment regimen he had been on? We decided to continue to have Will take his oral medications, but will not do further intrathecal chemo administration in the near future assuming this contributed somehow to the "episode." We don't know if the medications are helping any longer, but Will wants to continue and we'll honor this. He is still telling people that next year he'll go to Lourdes High School. *Please give us hope that he will make it there.*

April 1st dawned clear and cool. It was the first Sunday in April, and in these parts that means only one thing: the Fools Five Race in Lewiston. I had participated in this fundraiser race since 2005. This would make eight times I had raised money for cancer research and made the short pilgrimage over to Lewiston to join others united for the cause. This time, Katherine was committed to running the 1-mile race, and Liz and Will would come along to help cheer us on as I tackled the 5-mile race. The same feelings I'd had in the past came crowding back as we pulled up to the high school: anxiety, wondering if my body could stick out it out once again, and gladness at seeing thousands of people gathered in little groups, picking up their race packets, strapping the timing chips onto their shoes, pinning their numbers on their newly acquired race T-shirts, filling out stickers indicating they were running "In Honor of ____" or "In Memory of ____" and carefully placing them on their T-shirts in prominent places where they could be glimpsed by passersby. We moved slowly with the group from the high school a block away to where the crowd was gathering at the starting line. There was the ceremonial thank you to the organizers, a moving rendition of the "Star Spangled Banner" and the crowd of runners tensed as the starter raised his pistol. I lost sight of Katherine and Will and Liz as I heard the crack of the start pistol and the crowd of more than 3000 runners began to slowly surge forward. I started slowly, threading my way through the throng, reading the names on the jerseys remembering Grandma Betty and Uncle Bill and little Marie and thousands more. A legion of love and loss, both actual and anticipated, powerful and moving. The conditions were perfect for running and the miles slipped away with Jackson Browne and Styx to keep me company. Barely before I knew it, I turned the corner on the last mile – a straightaway to the finish line. I found an extra gear, and picked up the pace as the Olympic theme throbbed in my ears at just the right moment, a favorite tune Will and I shared. Then there they were at the finish line, Liz and Katherine and Will – with a big smile on his face – clapping to cheer me on as I crossed over. That's the reason I do it every year: I know he will be there to smile at me at the finish one more time and to help raise money to someday end all the suffering. A gracious bystander snapped a quick photo of us in our orange "Go Team Will" T-Shirts before the day drew to a close. In total, another $80,000 was raised to help fight cancer. It was an excellent day.

On April 2, Will had another appointment with Dr. Rao. After discussions about the all of the recent developments and test results, we decided it was best to proceed with Will receiving five consecutive days of intrathecal infusions of a chemo agent called Etopiside (VP-16). So, each afternoon this week, which was Will's Spring Break from school, Liz and Will made daily trips to Gonda 7 for the infusions. While it only took about an hour from arriving to finishing, Will said he wished he wouldn't have had to do this every day of his Spring Break. Who could blame him for feeling this way?

April 8, 2012 was Easter. Grandma and Grandpa Canan were here to join us in celebrating this important day. As luck would have it, I was also scheduled to lector and do one of the readings at Mass that day. It meant so much to be there together as we all crowded into the pew, the sunlight streaming in through the south-facing stained glass windows overhead. I thought back to Easter 2004, right after Will had been released from the hospital on Good Friday following his original surgery and recuperation, all the mingled joy at his return home and fear that he would not live to see another Easter. Now here we were, eight years later, celebrating Easter together. My Mom told me how proud she was that Will was truly engaged in the Mass, listening to the readings, saying the prayers, sharing the hymnal with her to sing the songs. I've had those talks with Will about getting to know God and I think he has taken some of that to heart. He knows how truly fragile his life is and how he may be called to meet his maker sooner than many of his peers. Developing that close relationship, so that he is prepared for when that time comes, is something that he has made a priority. I'm so proud of him for that. He has come to realize that at some point when you have endured the incredible hardships he has weathered, your faith and attendance at church change from an obligation to a comfort. Knowing that my parents understand that he has made that connection as well gives me comfort; I know that I've done at least one thing right as a parent, and I have my own parents to thank for that.

Will, Katherine, Mom and Dad at the Fools Five Road Race to raise money for cancer research, Lewiston, Minnesota – April 2012

– School Play

On April 14, Will awoke and felt pressure building inside of his head. He said it was there during the night, but he didn't get up to tell us! We went to the ER, where they did a head CT and found there was no sign of a brain bleed or any signs of swelling. By later in the day, the pressure had gone away. Allergies could have been a possibility for the feeling of pressure. We had previously discussed adding an additional chemo drug to the existing mix, Ara-C, to give Will a better chance that the chemo would have the desired effect, but after the pressure issue – and so that he would feel as well as possible in the final week of play practice before opening night – we collectively decided to defer giving the Ara-C indefinitely.

April 21, 2012 – The anticipation has been building all week as the family gathers to watch Will participate in the school play *Do Wop Wed Widing Hood*. The week began as we all gathered for Katherine's Confirmation, an important step that she has grown in her faith and is beginning to be recognized as an adult in the eyes of the church. It was a beautiful ceremony, though interrupted a bit toward the end when Ben, my 7-year-old nephew, ended up napping and snoring in the pew, which got Will and the rest of us near him laughing as quietly as possible. Will has been attending play practice on a daily basis. It's been hard for him to manage while he stays on a chemo regimen, tries to go to school and then attend a couple of hours of play practice. Dr. Rao, Will's oncologist and Donna Betcher, Will's nurse practitioner, join both sets of Will's grandparents, my sister Kathy, my brother-in-law Tom, their son Ben, and Liz, Katherine and me in the school gym. The lights slowly draw down, the curtain opens and the show has begun. The play is a modern take on the classic fairy tale, but set in the 1950s with Red Riding Hood in a kingdom where a host of suitors vie for the right to "woo" her. Will plays the role of Mr. Hood, Little Red Riding Hood's father. He's outfitted in an old flannel bathrobe and his life mainly seems to consist of curling up on the sofa with his "wife," the TV remote control firmly tucked in hand, while he watches old sitcoms and doles out quips of fatherly advice. The part about his relationship with the TV and the remote control is obviously a case of life imitating art since Will has such good control over the TV remote control at home. The surgery, the radiation and the chemo have taken a toll on his ability to remember all of his lines, so they have fixed a prop: a *TV Guide* book cover with his lines pasted and highlighted inside. There is a moment or two throughout where there is a pregnant pause as we wait, silently holding our breath that he will find his next line, but his dry wit comes through and the play comes off without a hitch. He is normally a rather shy young man; I give him credit to overcome his fears to stand up in front of a hundred plus people and act and deliver his lines loudly without a microphone where he knows he could have a lapse and fail, but then he has been walking the high wire without a net for quite a while now, so maybe I should not have worried. Grateful hugs from family and friends for a great performance. He has done well.

April 24, 2012 – Will indicated several weeks ago that he wanted to participate on the Lourdes High School 8th grade golf team. He knows several of the boys on the team and enjoys their company. Even better, his favorite teacher, Mark Arvold, the phy ed teacher at St. Francis, will be the assistant golf coach. It is good knowing that Mark's steady hand and reliable humor will be there to make things go smoothly out on the links. The night before the first match, I went through Will's golf bag, wanting it all to be perfect – golf balls in one pocket, tees in another, clumps of mud shined off the golf club heads. The day turned out to be a perfect one for golf: sunny, temperature in the low 70s, a light wind. We arranged to have a cart for Will, as it is getting harder for him after all the treatments to walk long distances. He lines it up on the first tee, a smooth swish of a backswing launches the ball down the fairway and we are headed after it. I walked along the course to watch as Liz drove the golf cart, kept score for the boys and, as the family golf expert, doled out advice on shots to Will as we went along. It was a bit of a tough day for the first time out, but he hit a couple of nice putts and his friends were full of encouragement when he had a tough lie in the rough and needed to find his way back to the fairway. He ended up with a 75 and a grin on his face. Will loves being part of a team, more than the average kid perhaps, because of the isolation that his illness creates. He looks forward to the next match at Willow Creek next week. It was yet another day that Liz and I could not miss; we were so pleased he was able to be a part of it.

May 7, 2012 – Will had an Avastin infusion today as we fight another day to keep the cancer gremlins at bay. One hour after his infusion was completed, he was at the baseball field for the first practice with his team. A hard day in some ways, as this is the last year that he will be able to play youth baseball. I agreed to help out Brian Cada, his longtime coach, as his assistant for a couple of days while his other assistant, Jim Ryan, attends a conference. As the players stepped up to Brian for introductions, all I could do was marvel at their size, a full foot or more taller than Will, and the bulging muscles gained in weeks or months of preparation. It was obvious that it was all Will could do to drag himself out onto the baseball field, a place he has always loved in the past. He did his best, but it was torture to watch him miss balls hit to him, or to watch balls sail over his head without any energy to run and catch them. I watched some of his new teammates who do not know Will and his story shake their heads slightly as they watched him struggle. It's the first time I really feared for his safety as I watched how fast these young men pitch and saw how far and how hard they can hit the ball. I see an errant pitch or lined fastball striking Will in the head leading to disaster. It made me wish again that he could be on a team of similarly abled kids fighting cancer who are shrugging off chemo for the umpteenth time, and see how he could shine. He told me on the way home after practice that this was the first time he felt he liked playing golf better than baseball. It's like turning your back on your first love. Though the spirit was willing, his body was too weak.

The next round of MRIs occurs Thursday and Friday and we get the results on May 15. It's undeniable that he's ebbing away slowly. I want to catch him and hold onto him so that cancer cannot have him, but I do not get to decide where he spends his future. *8th grade graduation is coming, a family trip to watch the Twins on Mother's Day, high school with the promise of a fresh start and new friends ... hang on ... please don't leave us yet, Will.*

May 13 – The week starts with Mother's Day. Will has made Liz a homemade card and gave it to her this morning, which she loved. Will also wanted her to deposit a fair amount of cash he'd built up in his reserve. He did spend some of it on himself, but then said, "Mom, we could keep the rest out of the bank and I can buy you some jewelry at one of the jewelry stores." This brought tears to her eyes. Will is always thinking of others, despite what he is going through. I have planned a special Mother's Day family trip on a beautiful sunny day to Target Field in Minneapolis to watch Will's beloved Twins take on the Toronto Blue Jays. A few hours soaking up the sun, working on some burgers and lemonade, watching one of the Twins rookies hit his first major league home run, and the Twins hold on to win 4-3. A respite from the worry about the upcoming MRI results on May 15. Liz and I toss and turn in bed on Monday night, the dread of what tomorrow will bring disturbing our peaceful slumbers.

On Tuesday, Dr. Rao unveils the new MRI results and the news is not good. While the chemo Will has been taking has likely slowed the rate of growth of the tumors, there is at least one new spot on his spine and two areas in the cerebellum of his brain where the tumors have grown further in size. Dr. Rao is apologetic; she does not have any further treatment options to offer. Will is stunned to silence. He willingly goes off down the hall for a few moments so that Liz and I can discuss things further. How much time does he have? When do we start hospice care? What kinds of symptoms will signal the end is near? Surely there must be something we can do. We've been at these kinds of roadblocks before but there has always been at least one more untried weapon in our cancer-fighting tool kit. Sure, he's slowed a little in energy, but he is relatively symptom-free. It's intuitively hard to grasp that he could go from his current condition to deceased in the matter of a few short months. Will does not go to school that day, or the next, or the next. He does not want to tell his friends that he may be out of options to treat his illness. He does not feel up to playing in his baseball game on Wednesday night. I'm an assistant coach this year, finally after years of waiting, and I ponder his absence as I serve as third base coach. What will he bring to this team? Will he rally them around him with his determination or will he get seriously hurt by one of the errant pitcher's fastballs and bring his season to a close virtually before it has begun?

Life blurred to Thursday. After Liz recovered from her shock, her anger kicked in and the Internet hummed with her searches. The predictable e-mails started to fly; doctors and parents from the cancer world weigh in with a treatment that worked for one child here, a "holding tumors in check" for another child but with serious side effects there. Dr. Wetmore was always so good to hold our hands and sort the serious from the downright dangerous or silly options. We hope and pray that Dr. Rao is up to the task. Liz and I end the workday by serving a meal on behalf of Brains Together for a Cure at the Hope Lodge for adult cancer patients. The setting is different, yet familiar. The small bodies with face masks and baseball caps to protect against infections have grown large and wrinkled with heads wrapped in colorful scarves; the crutches of the pediatric osteogenic sarcoma patients replaced by the walkers of adult cancer patients grown infirm after surgery and radiation and chemo, but the slightly sunken faces, hollow from little appetite after radiation, mark them as members of the cancer "club." They are uniformly grateful for the meal.

I finally rouse Will from his depression a bit tonight. He's still "got it" as he whips me in Hangman two games out of three. I ask about a trip he would like to take this summer. He mentions Yellowstone and so I plot out a possible trip to the great national park, knowing full well that yet another treatment regimen could prevent this dream from becoming reality. But we all have to have something to look forward to, even if you don't know how much time you have left, or the body gives up with nothing left to live for. Despite the current hardships, Will still very much wants to live and so we will continue the search for something, anything, to throw at this thing so he gets more time with us. Further discussions with Dr. Rao lead to a decision to start him on a drug called valproic acid. It's an anti-seizure medication that is showing some promise in treating kids with recurrent medulloblastoma. Will will start on a lower dosage and, if he tolerates it well, they will increase it and possibly add another oral chemo with it. If it can hold the cancer in check, we'll do whatever is needed.

Will in 8th grade class T-Shirt on Graduation Day from St. Francis of Assisi School, Rochester – May 2012

May 27, 2012 – It's the start of another important week in Will's life, the week when he leaves the familiar halls of St. Francis of Assisi School behind and graduates from 8th grade. Will has also been working on a class project as the end of his years at St. Francis draws closer. It involves the creation of a poster about himself entitled <u>Where Am I From?</u> His telling words as he reflects on what makes him tick go like this:

<u>I am from Rochester, Minnesota, the home of the Honkers.</u>

<u>I am from going to Twins games up at Target Field.</u>

<u>I am from golfing with Mr. Krenik and Mr. Arvold.</u>

<u>I am from watching the Packers at the Super Bowl.</u>

<u>I am from a great sense of humor and telling jokes.</u>

<u>I am from acting and singing and dancing in the school plays.</u>

<u>I am from St. Francis of Assisi School and Church.</u>

<u>I am from my dog and friend, Buddy.</u>

<u>I am from my favorite colors, orange and blue.</u>

<u>I am from playing outdoors on hot summer days and in the snow on cold winter days.</u>

<u>I am from being a part of (Class) 8b, the best and the beautiful.</u>

<u>I am Will Canan.</u>

It's Memorial Day, a couple of days before the family and friends start gathering here for the big event. I ask Will what he would like to do today and he would like to go to Quarry Hill Nature Center for a visit. We spent many happy autumn days there with Will and Katherine when the kids were littler for the Fall Festival, viewing the animals, making nature-oriented gifts, getting grab bags as the cool wind swirled the orange and yellow leaves around us. On the way over, I ask Will if he is looking forward to graduation and if he realizes what a great accomplishment it has been. He replies that he is looking forward to it but does not think it amounts to much compared to a high school graduation or a college graduation. Ah, but I tell him that few kids have had to overcome as much as he has to get here, to fight cancer every year of elementary school and junior high, to squeeze in studies with surgeries and radiation and chemo and baseball. He nods silently, the wheels turning slowly in that important head of his. At Quarry Hill, we linger at some of the exhibits. Will is focused on a carp that keeps opening his mouth in front of us, as if mouthing words only Will can hear. We watch the honeybees busily climb up the tube into their hives to deposit their precious honey; we take in the hummingbirds darting in and out around the feeder. We marvel at the 15-foot-long skin of a python, rough and menacing even stretched out flat. Finally we go for a stroll around the pond. The pond is larger now than it used to be; it's lined by a dirt path along the edge, uneven in spots. I notice that Will has difficulty picking his way down the path and seems tired by the time we have made it most of the way around the pond. His strength is ebbing. A couple of years ago, he would have made this walk without difficulty. A lump grows in my throat as I watch him struggle, but I say nothing. He has had enough and wants to head back. On the path back to the Nature Center sits a large box turtle, warming himself in the sunshine, seemingly oblivious to the dangerous place he has chosen to stretch his legs. Will seems worried that he has escaped from an exhibit, but I assure him he's just a regular resident of the park. Just for a second, I'm able to get Will to crouch down behind him and capture the moment. We head off down the path and our turtle friend heads for the pond and whatever awaits him there. A stop at Dairy Queen on the way back and we're home safe and sound. I'm thankful for the hour we shared and as I tuck Will into bed that night, he tells me that he is thankful for that time too. My heart overflows. *Time tick slower... please.*

May 30, 2012 – Will's last week of school. We are off today for his final class trip, a day at Valleyfair Amusement Park in the Twin Cities. The school bus leaves at 7:00 a.m. and it's hard now for Will to be up and ready to go that early, so he and I clamber into our car for the two hour trip at about 10 a.m. and off we go. Will's mostly quiet on the way up, playing his Nintendo DS. I think back to the 6th grade trip that started with his upset stomach and vomiting on the back of the school bus in Cannon Falls while I played catch-up in the chase car with clean clothes and an attitude that it would not spoil the rest of our day. We arrived a little after noon and found the St. Francis bus as kids were streaming back from the park to check in at lunchtime. But Will preferred to remain with me rather than his classmates, so we headed in and found a rib place for lunch. Will powered through four or five ribs and then, of course, was ready to hit the rides. We started slow with the Ferris wheel, a good chance to check out the rest of the park and plot our ride strategy. We followed that up with three roller coasters, ending with the Renegade, a "4" on the "5" scale. From the lurch up the first hill, I knew this one would not be boring. Roaring down from the top of the first hill, it felt like we were going about 50 miles per hour and I could feel my cheeks being pulled back as I glanced over and caught the hint of a grin on Will's face. By the end, we were both a little green around the gills, but satisfied that we had pushed our limits. I tried to get Will to engage his classmates as we ran into them throughout the afternoon, but he seemed reluctant and while they were pleasant to him, they did not seem eager to get him to join their groups either. I'm glad we got the chance to spend the afternoon together, but at the end, he did join a couple of friends before getting on the school bus for the ride back home. He has spent so much time with adults while in treatment that it may be easier for him to relate to them than to his classmates who have no idea what he it feels like to have surgery on your brain, or endure the pain of radiation or the side effects of chemotherapy. Nevertheless, as I followed the bus home, I was struck that the bus carried a very precious cargo, all of the young men and women from the 8th grade at St. Francis and their many hopes and dreams for the future. I wanted to call the bus driver and tell him to be extra careful, but it would have been redundant. They all made it home safe and sound. One day to go before graduation.

May 31, 2012 – Graduation Day. Liz and I thought so many times at difficult points in Will's journey that he would never live to see this day, but he proved us wrong with his will to survive, like he has so many times in the past. In the early afternoon, our extended family started to roll in: my Mom and Dad, my sisters Maureen and Kathy and their families, Liz's parents Joe and Pat, and her two nieces, Anna and Julia. I helped Will get into his new clothes, new dress shirt, dress pants, belt and dress shoes; it made him look so grown up despite his small stature. A fellow parishioner, who also has kids at St. Francis, unexpectedly offered to host our entire extended family at Victoria's, a local Italian restaurant, for a pre-graduation dinner; a very, very kind gesture for which we were extremely grateful. They had reserved a private room for our group, created a special menu of favorites just for us, decorated the room in Green Bay Packer memorabilia for our Packer fan, and created a huge graduation cake for Will too. It was perfect. We enjoyed catching up and savoring the anticipation of the ceremony soon to arrive. Then it was off to St. Francis and time to take our seats in the gym. The music commenced and the graduates processed in, Will near the front, a small smile visible on his face as he turned the corner and headed for his seat. The ceremony unfolded with music from the kids and a sermon from the priest … but I found my mind drifting to Will's diagnosis; those dark days after his first surgery; his return to kindergarten at St. Francis, still weak and going through rehab; the words of his first grade teacher, Robin Erickson, who said that when she saw that "little bald headed kid" in her class, she never thought she would see the day when he finished his time at St. Francis. Liz and I simply prayed that he would make it to the next day and the next, but believed it would all happen somehow. Graduation was a reaffirmation for me just how high he had risen to wage his battles and prevail, bloodied but unbroken. Then it was time to watch Will's name called, see him rise slowly from his chair, accept his diploma from the principal, firmly shake the hands of the priests and then return to his chair – a graduate, the moment we had all been waiting for. I felt as though my heart would burst with pride on seeing him with that diploma in his hand that he had worked so very hard for. Soon the graduates were filing out and formed a receiving line in the parking lot to thank all those people who made it all possible. Will was hard to spot amongst his much taller classmates, but I made my way through the line and got a quick hug and a kiss. After the family gathered for some quick pictures, "Dr. Jack" made his arrival and hopped up to his customary place on Will's lap for a moment – a necessary step to mark every triumph along the way of Will's journey. Then the whole group ambled down to the school cafeteria to meet the graduates and their parents over some cake and punch and extend our congratulations. Liz and I had felt that this opportunity to thank all of the parents in Will's class would not come again, so I drafted a letter pouring out our gratitude for the many ways they made the path a little easier for eight-plus years for Will and for our family. The class assembled for one last time on the stage, the kids calling for Will and putting him up front where he would not be lost in the photos; the camera flashes blazed away for a few seconds before the kids and families scattered. Some kids would join him at high school at Lourdes, hopefully; some were moving on to other city high schools, and so the school "family" was breaking up, not to be reconstituted again. A sadness set in once that realization became apparent. After last minute hugs and shouted promises to keep in touch, we drifted to our cars, bringing the evening to a close.

As the nighttime fell, Liz was reminded of the "Legend of the Hummingbirds," which goes something like this:

> Legends say that hummingbirds float free of time, carrying our hopes for love, joy and celebration. Hummingbirds open our eyes to the wonder of the world and inspire us to open our hearts to loved ones and friends. Like a hummingbird, we aspire to hover and savor each moment as it passes, embrace all that life has to offer and to celebrate the joy of everyday. The hummingbird's delicate grace reminds us that life is rich, beauty is everywhere, every personal connection has meaning and that laughter is life's sweetest creation.

Remember to always live in the moment, play in the moment and best of all, share in the moment.

The following day, Liz and I took the opportunity to meet with the school staff at St. Francis before they went their separate ways for the summer. It was a very emotional meeting for us. How do you properly thank the kind, giving, people who nurtured Will through the years, sent him get well cards and visited him in the hospital, took him to movies and plays, taught him how to cook ribs and to play golf, extended his assignments when cancer won the upper hand on a particular day and Will lacked the fight to tackle his homework, urging him onward through the challenge course at Eagle Bluff Environmental Learning Center and to learn as much as he could despite the many appointments that made it hard for him to be present as often as he wanted to, helped him when he learned to play the trumpet in the school band, encouraged him when he wanted to play on the school basketball team even though the chemo treatments sapped his ability to run up and down the court. The list goes on and on, and there are no bounds to the gratitude we feel toward the staff that made all this possible. It takes a village to raise a child and for nine years they were our village. It was cathartic to tell them this and be there so they could hear it from us in person. There were a number of eyes in the room that had teared up by the time we were finished. And while we have left St. Francis School behind as we see where God decides to take

Will next, we will always carry in our hearts the imprint left by the teachers at St. Francis and know that no matter what the future may bring for Will, they continue to cheer him on from afar. We know that we always have a place at St. Francis.

June 20 – This week started with Father's Day. Will made me a homemade card, which I'll treasure. Then he was careful to tell me as we waited for our dinner at a local restaurant that he forgot to give me the perfect Father's Day present, a T-shirt shredder. He enjoys my collection of T-shirts, especially the tie-dyed ones, so we all had a good belly laugh about that one. He is doing the best he can playing youth baseball for the last time this summer. It's becoming more of a challenge to chase the balls and run the bases, but he still managed to drive in a run and score a run in a game on June 19. We did not realize until later that it would be the last baseball game we would ever watch him play in.

I dropped Liz and Will off at the airport today in Minneapolis. They are bound for Bozeman, Montana where they will spend nine days at Camp Big Sky Kids and take in the wonders of Yellowstone National Park, Will's wish to see the amazing place to be unexpectedly fulfilled. One parent got to go, and since I got the Super Bowl trip, it was Liz's turn to go for the big event. It was an emotional parting, I hugged Will tightly as though I did not want to let him go, and I teared up. He is getting frail now, moving more slowly, as the cancer advances, and there is some unspoken fear that if he is out of my sight for too long I might not ever see him again. I got a tight hug and a kiss from Liz and a promise she would take good care of him, as she always does. They will have a great time. I just wish I could be there to watch his face as he takes in all of the new experiences, which he may never have again. Katherine and I will wait anxiously until their return when they can share the pictures and stories of their adventures.

Chapter 10 – Sunset and Preparation

Cancer can take away all of my physical abilities. It cannot touch my mind, it cannot touch my heart, and it cannot touch my soul.
– Jim Valvano

June 27-July 1, 2012 – With Liz and Will off to Montana, the house was quiet as Katherine and I worked and found some time to talk, just the two of us, about her job and about her upcoming trip to Camp Olson … and Will's illness. It was good to talk, heart to heart; it just never seems to happen when everybody else is here. Then Katherine was able to spend some time with her friends and I was off to the Boundary Waters for a few days with my friend, John Helmers, to paddle some quiet waters, savor the cool breeze and the sunshine, and see if we could catch a few fish. We were mostly out of range for our cell phones and so had no contact with the outside world. That isolation held some appeal for me; each little pod of our family was enjoying themselves in their own little worlds.

Will and Liz were having a great time at Camp Big Sky in Montana. They floated the Yellowstone River in a raft. They enjoyed visiting Yellowstone National Park, watching Old Faithful erupt, seeing abundant wildlife as they drove through the area – bison and their calves, a coyote, and elk. They participated in an amazing talent show by the kids, parents and staff. Will got up and told several jokes and had the audience laughing and some in tears. He also got up and danced on the stage with all of the kids at the end. They took a ski lift to the top of one of the mountains at Big Sky ski resort, snow covered but warm at about 8800 feet with an incredible view from the top. They learned how to fly fish and visited the Grizzly and Wolf Discovery Center. Will and the other kids got to hide food in the bear habitat before two huge grizzly bears came out to find it. They watched two young bear brothers, Grant and Roosevelt, frolicking about, as well as two different wolf packs up close behind large glass windows. They saw a funny musical called *Dirty Rotten Scoundrels*, performed by a local summer theatre group.

Later in the week, they enjoyed an overnight camping trip, taking horse- and mule-drawn wagons up to the campsite, which was surrounded by a rushing river, beautiful snow-capped mountains and open fields peppered with blooming native wildflowers. They slept in big canvas tents with cots inside, each with two sleeping bags to keep them warm. Liz was in the self-titled "Hot Flash Mamas" tent with five other mothers, which she enjoyed.

Following a great dinner prepared by local volunteers and a nice campfire with s'mores, they put on as much warm clothing as they could before bedding down for the night; their guide Harley was on dusk-to-dawn bear watch. The temperature got down to a chilly 26 degrees overnight. Will slept very soundly through the night. Liz had trouble sleeping, thinking about grizzlies and the cold, but enjoyed it nonetheless.

The next day, Will got sick to his stomach at the beginning of the evening meal but then felt much better after that. He slept well that night, but the next morning he spiked a fever and vomited again. This was a foreshadowing of things to come over the next few days. They visited the Bozeman ER, along with Dr. Dan, the camp doctor. It was very helpful having him drive them there and be with them in the ER. They checked Will's counts, which were fine, and gave him a dose of antibiotics and fluids and then dismissed him. He felt a little better, but his sense of balance still remained very off. The next day, Friday, June 29, after tearful goodbyes, they left for the airport to head back to Minnesota.

Once home, Will's condition continued to decline.

On Saturday, June 30, Will had 3-4 vomiting spells and wasn't able to keep food or liquids down. He required either Katherine or Liz to be right at his side, holding on to him, to steady him when he walked; he was also having some confusion, too. At 9 p.m. after another vomiting episode, which happened just as Will laid down for bed, Liz called 911 for the ambulance to come and transport Will to the ER. The CT scan taken upon his arrival showed that his ventricles were enlarged due to excess fluid on the brain, known as hydrocephalus. After being sent up to the Pediatric ICU at about 3:30 a.m. on Sunday, they drained 24 cc of cerebrospinal fluid using Will's Ommaya. A sample was sent to the lab for a culture. It came back showing some bacterial growth present in his CSF. They immediately started him on antibiotics. Then at 6 p.m. Sunday, they removed the Ommaya, the suspected source of the infection, and put in an external ventricular drain to continuously drain off excess CSF that was being generated.

All this time I had been out of cell phone range in the Boundary Waters.

On my way out of the Boundary Waters with John on Sunday, July 1, we got back in cell range. I received a frantic text message from Liz. She outlined briefly what had occurred and that something was obviously terribly wrong. When I was finally able to get a call through to her, Liz filled me in on the rest of the details about Will's infection of his cerebrospinal fluid and how this was affecting the flow of his CSF in and out of his brain. It was backing up and causing pressure in his brain; enough pressure that a couple more days and he likely would have died. John drove us back from the Boundary Waters at 85 miles per hour most of the way – without attracting the attention of law enforcement, mercifully. I arrived back just after they had taken Will back for surgery to remove the Ommaya reservoir. After a very quick and successful procedure, and some time in recovery, Will came back to us in the Pediatric ICU. As fate would have it, he was placed back into the very same room where his cancer journey had commenced eight years before. It took me off guard for a moment as I entered the room. All those memories came rushing back: Will's original surgery; his head wrapped in gauze and his skin so pale as he came back from surgery; the two weeks spent in that room amid the blinking lights, beeping monitors, the constant neuro checks; the not knowing then if he would live or die. Now, as the CSF culture was brewing in the laboratory, the doctors put Will on a couple of antibiotics until the specific type of bacteria could be identified. On Monday, they did another MRI of Will's head and spine. As we had feared, the tumors had grown further in both locations and so the valproic acid treatment regimen he had been on had failed. It was with great sadness that Dr. Rao told us that she had no other treatment regimen that offered any hope for Will and that we should focus on making his remaining time with us as comfortable as possible.

The day we had greatly feared for so long had finally arrived. Will had defied the odds so many times previously over the course of his illness that if one procedure or treatment failed, there always seemed to be another one waiting on the horizon to be tried and applied to give Will more time, but this time it was not to be. The feelings in my body coursed over me like waves: a profound despair that Will's time with us would finally be drawing to a close and yet some very small sense of relief that, at some point soon, Will would not have to endure the pain of yet another surgery opening up his poor scarred head, would not have to suffer through yet another round of chemotherapy or radiation with all of the horrible side effects. He would be free from his cancer at last.

We spent six days in the Peds ICU before they cleared up his infection, then they moved him for a couple of days to the regular pediatric floor in the hospital; they discharged him on July 9. I arranged for an indefinite leave of absence from work to be able to be home to help care for him during the remainder of his journey. The whole CSF infection ordeal left his body greatly weakened. While walking and climbing the stairs had not been simple for him before, they became a real challenge. As they had in 2004, though now to a lesser degree, Linda and Amy and the wonderful staff in the Rehab Department at the hospital worked with Will on exercises to help build his body back up; they were able to get him a walker and a special adapter to make getting up and down on the toilet easier. And we connected with the Mayo Hospice team so that we could start placing him on painkillers to stay ahead of the pain that the growth of the spinal tumors had already created.

July 9, 2012 – Today, Will, Liz and I are all back home; Katherine departed yesterday for Camp Olson and will return next week. My leave from the office still feels a little surreal. I have worked full-time for 23 years without ever taking more than one week off at a time; suddenly, I have the prospect of unknown weeks to months before I return. I now have the ability to focus solely on Will and meeting his needs in a way that was never possible when I was working. We watched a few cartoons together today, some of the ones I used to watch as a kid, Roadrunner and Elmer Fudd and Daffy Duck, laughing together at their silly antics. It makes me so very grateful that I closed my law practice in 2008 because, even with disability insurance, someone would have to take care of my clients; a law practice could not survive the extended absence of its sole practitioner, clients would only have so much patience before taking their business elsewhere. And I can work together with Liz to care for Will, in a way that I hope will bring us closer to each other at this very difficult time.

And what do we see as we look ahead? The prospect of creating a few more precious memories before Will leaves us; trying to manage the flood of visitors who want to come and wish him well and to thank him for touching their lives before the opportunity passes; watching the slow and painful decline of his body; planning a visitation, a funeral, burial at the cemetery, a tombstone and what words it should contain to try to describe the young man who fought his demons for more than half of his life, yet did not let it break his spirit. It's uncharted territory, as so much of Will's journey has been, but we will get through it with the help of our families and our friends and the medical staff at Mayo, hopefully with our sanity still mostly intact when it is all done. *Please hold Will's hand, Lord, and my family's as well that we may not stumble along the way.*

July 11, 2012 – Tonight is Will's last baseball game of the regular season. He is still unsteady on his feet, but is anxious to be there to cheer on his team from the dugout bench. As I walk out onto the field to take my usual position as third base coach, I become aware that I've already witnessed the last baseball game Will would ever play in; it just did not feel right not having him on the field this time. His last game was a typical game, but you always wish in retrospect that you would have caught it on video or paid closer attention if you would have known it was going to be the last one. Tonight, Will banters back and forth with Brian Cada and Jim Ryan, the fathers of two classmates from St. Francis who have been the coaches for Will and his friends ever since they first joined a baseball team. I look over and catch him smiling once or twice, although he is more silent than usual, which is more than understandable. Several of his teammates tell Will they hope he is feeling better soon. Team Ryan Windows and Siding fights hard, but comes up short in the end, 12-11. At the end of the game, the boys gather on the pitcher's mound and present Will with a baseball, signed by all the members of the team, which brings a smile that lights up his face from ear to ear. There is so much sorrow here that this may be the last time I ever see Will walk on a baseball field, but I'm swallowed up in joy for the moment. Brian gives me a big hug before we walk off the field and reminds me that his family is praying for Will and for all of us. Goodbyes are so very hard, especially when you have to say goodbye to a sport that Will has loved as passionately as he loves baseball. Another big bump in the road.

July 15, 2012 – Katherine is back home from camp and so it will be good to have some time for the four of us to share as a family. Admittedly, however, this new "waiting game" is very difficult. For so many years, we have waited. Waited for Will's treatments to be completed, waited for him to heal from the side effects, waited for the next round of MRIs and braced ourselves for news we did not want to hear. Though we often waited in the past for Will to get better after treatments, now we wait for him to get worse. There are only so many things that can done at home to stay busy – clean out the closets and the garage, touch up spots on the house that need paint – before you start to go a little stir crazy. And he is nowhere near as sick as he will get yet. We've been glad that Will has had a number of friends come over to visit this week. They've played cards, eaten the ingredients for s'mores intended for a future camping trip, and last night, three girls from his class brought pizza and chocolate chip cookies over for dinner. Liz and I sat outside on the deck so the kids could just be together. They talked about kindergarten memories – Natalie getting a bean stuck up her nose requiring an ER visit, and one of the boys having his toes and fingers painted by the girls with yellow nail polish. We're sure they talked about much more but, as Will said, "I could hardly get a word in with these three girls." He truly enjoyed spending time with them all. Walking is still a challenge. Will and Liz walked down to the corner to drop off some things at our neighbor's house; Will didn't want to use his wheelchair or walker. He said, "When I say I can walk, that means without either of those things." We both admired his continued desire for independence and his determination, even though he did need to hold on to Liz's arm off and on.

July 16, 2012 – Will had his first PT appointment today since being discharged from the hospital. He is still having difficulty climbing stairs, but Linda, his physical therapist, noticed some improvements in his abilities since last week and gave him some exercises to take home to work on. As we were waiting for his appointment today, I asked him what were the best and the worst things of his cancer journey so far, trying to get him to open up a little bit while we still can discuss these things. He told me that the best things were his Make-A-Wish Trip to Walt Disney World back in 2005 and our fishing trip to Alaska in 2007 – no big surprises there. He told me that the worst thing was the incontinence that he had just experienced as a side effect of the hydrocephalus, which has since abated. That took me by surprise. With all of the hard and painful things he has had to endure, it was the loss of dignity and the waking up wet in the morning that he hated the most. Mercifully, his ability to control his bladder returned when the CSF pressure went back down. If that was the worst thing, then perhaps he does not hate what lies ahead or, more likely, has simply chosen not to think about it. We'll find out soon enough.

July 17-18, 2012 – Will got his stitches out today from the July 1st surgery to remove his Ommaya. Dr. Hoover thought his incision was healing pretty well considering how much Will's head has already been through. Today we met with Dr. Rao and Donna. This appointment had a different feel to it. In the past, all of the oncology appointments were focused on how to come up with one more treatment that would buy us another few months, to halt that damn tumor in its tracks until it found a way to metastasize and start growing again. This time, for the first time, we were focused only on trying to treat the symptoms, rather than the illness, to find ways to stay ahead of the pain, to help Will with his balance issues and to try to move toward the end in a way that will preserve Will's dignity and give him some control over the process. We still found a little time to smile and laugh, despite the emotional pain palpable by all of us. On the way home, Will proceeded to tell us that when our van grunted a bit making it up a hill near our house, it sounded like it was "a mother giving birth." You had to smile at that one; the wheels in his head are still turning, even though his body is slowly starting to fail him. Tonight, Katherine and Liz were out so it was the boys' night at home. I finally persuaded Will to join me in looking at some old photo albums of his amazing life. Those glossy pages were full of many happy times: Will gleaming as a toddler with our old dog Thoreau, laughing as he hugged Katherine and Liz, birthday parties, trick or treat costumes, growing his sunflowers and vacations by the water. He saw his first baseball team and remarked that baseball was all "so easy then." He enjoyed looking through the albums, but it was all I could do to choke back the tears as I watched my little boy, whose life started so happily and full of promise, become the young man whose smiles are fading along with his memory of his treasured past and his ability to climb the stairs up to his bedroom. Bittersweet to take it all in…

July 22, 2012 – Today is a day to remember, one of many in Will's life, as his participation in Rochester youth baseball officially came to an end. The day started with 10:00 Mass at St. Francis. Something tells me that the times he will be there with his family in the future will be limited. He is unable to kneel now at the appropriate times; he sits instead. I glanced down at him and Katherine after Communion and caught a glimpse of his head bowed in prayer. What conversations does he have with God at a time such as this? "Why me? Why do I suffer before I lose this fight? Calm me for I am afraid for what is to come?" The tears begin to flow as I think about this and press my own prayers behind closed eyes that there will be deliverance soon from the enormous burden that Will carries, which will only get harder in the days to come.

With church over, it was off to the baseball field. His team, Ryan Windows and Siding, played hard and won third place in the consolation round of the RYBA tournament. Will was on the bench in the dugout cheering his team on to victory. I know it tore him up inside that he was unable to be out there on the field playing, but he kept his disappointment to himself. It was very emotional at the end of the game. Will is struggling to walk now as his legs are no longer consistently doing what his mind is telling them to do, so I tried to keep him pointed in the right direction as he slapped the hands of the opposing team to wish them a "good game." He stood in line to receive his trophy from his coaches, Brian Cada and Jim Ryan, and Brian gave him a huge hug, which brought tears to my eyes. Brian and Jim have been patient stewards of the St. Francis boys on the baseball team, reaching all the way back to the "Grasshoppers" when the team was in first grade, teaching them the fundamentals of the game and most importantly how to be good sportsmen and conduct themselves well, on and off the field. We are forever indebted to them for the many hours they spent working with Will and his teammates to improve their skills and lead them. It was hard to accept that these many years were coming to an end today. Will's left leg gave out completely shortly after he received his trophy. We steered him into a chair while we shared some refreshments, reflected back on the day and the year, and caught up on how the other St. Francis boys were doing in their games for teams at other levels. When we got up to leave, Will's legs gave out again on the way back to the car; I carried him on my back the rest of the way. When we got home, he wanted to crawl from the garage to the foot of the stairs up to his bedroom to show he could still get himself where he needed to go. He did make it, but the effort tired him out and I cajoled his tired body up the stairs and into bed for a nap. A wheelchair cannot be far behind now as the cancer continues to start to spread to vital control centers in his brain. Will has an assignment for his Lourdes freshman English class. Before the start of school, he needs to read the book entitled, *Chains;* we continue to read it together. How will this story end? Will he get to reach the conclusion? Will he be able to remember the story or the characters if we finish it? We will find out soon enough. *How far is heaven?* (A nod to the Los Lonely Boys.) *Why does the road to get there have to be so difficult with Will losing seemingly one more vital function daily that makes him human and gives him dignity and a reason to live?*

July 23, 2012 – I made my periodic three-month trek back to the dental chair today. Teresa, my usual dental hygienist, had some surgery and was out on leave, and so Tara had the honors today. I share a hereditary predisposition for receding gum lines with my Dad. Combine that with a less-than-stellar record of teeth cleaning in my

20s, plus eight years of Will's cancer battles, and it means trouble in my mouth. Tara gets the nitrous oxide flowing to take the edge off the scraping, which is like nails on a blackboard at times and I settle down under the giant spotlight for an hour of bliss. There is no hiding from a dental hygienist. Every spot where you have not brushed, flossed or picked as regularly as you should have is immediately exposed under the glow of that beaming eye hanging over the dental chair. It always leaves me feeling naked and inadequate; although I have done what I can every morning and night to take care of my teeth and gums, there is always some place where the dental gremlins have hidden away. How unlike Will's cancer. Sure, there are the large spots that show up on an MRI where, in the past, surgery or radiation or chemo could be directed; but there are so many more spots where the cancer cells float free in the CSF, waiting for the cranial currents to carry them away to distant locations in the ocean coursing throughout the body. No ability to home in on those spots and fix them before the next visit in order to find the next set of problems you may have missed. Someday soon I hope the scientists and doctors will have that ability, even if you have to be exposed to the harsh glare of the spotlight to make it possible.

After Will's baseball tournament on July 22, we had noticed that his balance was growing steadily worse. He had begun vomiting repeatedly and his short-term memory had declined further, all signs that his hydrocephalus had likely returned. We took him in on July 23 for a CT scan. A follow-up appointment with Dr. Rao confirmed that Will, indeed, had hydrocephalus once again ... though he still had his sense of humor. Sitting in Dr. Rao's office, in the midst of Will's sleepiness and nausea, I moved from the long seat so that Will could stretch out with his head resting on Liz's lap. But, as I did this, Will said, "But ooh Dad, your butt was sitting here!" causing the room to fill with laughter for just a moment. Very few kids in Will's type of situation had been able to avoid installation of a permanent shunt to drain off excess CSF. We discussed this with Dr. Rao and with Dr. Wetjen, Will's surgeon from Mayo, and decided it would be best to install the shunt.

Dr. Wetjen completed this surgery successfully on July 24; Will was released to return home on July 25. I noted some improvement in his balance and in his ability to climb the stairs after he returned home, signs that were very welcome at this late stage in the game. Dr. Wetjen warned us, however, that in some cases the shunts were prone to becoming clogged with clumps of cancer cells, which could cause the

CSF to start backing up in Will's brain once again. There was no solution for this problem except for another surgery to clear the blockage.

Will continues to be tired and is taking long naps in the afternoons. He was cheered when his former principal, Barb Plenge, stopped by with a meal on Friday, which led to another amusing exchange. Will mentioned to her that Mr. Arvold wanted to take him out for ice cream. Barb said, "Why don't you have him bring over his smoker and make you ribs?" Will paused for just a moment and said, "He'd probably make me pay for the meat." Barb laughed and said, "Tell him to put it on your tab."

July 29, 2012 – My sister Kathy, her husband Tom, and their 7-year-old son Ben visited for a couple of days, as did my parents, Mike and Jean Canan. They came to support us at this difficult time, and to celebrate my Dad's 80th birthday. My dad enjoyed reading several chapters of the freshman English book, *Chains,* to Will. It is a riveting book about a slave at the time of the Revolutionary War trying to care for her sister and find freedom for them both, while the chaos of war rages around them. There are some parallels in there with Will's cancer battles. Will's freedom – in what form will it come? Will we be free when he is free and the battle done?

On August 1st, Will had an appointment with Dr. Rao. His strength continues to remain strong and the tremor in his left hand even seemed better today to all of us. She encouraged Will to take it slow when getting up to walk and not make quick turns/movements because he loses his balance and falls easily. She told Will that his brain doesn't react as quickly as it used to and doesn't always know "what to do" when he gets up too fast. Will said he would try to remember this. We don't want to discourage him from walking, but we do want him to be careful and not risk falling. He also still isn't having pain anywhere, which is a blessing.

August 5, 2012 – We had planned a special vacation in Wisconsin several months ago, before we knew that Will was entering the final stages of his illness. It was supposed to have included a trip to Milwaukee to visit the Wisconsin State Fair and see a concert by ventriloquist Jeff Dunham. This was to be followed by a trip up to Green Bay to attend Packer Family Night at Lambeau Field. Will is in tune with the weakened state of his body lately; he felt that the Jeff

Dunham concert would be too much. I sent the concert tickets to my sister-in-law Patti Canan to enjoy in our place. Later, when we linked up with my brother Steve and Patti, she produced a "Walter" doll that she had fought tooth and nail to obtain for Will. We appreciated that kind gesture greatly.

We altered our plans and made the trip directly over to Green Bay where we were to meet our Packer fan friends Marcia and Gary Fritzmeier; we drove through the parched cornfields of central Wisconsin that had been enduring a severe drought for many weeks. We arrived in Green Bay on Thursday, the day before the Packer Family event, and enjoyed a great meal at the Stadium View Bar and Grill where we hooked up with our friend, Larry Weyers, the treasurer of the Packers. Larry had pulled a number of strings to get us sideline passes to be on the field for the event; in addition, he gave us club suite passes so we would have nice air-conditioned accommodations for the remainder of the event after our time on the sidelines. To cap it all off, he arranged for the highlight of the evening: a chance for Will to meet Packer quarterback Aaron Rodgers one-on-one and have his picture taken with him.

When we awoke on Friday morning, Will had blood on his pillow; we initially assumed that he had had a nosebleed during the night. In reality, we learned later in the day when Liz was bathing Will, that he had gotten up to go to the bathroom during the night, had lost his balance and had struck the top of his head hard on the bathroom door. The blow to his head reopened the incision site from his recent surgery and left a gaping wound, thus the blood loss. So, in the middle of the afternoon, we headed for the ER at a Green Bay hospital, where we waited nearly five hours for their neurosurgeon to finish operating on an aneurysm before he was able to see us. The deep wound would require stitches, but they ultimately decided that Will did not have enough skin on his scalp to suture it closed. Consequently, they cleaned it and covered it and sent us out the door. We had missed the game and the chance for Will to meet Aaron Rodgers. We were very disappointed, although Katherine was at least able to attend the game with Gary and Marcia.

It's a cruel irony that the doctors could not even fix the problem, compounding the disappointment that Will had to miss the game. Will needs something, anything to look forward to; it's a reason to keep getting out of bed in the morning and not give up. It was a sad trip back, knowing that in all likelihood this will be our last trip outside of Rochester as a family. We have so enjoyed the time spent together on all our family trips; we've enjoyed the unique experiences that Will's illness made possible for him, and often for all of us as well. Just one more chapter of Will's book that is drawing to a close. When do you cross the line from living to dying? What goals become possible each day as your physical abilities slip away? When do you just start marking time when the end of your life is all that is looming ahead? With the only possible exception of the start of high school a few weeks away, Will seems to be flirting with that "line" now. It's hard when you want to make more memories in the precious time left and Will mostly just wants to watch reruns on television.

Will, please let me in, let me know what you are thinking about, what you have learned on the journey before this disease robs me of that opportunity to learn a bit more, some pearl of wisdom you have gleaned that others may relish when you live on only in our collective memories.

August 7 – Will is definitely having difficulty now controlling his legs and walking normally. You can see from his furrowed brow and pursed lips that his brain is intently trying to tell his legs what to do, but they aren't listening, and it is proving now to be a challenge just to walk from the couch in the great room to the first floor bathroom. Will is now unable to make it up the stairs to the second floor without stopping to rest and has begun crawling up the remainder of the steps when he gets to the landing. He has become incontinent now at night and so he has begun to wear Depends to bed, which has solved the concern about him getting up in the middle of the night to go the bathroom and falling. Liz and I have pulled his mattress into our room and Will seems OK with the change.

The losses from now on are real losses of dignity. To a young man who overcame a massive brain resection eight years ago to relearn how to walk again and to regain control over his bowels, it's a bitter pill to swallow to see that hard won gain lost again, never to return. To watch Will crawl up those stairs to his room – full of his treasured sports memorabilia and self-built Lego creations that he is justifiably so proud of – tears me up inside.

We go in tomorrow for surgery to close the wound that Will got over the weekend in Green Bay. It's disconcerting to see this huge wound with Will's skull clearly showing through at the bottom of it. We worry about the risk of infection while it remains open; we worry about the risk of infection once they suture it closed. His life is becoming so precarious now that a serious infection could claim it before the cancer does. We played a game of "Sorry" at the kitchen table tonight and, for just a few moments, it was like the old days in happier times. *Prayers for Dr. Wetjen and his team tomorrow. Please let Will's surgery be successful so that we have more time to share.*

August 8-9, 2012 – Will is the first case on the day's docket for Dr. Wetjen and his plastic surgeon counterpart, Dr. Nardini. We are scheduled to show up at the ungodly hour of 5:30 a.m. The sun is glimmering below the horizon as we head east toward Saint Marys Hospital. We are mostly silent for this drive, lost in thought, nothing worthwhile to say that will ease the hurt or make sense out of what no longer makes any sense. We ease Will from the car into a rickety wheelchair, then trundle off to the pediatric surgical prep area. How many times have we made this walk before today? It is likely we will not be making it again. We help Will out of his clothes and into a surgical gown, through the endless prep questions (Will is never going to be with us long enough to cause the surgeons headaches due to excessive alcohol use or body piercings or dentures or all of the other things that can cause problems when the cutters are delving into your body), then onto a surgical gurney for the trip to the operating room, past the blinking monitors and huddled groups conversing in the hallways in blue scrubs, to the brightly lit cocoon where they will "put Will back together again" in the words of one of the nurses, as if he is some juvenile Humpty Dumpty fallen off the wall who can be made whole with a little time and effort. Liz and I kiss him gently on the cheek and with a quick squeeze of his hands, the propofol does its magic and Will's eyes roll back into his head and we step out to let the surgeons do their work.

About three hours later, Will is back in recovery. The wound first created only five weeks previously, then reopened in Green Bay, has been stitched closed with a little creative work from Dr. Nardini using an inflated breast implant under Will's skin to stretch it just enough so they can close the wound. Will's head is swathed in gauze, looking vaguely like a turban made by Johnson and Johnson, but tighter to keep the swelling under control. The decision is made to keep Will in the hospital overnight for observation, one more time for the pills and neuro checks every four hours, the rounds of nurses and residents and doctors who mean well but rob Will of the rest he so desperately needs. I toss and turn during the night on the rock hard bed despite my best camping pad. I know somehow that the Will who leaves the hospital will not be the same one who entered it.

This afternoon, after a shower to clean his body so in need of refreshment, and a long nap, I ease the van up to the front door of the hospital only to learn that Will's legs have now stopped functioning totally and he has become completely incontinent. When we arrive home, I gently scoop him up out of the van seat, carry him up the garage stairs into the house and set him down into the yellow leather chair in our great room. His legs have become like two large branches; he can move his toes and move his legs a bit like branches swaying in the wind uncontrolled, but the ability for those legs to carry him across the room, down to the basement to the pool table or the Wii console where "Mario Kart" awaits, up to his bedroom or down the street to take his favorite dog Buddy for a stroll around the block is gone forever. We who have working appendages tend to take for granted the fact that they mostly do what they are supposed to do. It's like Will has suddenly been in a serious car or diving accident and has become a paraplegic. He's becoming trapped in his own body. That would be bad enough, though we could adjust to that with the right set of wheels and tools, but his cancer is still hungry to consume more when the opportunity comes. The fact that he will no longer have control over his bladder and bowels is hard to accept, too; in a sense we have moved backward to when he was an infant again when he was just learning how to direct the functions of his body. But Will does not dwell on either of these newest setbacks; we watch the Packers lose a pre-season game to the Chargers and then I carry his slumping body up the stairs to his mattress on the floor of our room and Liz and I tuck him in for the night. He is starting to slip away from us. The pace just picked up today and we have to run faster to keep up.

August 10, 2012 – A large truck pulled up to the house today, carrying two men and a hospital bed. The men carried in the bed, set the pieces down gingerly in the great room, and spent the next hour putting it together, pieces of a giant metallic jigsaw puzzle. When the puzzle was complete, a large hospital bed sat in the great room in front of the television set. This will be the place where Will spends much of the remainder of his days on Earth, with his head elevated enough to take in old episodes of *Good Luck Charlie* on Disney, and *Victorious* and *iCarly* on Nick that he has already seen dozens of times before. Because Will's new hospital bed lacks the proper pads and sheets, Liz and I decide that he will sleep one more night on his old mattress, and in his own bedroom. We move the mattress off the floor of our bedroom back into his room for one last night. As evening falls, we gather around the TV to watch the coverage of the Olympics, as we have often in the past couple of weeks, marveling at the speed and ability of the superhumans who make their way around the track in London. I can't help wonder what is going through Will's mind as he watches this, the juxtaposition of the fastest humans on the planet whose legs and joints move perfectly with fluid motion, and his own legs, unwilling to do the simple bidding of his mind to move them across the room so that he can join us, as he always used to, at the dinner table for our evening meal. When the last race is run, I carry him up the stairs. Liz and I tuck Will into his bed in his room and kiss him good night as we have thousands of times before, but this is the last time he will spend the night in his own bed in his own room, watched over by the larger than life personas of Derek Jeter and Justin Morneau and Aaron Rodgers. Tomorrow the room will seem less his, as he cannot rise to claim it as he has in the past; another comforting ritual plucked away not to return.

August 11, 2012 – Today I return briefly to Wisconsin with my parents to attend my 30th high school class reunion. Thirty years removed from 12 formative years with the people who got to know me well in my youth. As I walked into the Darboy Club, where the reunion was being held, I see a mass of middle-aged people, the outlines from 30 years ago blurred now as hair has receded and started turning gray, and the middles have expanded. I see several heads turn when I enter the room and smiles creep across a few faces. It's hard to explain the bond I have with my former classmates. Some of us entered the hallowed halls at Holy Name of Jesus Elementary School, Kimberly, Wisconsin, in the fall of 1970, as the Vietnam War raged halfway across the world. The Sisters were strict, but fair and caring; they instilled in us a respect for our faith and for each other, in addition to the readin', writin' and 'rithmetic. We shared happy and sad times together; Christmas concerts and school plays; four square on the playground; hot dog and Spanish hamburger days; CYO basketball; paper footballs flicked at finger goalposts; the trials of a sweating principal hunched beside his overhead projector trying to teach sex ed to the class of 6th grade boys; the polyester plaid pants in vogue in that time, which most try now to forget. We went on to join the public school kids in 7th grade and for high school starting in 9th grade. I made friends there, too, as we began to spread our wings and learn about what life would be like. But those bonds forged so long ago endure. I know that I can walk in to a room of my former classmates and get the biggest smiles and the biggest hugs; they give me the sincerest wishes of better times for Will and for my family that I can get anywhere on Earth. And why is that? They knew me when my soul was being formed, when I was becoming the person I would be; I watched them being formed as well, and so we know how each one is made up. That leads to an understanding and empathy that cannot be easily recreated. Our reunion celebration began at 6 p.m. and before we knew it, the bar staff was turning the lights off on us repeatedly at 1:00 a.m., trying to kick us out because several of us did not want the evening to end. Sue Hiroskey, and Paula Schnese and Jill Vander Zanden, John Van Herwyen, Bob Lewandowski and Andy Minten – we shared lots of tight hugs and tears as we said our goodbyes and the evening came to a close. They feel my pain regarding Will and his impending loss deeply. They give me hope that, with their help, we will survive this cataclysm and rise again.

August 15, 2012 – It's been a wish of mine for some time that Will could receive the Sacraments of the Anointing of the Sick and Confirmation. The Sacrament of the Anointing of the Sick is given by the Church to those who are seriously ill and at risk of dying to give them strength as they face the trials of their illness and to prepare them for the end of their time here on Earth. Confirmation is an outward sign that the person has become mature enough to be recognized as an adult member of the Church. It was arranged that Father Mark McNea, our pastor at St. Francis, and Barb Plenge, the only principal Will has ever had in all his years at St. Francis School, would help with administration of the Sacraments; Barb would also serve as his Confirmation sponsor. Will needed to choose the name of a saint for his Confirmation name. Given Will's fragile state, I did some research for him and suggested that he choose St. Peregrine Lazioli as his Confirmation saint. St. Peregrine is the patron saint of those fighting cancer. After his conversion as a young man, he decided as his penance that he would stand rather than sit whenever possible. Eventually, St. Peregrine developed cancer in his leg. The night before he was to have his leg amputated, to stop the growth of the cancer, he prayed fervently for help and received a vision of Christ touching his leg, which healed him. Given Will's situation, we both decided that this would be a good choice for a patron saint. The

222

Sacraments were conferred at home, with Will sitting comfortably in his wheelchair. The only other people present were Liz, Katherine and I. Father prayed for Will and anointed him on his forehead and on the palms of his hands as a sign of God's love for Will. The photo taken just afterward shows the impact it had on Will. His smile suggests it's as if God had slipped in and shouldered some of the burden. It was a moving experience for all of us, and another step forward to prepare Will spiritually for what lies ahead.

The following day, my good friend, County Parks Director Tom Ryan, invited us to come out to spend the evening at Oxbow Park. Liz and Katherine decided at the last moment to join us and so we loaded Will and his wheelchair into the van with some warm blankets and food to make s'mores and headed out. Tom was waiting at the zoo to meet us when we arrived. We got Will out of van and settled into his wheelchair. Tom took the controls and off we went. Our first stop was at the wild bird exhibit, where we marveled at the bald eagles. Tom slipped away for a moment and returned with special gloves so that Will could have the opportunity to hold one of the owls. The owl beat one wing furiously initially; once settled a bit on Will's gloved right hand, it began to calm down and slowly turn his head to take in these large strange new creatures next to him. A small grin began to grow on Will's face as he gave the same once-over to the owl. They shared a similar hardship, the owl having lost a wing and his ability to fly from place to place, Will recently having lost his ability to walk and get from place to place. Kindred spirits, dependent on the goodwill of others to survive – maybe that's why they seemed to appreciate each other. Soon we continued our stroll around the zoo as the sun crept lower in the western sky, watching the animals like the wolves and the black bear communicate in their special way, getting ready to bed down for the night. The sun was setting as we finished our tour. Tom rolled out two ATVs, which we then rode up to a remote spot in the park for a campfire and s'mores; we shared stories and laughter in the dancing light of the roaring fire as darkness closed in around us and the coyotes in the park shared a plaintive howl. Not a true campout, but our last campfire, bringing back memories of earlier campfires shared. Thanks so much to our buddy Tom to make this simple evening special.

August 23-24, 2012 – On Thursday, we attended freshman orientation at Lourdes High School. Liz and I had a meeting on Wednesday with the school staff, school nurses and hospice team to discuss Will's school year. It was agreed that Will would have only two classes, Religion with Mrs. Hendrickson and English/Lit with Mrs. Falvey. He would attend from 10-11:30 in the mornings, the best time of the day for Will. Katherine would be available to meet us when we arrived at the school door; she would get Will to his locker and his first class. Several of Will's classmates were tapped to serve as his buddies to ensure that he got to where he needed to go; they would get him down to the lunchroom on the days he wanted to stay for lunch with his class. Plans were put in place if Will had a medical emergency and the hospice team needed to be called.

Orientation was a blur for Will. It was shortened for him from about three hours to only one hour. Katherine took charge once we got Will unloaded from the van and into his wheelchair; she gave Will a little tour around the high school. Then we spent some time showing Will his new locker. We talked to Jerry, the maintenance guy, about lowering the shelf so Will could reach it in his wheelchair. They assigned him a combination for his locker but there is no way, given his short-term memory loss, that he could remember it; we will find a way to make sure it gets opened. Will enjoyed meeting Mrs. Falvey and Mrs. Hendrickson, knowing that they would have a small table that his wheelchair could fit under. It was heartwarming, too, to see Will's classmates from St. Francis say hello as they saw him gliding down the halls in his wheelchair. But I could see from the blank look on Will's face that the challenges here, even with this simplified schedule, would be great. As the tumors grow in his brain and spinal column, they would surely interfere with the smooth functioning of messages trying to get around his body. He seemed to have difficulty processing what he was being told, although fatigue certainly was a contributing factor as well.

How do you spend your time when you likely only have weeks to live? School will give Will a chance to be with his friends, to see a little of what high school life is like. Any knowledge he will learn in the morning will likely be lost by the time he arrives home after lunch. He will have no homework to worry about, unless he wants to do some. It will give the other kids who don't know Will and his story a chance to get to know him, to give thanks for the blessings of good health they take for granted, to serve someone else who will need their help to survive in school day to day.

Today, four of his female classmates from St. Francis – Skylar Drefcinski,

Miranda Hawkinson, Abigail Thompson, and Nora Haas – and two of their moms came over to visit Will and brought lunch. They fluttered around Will like a flock of young birds, chattering away about everything under the sun; Will mostly listened and chimed in with his dry wit now and then. They had brought fingernail polish and managed to talk Will into letting them paint one of his fingernails. Will, the boy who has developed the patience of Job, laid on his hospital bed while the flock hovered around him. They painted his index fingernail blue and admired their handiwork when they were finished. Then the flock flew off and gave our little bird a chance to take a rest in his nest. Before dropping off to sleep, Will acknowledged that the girls in his class had really taken an interest in visiting him and coming over to cheer him up; he was grateful for that. We were too. I just hope it continues once the hustle and bustle of school begins so that Will does not feel left on the sidelines, hindered by the limits that his failing body are placing on him. I trust in the kids who have known Will for so long; they will remember to count him in, when possible, as long as his health permits.

August 25, 2012 – As I spend three hours on the road, driving to and from an away soccer game for Katherine, I reflect a little about Will's current situation. It's become hard to talk to Will and I haven't been able to put my finger on just why. It's dawned on me it's partially because we can only seem to talk about the present now. We struggle to talk about the past because Will's severe memory problems often mean that he has little or no memory of his rich past and so I can't refer to a past event because it will mean little or nothing to Will. We have trouble talking about the future because what Will has left is growing short; with the failure of his body in recent weeks, there is little here on Earth that he looks forward to, even if he could remember a favorite upcoming event for a while after we discuss it. We've talked in passing about the time he will be spending in heaven with God once he has shed his earthly body and left his cancer behind, but he still prefers to dwell in the here and now. That leaves only the present, where his cancer devours him, bit by bit, leaving less today than he had yesterday. The spinal cord tumors send waves of pain from his lower back whenever we change his position. His beloved Minnesota Twins are mired in last place, and he seems to find solace only in old TV episodes on Disney Channel and Nick, which he is having difficulty seeing, perhaps because of the cataracts caused by the radiation treatments over the years. He still enjoys eating, and is putting on weight now since he is not getting exercise.

But when have you taken away enough of his life that he is just existing? Does his life still have inherent value if we treasure it and work hard to preserve what he still has, even if he does not value it any longer? Is it worthwhile if he is still here to greet old classmates and teachers and friends, and tug at their heartstrings, when they see his current state, if he does not remember the ties that brought them together in the first place? It truly makes you question what makes us alive. How we wish that Will still had a past and a future. The deep conversations are still straining to spill out of me about what he thinks about his life and whether he has learned any lessons to share with the rest of us ... before his voice is stilled forever.

August 27, 2012 – First day of school for Will at Lourdes High School. When Dr. Rao told us at the beginning of July that there were no more treatments available for Will and that we would simply be letting the cancer take its course, I did not know if this day would ever come. But it is here – a warm, sunny day full of promise. Katherine is up early, catching a ride to school from a classmate because getting a ride to school from Dad isn't cool anymore. Will awakens about 9:00 a.m. and the familiar routines of the last couple of weeks begin in earnest: make sure that his undergarments are fresh, help him wriggle into his polo shirt and blue shorts, then gently guide him into the wheelchair and over to the table for some breakfast before the time arrives to depart for school. We gather up his school supplies, roll him gently down the front steps and out to the van, lift him up into the van trying to be careful not to bump his still-healing head incision in the process, fold up the wheelchair and lift it into the van; off we go. As we head downtown, I think back to other first days of school, for the last 13 years, dating back to Katherine's days in preschool, all spent at St. Francis School: dropping them off with their backpacks, giving them goodbye kisses and wishing them a good first day, and watching them walk off to the school door to join their classmates, most together since kindergarten. Today we turn off to head to Lourdes High School, pull into a handicapped parking space, get Will into his wheelchair and roll him over to the school sign to snap a few first day of school pictures as we wait for Katherine to appear and take Will to the classroom for his first class. It feels strange, as it should: a new school, Will unable to walk to get into the building. But there are smiles to greet us at the door as Katherine and her friends appear to gather Will and his things; they slowly push Will down the hallway out of sight. Liz and I wait in a small conference room in the school office for Will to complete his two classes. An hour and a half passes quickly and we venture down to the English classroom where a smiling Mrs. Falvey is talking to Will who is sitting at a table near the front of the room. She assures us that everything has gone smoothly and, after a brief exchange, we roll Will out, back down to his locker to store his books until tomorrow, and then out to the van to repeat the process to get him back home. We sat down for some lunch before Will took his afternoon nap and the conversation turned toward the day at school. Will says that he didn't like it, but was unable to say exactly what he did not like or what he would change to make it a better experience. The sad reality is that with Will's cancer robbing him of his short term memory, much of what the teacher has probably said at the beginning of the period has been lost from his memory by later in the class, and so there is no foundation of information that Will can build on to make sense of what he is seeing and hearing in class. It is bound to be a confusing exercise, unless perhaps there is some kernel of knowledge that corresponds to something already held in his long-term memory that he can connect. So I wonder a bit why he is there. It's hard to talk to the other kids and make new friends when they have no frame of reference for what he is facing, and when he cannot recall their names or information personal to each of them. It's hard for him to talk to the teachers for the same reason, though perhaps there are some nuggets of wisdom in Religion class that will resonate when he hears them at school, however briefly. Perhaps he is there to help the other kids learn empathy, and recognize in Will a unique soul and a beauty that shines through, even as the essence of what made him who is recedes like the waning tide of the ocean. I'm sure we'll understand more as the days ahead unfold. This evening, we had Katherine's best friend Anna Sutherland and her mother Laurie over for dinner. As dinner was winding down, Katherine was complaining about how unfair a set of new rules at school was and in a pause in the conversation, Will simply said quietly, "Life is hard," looking over at Katherine. It cut me to the quick. Katherine has nothing to complain about, when you consider what Will is grappling with and, for just a moment, there was silence as we all felt the power of his understated words.

August 29, 2012 – Will awoke this morning and it was immediately evident that cancer had stolen more from his poor body. He had difficulty swallowing his breakfast and ended up vomiting it up on his shirt. Then, when he was in his wheelchair, it became apparent that he could no longer hold either his torso or his head upright without support. We noted that he was losing control of his arms and hands;

he struggled to find a way to get a spoon up to his mouth to feed himself breakfast. Katherine helped feed him his dinner tonight; she is so careful about not hurting him and asking him if he's in any pain. She is so tender with him, but I can see the sadness and pain in her eyes and the look asking "why is this happening to my brother?" ... We are all feeling this way. Today we also moved Will's twin bed downstairs into the great room so that one of us can sleep near him in case he needs help during the night. Each time we pass his room, now void of a bed, the sense of loss, sadness, despair and anger is profound.

With these additional changes, there is no way Will can handle high school, even on a reduced schedule. And so, without warning, his high school experience, all of two days, is over. We are indebted to the teachers and staff at Lourdes High School who worked hard to make his brief time there special. His freshman classmates will move on, meeting new friends, going to football games and school dances; our son will not be there to join them. I pray that they remember Will as they move through high school – remember his spirit and his dreams of joining them unfulfilled, and remember that their worst day there will likely never approach the worst days that Will endured to get to have his two days of high school. How much more can Will be expected to give? Everything, of course. His cancer will not be satiated until it has devoured Will. I'm thankful that his pain at this point is still being managed pretty well. *Please God, don't make him suffer as all that makes him human, and the Will we know and love, is gone.*

August 30-31, 2012 – Will got a visit tonight from Dr. Rao, Donna Betcher, and Dr. Khan, who is the oncologist assigned to help with the hospice program. It was a routine visit, mainly to check on the decline in Will's condition, but also to determine why his stomach and abdomen had become so hard and distended. The medical staff huddled around Will discussing his condition when they paused for a moment and he looked them in the eye and asked them collectively, "When will I get 100% better?" I watched as Will stopped three world-class medical professionals in their tracks; there was a long pause as they grappled for an answer. Eventually, they gently explained to Will that he would not be getting better. He vaguely remembered that and accepted his fate once again, but it took our breath away for a moment. Liz and I later told Will what a wonderful, remarkable son he is and will always be to us; how many, many lives he has touched; we reassured him that he was going to heaven to be re-united with our first dog, Thoreau, and that we will meet him there someday; that he will always be with us and us with him; and that we will miss him terribly, but we'll be OK. Liz asked him if he was afraid of dying and he said, "No." Then he said, "Mom, you're sprinkling me with your tears. Please stop." Will had small tears in the corners of his eyes as Liz got up to leave the room as the tears flowed down her face. *Oh, Will, that we could change the past, and we could fix you and restore the health you once had long ago.*

Then today, we were blessed when half of the Lourdes High School football team showed up in their jerseys at our front door a few hours before the season opener against Hayfield. It was the end of the first week of school and, despite homework and the impending start of football, some of the young men on the team, mostly former St. Francis students, had heard about Will and losing his battle to remain in school. They came over *en masse* to try to cheer Will up a bit, to shake his hand and wish him well. It brought tears to our eyes to see their large strong bodies gather around Will's bed where he lay with his strength slowly ebbing away. They posed for a quick picture before they said their goodbyes and headed off for the football field. They are raising young men and women of character at Lourdes High School who are never too busy to remember someone less fortunate than themselves. How I wish that Will could still be there making his way through the halls to his classes and learning some of those same fine lessons.

September 2-3, 2012 – My parents and Liz's parents arrive for a visit. It's a hard one as they do not know if this will be the last time they see Will alive, since no one knows the timeframe of how much time Will has left. Will's principal, Barb Plenge, stops by to bring Will Holy Communion and a St. Peregrine medal on a chain so that he will always have something of his patron saint, the cancer fighter, with him. She also tells us that Will's painted blue fingernail has gone "viral." Back in August, when the girls convinced Will they should paint his fingernails, and he acquiesced to one nail painted blue, little did anyone know that this outward sign would become a phenomenon. It became a small gesture of solidarity, one blue fingernail at a time. It showed up first on the index finger of one of Will's male 8th grade teachers at St. Francis, and was later observed spreading quickly through the faculty, male and female. The teachers have become the students as they learn from Will as he fights this final battle.

After a delicious dinner, we gather in the great room for a viewing of the photo movie of Will's life that I have been working on for the past couple of months. It's fun to watch as the movie begins to unfold with Will's baby pictures – glimpses of a time before cancer touched his life. There are smiles as the happy events, the trips to Disney World and Alaska, roll by. Some tears are quickly wiped away when Will's gaunt body, following his first surgery and treatment, appears in photos and we see how many of those photos over the years show Will's bald head. At times it seems like he was always in treatment, but he kept smiling for the photos nonetheless. I started the happy music at the beginning and kept the more somber music, including Will's personal favorite, "Let It Be" by the Beatles, toward the end as the havoc wreaked by his illness reached a crescendo. A very quick 1 hour and 22 minutes. Too many Kodak moments to sort through to find only the very best, which is a nice problem to have. In the end, it seems well received, even if everybody found fault with some part of the music. Oh well.

The next day, we were fortunate to have a photo shoot with Cat Thisius, arranged by Sara Ovist, one of my co-workers at the County. Cat came in and immediately took charge, transforming our great room into a photo studio in a matter of minutes. She had some great ideas for photos, including several involving our hands and our feet, and Will holding some of the collected sports memorabilia that meant the most to him. Both sets of grandparents got to be part of the photos, which meant a great deal to us and to them. Will was in some pain, but did not complain at all and smiled repeatedly when asked, even though the session quickly wore him out. Buddy would not cooperate, but I carried him into the great room and set him on the couch so he could be a part of it all in the end. We can hardly wait to get the pictures back so these moments are captured for eternity.

Before my parents depart for home, Mom tells me about a conversation she had with Will a few weeks earlier. They were sitting together on the couch watching a team from Brazil play soccer. Will said to her, "Grandma, I would like to go to a country like Brazil someday and be a missionary." Grandma asked him why he would like to do that. He replied, "to help poor people there." Grandma said to him, "Will, you are already a missionary here in our own country. That is because your goodness and kindness and trust in God have influenced so many people, young and old, to try to follow the wonderful example you have set for them." Wise words from Grandma.

On September 8, Father McNea stopped by to give Will his Confirmation Certificate and also offer Communion if Will wanted it. After visiting a while, Will said, "Do you have any of those (Communion wafers) on you?" Father smiled and said, "yes," and pulled the pyx in which he carried them out of his pocket. Will's candor and dry sense of humor remain.

On September 9, John DeRouin, fondly known by most of his former students as "Mr. D," stopped in to visit Will. John was a wonderful 4th grade teacher at St. Francis who both Katherine and Will were lucky to have. We had a great visit and John promised to drop by with some fresh goat cheese soon for us to try. He's raising goats and gets about three gallons of milk/day so he's got to do something with it besides drink it! When John came in and hugged Will, he sat down and asked Will one of his favorite memories from St. Francis. Will said, "Having you as a teacher." This brought tears to our eyes and John said gently, "Thank you, Will, for saying that. I needed to hear it from you." We hope he comes to visit again soon.

September 11-12, 2012 – September 11, an iconic day laden with symbolism, when the embodiment of evil led to the deaths of innocents, a day when we reflect on those who gave their lives that the rest of us might be free. Will is riveted watching a special with me on National Geographic about the events of that fateful day; he was only three-years-old and too little to remember how that day became seared into our collective memories. But the survivors found ways to remember those whom they lost, how to cope with being left behind and stitch together the tatters of their lives so they could go on living; a good metaphor as Will's journey winds down. I beg him to play Mario Kart with me today; then almost immediately, I regret my decision as it is evident how much Will has lost in recent weeks. In past video racing bouts, Will almost always came out on top with ease, the hand-eye coordination there at his command when he called upon it; a win always gave me something to keep striving for. Today, it was no contest. Will struggled to hold the wheel containing the Wii remote controls that were needed to drive the cars; he struggled to turn it to get his car to go where he had willed it to go a hundred times before and spent three races slowly swinging in and out of the various racetracks, finishing in last place. I won, but it made me sick to my stomach. Not surprisingly, after three races, Will said he was done with Mario Kart. The universe of activities I enjoyed with Will shrinks by one more.

On September 12, 2012, Will slept for an exceedingly long time – a period of 16 hours from the preceding evening. Will's cousin Molly stopped by to visit today and prayed fervently for healing for Will and for all of us. We noticed for the first time that Will has started to slur his words slightly and is having difficulty speaking, which is compounding the existing difficulty he is already having thinking clearly. He is also spending much more time with a blank stare on his face, his usual wit laid aside. He did tell me today that "I'm your son, so it's my job to boss you around," which brought a smile to my face. Katherine took some extra time helping to care for Will tonight, feeding him his ice cream, cleaning him up and getting him ready for bed. Katherine told him that his skin was soft as she wiped away a remnant of his ice cream; he responded, "of course it is, I'm a kid." She will be coming home tomorrow afternoon to spend some extra time with Will. There is a sense among all three of us that Will's time with us is short before the side effects caused by tumor growth will wipe out what makes Will the unique, witty and beloved young man that he is. There is a sense that the fine porcelain figure that is Will has been dropped and shattered into a thousand pieces. We are powerless to find a way to fit the pieces back together again, to remake him as he was.

On September 13, Will received some wonderful gifts, which will be always cherished. The Minnesota Twins sent a package containing a Twins hat, an autographed Joe Mauer jersey in Joe's size (48), and a baseball, autographed by Justin Morneau, in a case. The card said, "We're thinking of you Will. You're an inspiration to many and we wish we could see your reaction when you opened this gift. [signed] Your friends in the Clubhouse of the Minnesota Twins." Will was thrilled with these gifts. What a class act the Twins have been, continue to be and will always be. Thank you to everyone who made this possible. Katherine hoped that the jersey had actually been worn by Joe – complete with grass and dirt stains and smelled like Joe (a girl can dream, can't she?) – but it is brand new.

On September 16, we were visited by Deb Hatzenbihler (who "runs" the school office at St. Francis), and teachers Brian Krenik (Will's 3rd grade teacher) and Shannon Weick (his 2nd grade teacher). Deb brought Will a "Tardy Slip" because he was late in coming by the office to pay them a visit. They also brought an album of photos of students and staff at St. Francis who had painted their nails blue in support of Will, which also included some reflections about Will by members of the staff. Monica Steinmetz, Will's 6th grade teacher, wrote one that we felt really captured the essence of Will and his impact on others:

> *Will…. you have been a master teacher to me..*
>
> *a teacher of simplicity – enjoy the simple moments of sunshine, quiet, and beauty*
>
> *a teacher of friendship – treat one another with genuine compassion*
>
> *a teacher of laughter – have fun, practice sarcasm and keep it positive*
>
> *a teacher of courage – God will provide*
>
> *a teacher of family – one of the greatest gifts given to us by God*
>
> *a teacher of determination – the sheer will to carry on even in tough times*
>
> *a teacher of love – allow yourself to love unconditionally and allow yourself to be surrounded by love*
>
> *a teacher of faith and trust – you walked this walk every day, Will, and have taught me to do the same.*
>
> *To my master teacher – you are a marvel.*
>
> *In thanksgiving for you – Mrs. Steinmetz, September, 2012*

September 19, 2012 – This sunny, cool day began with a visit from the nice guy at Apria, the home health care agency, bringing us oxygen for Will. He gingerly rolled the oxygen concentrator and half a dozen canisters of compressed oxygen off his delivery truck and into our garage. Liz and I spent the next half hour learning all about how to run and maintain an oxygen concentrator, and backup oxygen from the portable tanks in the event of a power failure. Will has been having some shortness of breath lately, and having oxygen available for him to use at the house when he needs it is the next step. It's a reminder that Will's last hours, when the vital organs of his body begin shutting down, are approaching. It's been hard to watch him battle his cancer; it's going to be devastating when he starts to have enough trouble breathing that he will need supplemental oxygen. I don't want him to have to struggle to breathe.

It's also hard because today my Mom and Dad believe it will be their final visit with Will. For a while before they leave, the house is quiet. My Mom and I sit together on the couch, crying softly, holding hands, looking at Will sleep in his hospital bed, watching his chest rise and fall as he slumbers. We reflect back to the final days they endured when my brother Dave lost his battle 40 years ago, but the pain is still there, lying just under the surface. My Mom reassures me that we have done everything possible to fight his cancer and enable Will to try to live as happy and healthy a life as he could under the circumstances. I know this, but final goodbyes are still hard, knowing this is the last time, in all likelihood, that they will see Will alive. My Dad is at a loss for words, but does his best and tells Will he loves him as he says goodbye. My Mom spends a tearful few moments with Will, stroking his hand, telling him how much she and Grandpa love him, what a good grandson he has been and what a wonderful life he has lived, and whispering in his ear that his Dad loves him very much as well. Will listens, his stare partially blank as it takes a moment for the words to pass through his brain where the cancer cells are wreaking havoc and interrupting the nerve messages through his brain, trying to make sense of it all. Then it clicks and he smiles and says, "Thank you Grandma" and gives her a hug goodbye. A "see you later" falls flat for the first time as there will no "later," not until we all hopefully meet Will again in heaven. Only God knows when that will be. I'm grateful for the love poured on Will and Katherine by my parents and by Liz's parents; it has helped shape them into the fine persons they have become.

On September 21, Will's psychologist, Daniel, and Mark Arvold stopped by in the late afternoon. Upon hearing their voices, Will woke up and had an engaging conversation with them both. He also told Liz at one point to stop asking him if he needed anything as she was annoying him. Of course, he allowed Dan to give him water. Will did eat some soup while talking with the guys. Liz was touched by a comment made by Dan, who is a very thoughtful, articulate person and a man of few words. When he was introduced to Mark, he said, "Hi. I'm Daniel and Will's been my teacher for the past two years." A statement profound and so true. Will has been a teacher to so many over the years.

September 22, 2012 – Another hard day: Uncle Tom and Aunt Kathy and Ben Biskupski arrive for a visit. Will is asleep most of the day, though he wakes up briefly shortly before they leave to enjoy some blue Cookie Monster Ice Cream from Flapdoodles and a chat with them. Tom and Kathy are devastated, leaving with bone crushing hugs and teary faces. Doug and Betsie Holtan and Alan Horn also stopped by today. Alan says he is there on behalf of all of the people who want to come, but won't because they don't know what to say. That comment speaks volumes: no one knows what to say. We have passed the stage where we can rage and be angry that Will is going to die and leave us; anger does us no good at this point. All we need is for people who know Will and know us well to show up with open arms, ready to give us a collective big hug and hold our hands as we walk the rest of the way on Will's journey. Will is sleeping nearly 20 hours a day now; he only wakes up long enough to eat a bit before descending back into a fitful slumber. He is talking in his sleep now; oddly his speech when he dreams is clearer than his speech when he is wide awake, at one point asking me if I have completed his Spanish assignment. Liz and I have begun taking turns sleeping in the great room next to him. He has been having shortness of breath and the oxygen concentrator is ready next to his bed if cancer begins to steal one more essential function from him.

The maple trees outside the picture window are dressing in Will's favorite color, orange, as evening settles in. The first frost of the season is expected tonight, bringing the season when all the plants will cease to grow to an end for the year. The Earth is getting ready for its long winter sleep and so, in a sense, is Will. Both hold the promise of new life when the time is right.

September 23, 2012 – We were honored to have several visitors today. First, Chris and Stacy Brent stopped by with a delicious meal, which we very much appreciated as it allows us to spend more time meeting Will's needs. Then Brent and Katie Boggust and the Viggiano family (minus Gracie) stopped by to see Will. It was hard for them to see the changes that the past few days have brought, but Will smiled several times as he spoke with them. Just before they departed, Will had us all gather around his bed, hold hands and recite with him the Prayer of St. Francis. The prayer is inscribed on the wall in the St. Francis School cafeteria; he read it every day as he ate his lunch and committed it to memory. It was an extremely powerful moment. Although it was hard at times to understand Will as he led us through the prayer, there was no mistaking the passion that he felt for the message it conveys.

Prayer of Saint Francis of Assisi

Lord, make me an instrument of your peace.
Where there is hatred, let me sow love;
where there is injury, pardon;
where there is doubt, faith;
where there is despair, hope;
where there is darkness, light;
and where there is sadness, joy.

O Divine Master, grant that I may not so much seek
to be consoled as to console;
to be understood as to understand;
to be loved as to love.
For it is in giving that we receive;
it is in pardoning that we are pardoned;
and it is in dying that we are born to eternal life. Amen

There was a long pause as he finished and the impact of his prophetic words slowly sank in. It made me think of a passage from the Book of Isaiah (Chapter 11) in the Bible where it says in part that "the wolf shall dwell with the lamb, and the leopard shall lie down with the kid … and a little child shall lead them." Will was in the lead today, perhaps in a moment when we least expected it, and we were the students with much yet to learn.

After everyone left, it was just the four of us – our family – together for some peaceful, tender moments with Will. The emotions over the past several days (more like years) have accumulated inside Katherine and she was able to release some and share a beautiful conversation with Will. During the conversation, Will was patting her shoulder saying, "It's OK Katherine. It's OK." After they finished talking, Will, in true style, said, "See ya later toots." Never before has he called Katherine this, and we all burst out laughing.

September 26, 2012 – Will has slept for most of the day. He says he's in no pain (thank God for that blessing). He is having more difficulty swallowing. He chews his food for a long time and then it's as if he doesn't know that the next step is to swallow. He still feeds himself as much as he can, but we have to be right there to ensure he doesn't put too much food in his mouth. His speech continues to be a little slurred;

however, when he talks in his sleep at night, his speech is still as clear as ever. Go figure!

For the first time in weeks he is interested in using his iPad when he wakes briefly in the afternoon. I ran up to his room to retrieve it for him. I brought it back, propped it up on a pillow in front of him, and he is able, with a little help, to still play Tree World, one of his favorite game apps, for a while. Then I help him pull up his music. I click the Beatles icon, and the strains of Will's favorite song, "Let It Be," drift up from his lap. He smiles, just a little, as he hears it. After listening to a little more music, however, the iPad falls from his grip onto the bed. He is finished.

He is restless tonight, which is unlike him. He tells Katherine, "I don't feel right" and, for the first time, refuses to take his medications before dropping off to sleep for the night. I'm obsessing that this is the beginning of the end, so I retreat to the "man cave" in the basement and pop *A River Runs Through It* into the DVD player. Why? Will and Liz visited the location where the fly fishing scenes in the movie were shot during their trip to Montana this summer. I love the beautiful scenery of the mountains and the rivers and the storyline – a brother's story about the difficult life and the death of his brother, whom he loves dearly. It's a theme I can relate to well right now. *Please keep him safe, God, through the night.*

Meanwhile, the blue nail phenomenon has taken off. It started slowly with the staff and some students at St. Francis. I put a post on Will's Facebook page, challenging the people who have been following Will's progress to post pictures of themselves with their right index finger painted blue as a show of support, and it has taken off. As of the time I write this, there are over 1000 people – and seven dogs – in 20 states and two foreign countries who have done this for Will. Many of them have never met our special young man, but all have been moved by his fight nonetheless. They include students of all ages, schools of dance, Girl Scout and Brownie Troops, the administrative office staff for Donald Trump, and the rock band Paul Revere and the Raiders, among others. It's an amazing show of support for Will, right at the time when the battle seems to be nearing the end. I've told Will of this support and all the people he has touched. I think he understands; I hope and pray that he does and does not leave us without knowing about his incredible "Blue Crew." If only we could harness all of that energy and goodwill and use it to save his life so he could be here with his family until it is our time to depart together.

On the evening of September 27, some of the Camp Jornada crew stopped by and put flamingos in our yard, which was always a "start of camp" tradition. They presented us with a beautiful quilt for Will. It contains cloth blocks of pictures that campers made back in 2007 and Cheryl, one of the former camp staff, sewed them into a beautiful quilt. Cheryl said that yesterday morning, when she took the quilt out of the closet, the square facing her was Will's square – a baseball diamond with the words "home run" written on it. She took that as a sign that the quilt should go to Will.

On September 28, Will is peacefully sleeping beneath a beautiful white angel sculpture, given by the Dearani Family. The wings are made out of driftwood; there is a head (no face) and beautiful white clothing. Ann Dearani also had a blue nail painted on one of the angel's hands, so the angel would "go blue for Will." Ann told us that these angels are made by a woman from the East Coast, whose 10-year-old son was killed in a car accident; crafting these angels brought her some sense of peace. The Dearani's son, Patrick, brought one for Will, and they hope it brings some peace to us. There is something comforting about this angel each time we look at it. Patrick, thank you for sharing one of your angels with Will.

September 29, 2012 – Will had a restless night, and his breathing seemed labored, so in the morning we decided to put Will on oxygen. It seemed to help his breathing and help him relax. He ended up sleeping most of the morning and afternoon, often with his eyes partially open, suspended in a state somewhere between sleep and semi-consciousness. Looking at Will with the oxygen cannula in his nose makes the end of his journey seem that much closer. Breathing is yet another "given" taken for granted, which Will now labors to achieve.

In the early evening, his former phy ed teacher, Mark Arvold, and his wife Jayne, brought over a wonderful homecooked dinner. After unpacking the food, Mark came over to Will's bed and began to talk to him about his time in phy ed class at St. Francis – the games that were fun, the kids who always seemed to get into trouble, about how Will used to come to his office and bum candy from him and hang out before drifting back to class. Will seemed to rouse himself from his

Camp Jornada Quilt with blocks made by Will and other campers back in Summer 2007 – September 2012

semi-conscious state, listening intently to Mark's questions and trying to clear away the cobwebs and give answers. To me, it seemed nothing short of almost miraculous. Will, who was slipping toward the brink, was pulled back again for just a few moments. The effort, however, wore him out, and he slumbered soon after Mark and Jayne left. He did rouse just long enough to view Katherine, beautiful in her black Homecoming dress, and meet her date for the evening, Zach Hebl, who was gracious to meet Will for the first time under such trying circumstances.

Late in the evening, the din in the darkened great room is a little louder now with the mattress aerator and the oxygen machine, each softly buzzing trying to cancel each other out, but neither can reach Will. He doesn't know that the "Go Blue for Will" phenomenon is still growing. Friend Ben Viggiano orchestrated a mass blue nail painting for students at Mayo High School. Nearly 300 people participated and joined together for a picture with a sign "Go Blue for Will." Now we have heard that the band at Century High School, the football team at Pine Island High School, and members of the soccer team at Austin High School have all gone blue for Will. The list continues to grow: over 1300 people in 22 states, 4 foreign countries, most of whom have never met and will never meet Will. Why do they do it? It's become a movement; maybe it's just a cool thing to do. But I hope that the real reason doesn't get lost somewhere along the way. I hope that everyone with a painted blue fingernail personally does something kind for someone fighting cancer. That will be the best way to honor Will when this is all said and done, even if they never got to know the incredible person that Will is, face to face.

October 2 – Dianne Isaacson, Will's hospice nurse, stopped by today for her regular twice weekly visits. After changing out Will's catheter for a new one and giving him a sponge bath in bed, he dropped off to sleep. She came into the living room for a chat with Liz and me. She's been a hospice nurse for a lot of years, and with that experience comes the insight that regular people lack. She told us that she noticed some new signs today – changes in Will's finger and toe nails, change in the coloring of his skin, and new challenges with swallowing – which led her to conclude that Will's very long journey is close to reaching its end. We hugged her tightly as we said our goodbyes today.

Will was restless when he woke later in the afternoon. Then we noticed that he was starting to have involuntary twitching in his hands, feet and on his torso, symptoms that had not occurred before. Hospice has a second line of defense with regard to drugs when the end is nearing, including Ativan to help Will's body relax. Liz got the OK to slip some of the Ativan pills under Will's tongue. Soon the twitching/seizure start to lessen and eventually stopped. Liz then slipped out to pick up dinner at Chipotle, which left me alone in the house with Will for a little while. He was awake, lying in his bed and staring at me vacantly with those big, beautiful blue eyes of his. I got down on my knees next to the bed and took Will's hand and I prayed aloud to God so that Will could hear. I told God about what an amazing son he has been to us, about how he has touched the lives of so many people in ways we could little comprehend, about how I wanted God to know how much we loved him. I asked God to take away his suffering and to take care of him in heaven. I told Will again how heaven would be a new beginning, a place where he would leave his cancer and his failing earthly body behind and his soul would be free. I said that although Liz and Katherine and I would miss him every day for the rest of our lives, God would take care of him and us. When I was done, I opened my eyes and could hardly see him through all the tears. Will said quite clearly, "thank you for sharing that with me."

Perhaps it was Divine Intervention that not more than five minutes later, Father Tom Loomis, Will's favorite priest, was standing outside our door to say hello. He came in and spoke with Will, who recognized him immediately. A smile curved across Will's face as they engaged in a quick conversation before Will dropped off to sleep once more. Father Tom was happy to take some tater tot hotdish and chocolate covered peanuts off our hands as he listened to Liz and me talk a bit about the trials of the past few weeks. He reassured us that we had done a great job taking care of Will and meeting his needs during his illness. After a quick blessing and a big bear hug, he was off. *Lord, strengthen our fortitude against the coming fight, and thanks for sending your messenger at just the right time to bolster us at a hard time.*

October 4 – The Feast of St. Francis of Assisi in the Church calendar, when the humble Italian saint was born into heaven. Visits from family and dear friends are becoming more emotional, knowing that this could be their final goodbye to Will until we all meet again someday. Marcia, Gary and Jack came over yesterday. Jack climbed up onto Will's bed and curled up beside him with his head between his paws. Will put his hand on Jack and gently stroked him. He and Jack have been on this journey together for the entire 8½ years; his pawprints have marked many of the milestones along the way and we are eternally grateful for that.

The Gades stopped by to visit Will. Mitch had made Will a collection of his football photos, mounted on a styrofoam cylinder, along with his wrist tape with "WC" on it that he's worn in past games and will continue to wear. Will spent quite a bit of time studying it and trying to talk to Mitch, but it's become too hard to understand him now. We were unable to know what he was trying to say. Then each of the Gade family members spent their time at his bedside talking to him quietly, saying what they wanted to say and ending each conversation with, "I love you." We could not ever ask for better friends than the Gades. They have helped us through the darkest of times and celebrated the victories with us as well. We know they'll continue to be by our side in the future. We love you Chris, Marne, Meredith and Mitch.

October 6 – We passed a milestone this week. October 4 was the 10-year anniversary of moving into our "new" home. It had been such a happy day, watching the kids run around the new house with our former dog, Thoreau, picking out their new bedrooms and the colors and borders they wanted to put up in their rooms. Will was just four-years-old and cancer had not yet found us. Oh, to be able to go back and pursue the road not taken, the path that did not contain cancer for Will. That road today included the annual "Brains Together for a Cure Walk." At the event, Dan O'Hara, who lost his daughter, Shannon, to a brain tumor nine months ago, spoke movingly about Shannon and the powerful effect she had on people in her life before her journey ended. He also asked people in the audience who had painted their fingers blue in support of Will to raise their fingers and be counted. We needed to be home caring for Will, but we understand it was a powerful testament to the compassion felt by local brain tumor families for our Will.

Things also really started to get to me today, for some reason; a million little things that added up to a big thing. "Tired" is the best description I could give the day: tired of sleeping on the couch in the great room, with Liz in another bed nearby, and Will between us in his hospital bed clinging to life; tired of trying to balance the caregiving of Will with Liz as too many months of being emotionally on edge were taking their toll; tired of being away from work for three months now, with the stable routine and supportive coworkers that could help ease the tension that hangs in the air in the house; tired of having extended family present, even though Liz and I each needed them now for emotional support as Will's life hangs in the balance; tired of lacking the temptation to stop eating too much of the delicious food brought by all the kind people trying to help (and feeling my pants growing a bit tighter by the day); tired of all the visitors to the house who made Buddy bark and disturbed Will from his slumber in bed; tired of the funeral preparations in which ideas were floated but no final decisions could be made; tired of the struggles Will was having communicating with us as the cancer crept further into vital areas of his brain controlling his speech; tired of seeing Will suffer, day after day. Tired, tired, tired. It helped a bit to have my parents start helping to edit my book today, as I look forward to the day when I can share Will's story with others and raise money to help families battling cancer, but my reserves are being taxed to their limits. Will has it a million times harder than I do, so I should not have anything to be tired about; I need to grin and bear it. *God, help me keep holding it together.*

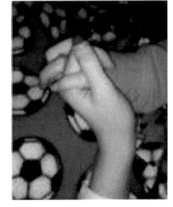

Will and Katherine sharing a quiet moment together at our home – October 2012

October 8 – Katherine went to school today, but spent a lot of time at Will's bedside when she got home. He asks for her. They hold hands in a way unique to the two of them. Their fingers are threaded between each other's, almost the way you would fold your hands when you would pray. Will only holds her hand in this way, no one else's. He also looks right into her eyes and they don't even have to speak any words. You can see the love being exchanged between them. Katherine holds his hand and gently rubs his shoulder or his head. She told Liz last night, "Mom, I don't feel like I can leave his bedside." She has such a tender heart for Will and this is such a load for her to carry, along with trying to stay focused on school. She's doing an amazing job and we are so grateful to everyone at Lourdes for their support and understanding.

Our dog, Buddy, has been reluctant to enter the great room where Will lays in his hospital bed, intimidated by the size of the bed, and the whirring noises from the air circulator on the mattress and the oxygen machine. Knowing that Will's time with us was growing short, while I had Liz and Katherine gathered around Will's bed, I picked up all 85 pounds of Buddy and brought him into the semi-darkness and placed him next to Will on his bed. Will's strength had been failing for some time, as he has gone without anything significant to eat or drink for nearly two weeks now but, with some help, I was able to guide his hand to stroke Buddy on the head and rub him under the chin for a little while. Buddy was petrified, of course, being up on the bed, but sat still as a statue while Will caressed him. It was a priceless moment as the four of us gathered around Buddy; perhaps Will knew his time was drawing near and he wanted to say goodbye to Buddy. We all cried a little as we huddled there, feeling the end of Will's time with us lurking just out of reach.

On October 9, Will started having difficulty breathing and lapsed into semi-consciousness. Liz and I kept vigil over him at night, as we had for the past week. In one corner of the great room, Liz slept on the twin bed that formerly was in Will's bedroom; on the other side of the room, I slept on the couch. Once Will was no longer conscious, he was no longer able to swallow his pills. After discussions with Dianne, Will's hospice nurse, we decided that we needed to give him only medications he could absorb without swallowing: Ativan, to help him relax and help him breathe better, and morphine to take the edge off the pain he had been having in his neck and lower back. Liz and I set the alarm on my phone to ring, once every hour to administer the morphine, once every two hours to administer the Ativan. It was frightening to us to awaken so often during the night to give these medicines to our son, who was no longer able to swallow them and who could no longer focus on us nor give us any feedback as he received them. Will also developed sleep apnea at this time. The pauses between his breaths grew longer and longer; Liz and I lay in our beds collectively holding our own breaths as we waited/prayed for Will to take another breath, time and time again. Finally, at 3:30 a.m. I was convinced I could sleep no longer. I climbed into a chair and sat next to Will's bed and stroked his hand until the morning light crept in through the east window. It helped me some. I'd like to think that somewhere through the haze of Will's semi-consciousness it helped him a little bit, too.

Dawn broke on October 10. Will's best friend, Joey Viggiano, came over and spent some precious time with him. Joey sat by his bed, held Will's hand and shed some tears. Joey talked with us a little, about all the fun he had with Will and how Will was his best friend, and how he would always miss him. Our hospice nurse Dianne also came in the morning to help. As she turned Will on his side to clean him, she alerted us that doing so could cause his life to end. We gathered around Will as she turned him. For at least a minute, Will did not take a breath. The tension in the room was palpable but, finally, Will breathed in and Dianne was able to finish cleaning him up. Will's breathing became increasingly more labored as the day wore on, the air raspy as it left his drying mouth and he struggled to breathe. At one point, Dianne wanted to increase Will's dosage of morphine. I misunderstood and thought for a moment that this was to be a lethal dose of morphine, one that would hasten his death. I could not consent to a decision that would hasten Will's death, despite the circumstances and told Liz she would have to authorize this. I could not do this in good conscience. Dianne quickly clarified that the dose would only make Will more comfortable and would not hasten his death. Relieved, of that worry we proceeded to administer the higher dose to Will.

After darkness had set in, Liz, Katherine, my parents and Liz's parents, and I gathered around Will's bedside and held his hands. The lights were turned down low and music played softly in the background. With his precious iPad close by, we listened to some favorite music that Will had loaded onto it: Rascal Flatts, the Beatles, songs from *Glee*, and, of course, the theme from *Star Wars*, among others. It felt right. We were all right where we needed to be. It was all in God's hands how much longer Will would get to stay, but he was surrounded by the people he loves. When he goes, it will be with the knowledge that many people have showed how much they care about him and that he made a real difference while he was here. You can't ask for much more than that.

Liz and I did not think he would make through the night. I dropped on my knees at bedtime to pray next to Will's bed. The room was dark except for the light from the behind the laundry room door. The only sounds were the steady *click-bahhhh, click-bahhhh* of the oxygen machine as it delivered precious oxygen to Will; the gentle whir of the air circulator as it moved the air under Will's failing, fragile body; and the lengthy pauses and rasp from Will's throat as he struggled for each breath. I prayed silently. I asked God to deliver my son from his suffering; I thanked God for the short time we got to spend here with Will on Earth; and I prayed that he would take him straight to heaven. Then I climbed onto the couch for another difficult night.

We were up every hour once again over the course of the night, Liz and I taking turns delivering the morphine and Ativan inside Will's increasingly drying cheek and gum. We were surprised that morning dawned once again and Will was still with us, though his breathing had become less labored and quieter.

October 11 – Dianne arrived in the morning once again, surprised also that Will continued to hang on. We reminded her that he had always been a fighter. His coloring became increasingly paler. At our request, Dianne began shaving Will, removing the stubble that had grown on his teenage face over the past several months. In the middle of being shaved, Will's breathing stopped completely. We gathered around Will's bedside. As Katherine leaned over tearfully at his bedside and told Will what a good brother he had been, and how she did not want him to suffer any longer and that happiness awaited him in heaven, Will was called by God to return to heaven at 10 a.m. October 11, 2012. He passed away peacefully surrounded by his mother Liz, sister Katherine, his Dad Tom, his paternal grandparents, Mike and Jean Canan, and his maternal grandparents, Joe and Pat Levy, as well as his hospice nurse, Dianne Isaacson, who took such wonderful care of him in his last months.

It was stunning. Will's 8½ year battle with cancer was over. He had left his earthly body and his cancer, multiple surgeries, radiation, chemotherapy, and all of the pain and side effects that went along with it behind. We loved his earthly body and the humanity it contained along with his cancer. This was gone now. His soul was free, free to leave for heaven where all of his friends who had fought their unsuccessful battles in the cancer wars had blazed a trail before him. In a flash, he was no longer there. There was nothing left to hold onto, the spark that made him special gone. The recognition of this hit us all very solidly, sobbing hard, holding each other tightly as well as Will's hands, stroking his hair, giving him gentle kisses on the forehead. The rest of the morning was a blur. It seemed absurd, retrieving Will's medications from various places throughout the house and mixing them with kitty litter to neutralize them: there were so many from his war, it was hard to fathom how we had ever gotten him to swallow them all without complaint. The gentlemen from Macken Funeral Home arrived. I gently scooped Will into my arms, Liz supported his head, and together we carried him gingerly out the door and down the garage stairs, placing him lovingly on the gurney. We watched as they strapped his body to the gurney, then respectfully covered Will with a sheet and zipped him into a bag to transport him to the funeral home. The SUV eased out of the driveway and Liz and I held onto each other, sobbing, as Will left our home for the last time and vanished around the corner, out of sight. Later we watched the guys from the home health care agency disassemble his bed, and remove it from our home. As the last piece headed out the door to the truck, I was suddenly cognizant that they took with them the last signs of Will's fight – that bed where he spent the final weeks of his life. I felt the emptiness of the big space in our great room where the bed had been; it was symbolic of the large hole in our hearts since Will had left our lives. Quiet enveloped the room as the constant chatter of the oxygen machine and bed air circulator was gone now, along with him. Sitting at dinner tonight with Liz and my in-laws, I was aware of the absence of Will from the house. I had the sensation that he was merely over playing at a friend's house and having dinner, and would be walking back in through the front door, with that wry smile of his, ready to tell us about the things that had happened that day, ready to be tucked in at night as we had every night for the past 14-plus years. Knowing that he will never walk back through that door and into our lives leaves a chasm that will never be filled.

Chapter 11 – Will's Visitation, Funeral and Aftermath

Children are the hands by which we take hold of heaven.
– Henry Ward Beecher

October 14-15, 2012 – October 14 was the day of Will's visitation. There were so many details that needed to be attended to in order to make this event possible. Liz and I slept poorly that first night after Will died, tossing and turning, knowing that for the first time he did not sleep close by. The next two days were a blur, meeting with the funeral home directors and our pastor, to get everything all in order. Our friends, Shanna and Sherrie Decker, came over and took charge of the photo tributes. By 4 a.m., they had turned a huge, disorganized stack of photos into a series of large display boards that proudly and colorfully displayed Will's life, his school years, his sports interests and much more. Will's artwork and sports memorabilia, pieces he had written, memory boxes for people to jot down memories of Will to share with us, helped complete the picture of his life. All of this material was lovingly displayed on tables and on easels in the chapel at Macken Funeral Home in Rochester; a large-screen TV played the photo movie of Will's life that I had created, complete with the music Will loved, "Let It Be" by the Beatles, plenty of Rascal Flatts and tunes from the cast of *Glee*. The funeral home did a wonderful job preparing Will for his reviewal. He looked serene as he lay in his casket, merely asleep and about to awaken from a nap that could somehow bring him back into our lives. His casket was framed by large bouquets of flowers, with plenty of orange blooms. His trusted driftwood guardian angel from home, which had kept vigil over his bed during the final month of his long fight, hovered over the head of his casket, protecting him once again.

Before the doors opened to the public, we gathered for a short prayer with Father McNea, to remember Will and pray for the repose of his soul. With heads bowed, we faced the calm before the storm of people. The queue of mourners waiting outside to come in and pay their respects was astonishing. The visitation was scheduled to last for three hours. At one point, the line of people outside the doors was so long that it would take two hours just for them to reach the front. I expected to feel that the whole experience would be emotionally draining as I stood next to Liz and Katherine to greet people. On the contrary, I found it to be comforting and sustaining. There were so many people: family and old friends, from near and far away; colleagues from work; parishioners from St. Francis; teachers and classmates of Will and Katherine's from St. Francis and Lourdes High School. There were so many hugs when just a handshake seemed wholly inadequate in the sea of emotions coursing through the room. Many people lingered after having gone through the receiving line, cognizant that they were witnessing something quite special and beautiful that would touch their hearts and leave them not quite the same. The three hours flew by and still there were people in line waiting to see Will and us. Then abruptly, it was over. I did not want to let the moment go. I spent some time alone with Will by his casket, knowing that this would be the last time I would have one-on-one time with him, face to face, talking to him, while his favorite music played softly in the background. I told him about how proud I was of him and of the effect he had on so many people; about how I was going to miss the million little things that a father and son share that only they know intimately, like playing catch and watching him play baseball, working on our coin collections, taking those camping trips where we witnessed the wonder of God's creation as we hiked to the top of Brady's Bluff and other adventures; about how I was going to miss his quiet strength and dry sense of humor that put others at ease. I'd like to think that he heard some of this from his new home in the heavens. We left Macken's chapel and went home to prepare for the next day.

On October 15, the day began with a quiet moment. At my request, the funeral home brought Will to St. Francis of Assisi Church. There, in the darkened stillness of the church, with my Mom and Dad and sister Maureen gathered around, we placed our hands on the smooth dark wood of Will's casket, around his head lying just beneath, and we prayed. I talked to Will and to God about that holy place where Will had first come to know, love, and serve God: where he had attended Mass and Sunday school; then as Will grew older, the place where he attended school Masses, read petitions and Sacred Scripture from the pulpit, put on his server's garments and served Mass; the place where his family prayed when we got bad news in the cancer wars, prayed for healing for Will and for strength for the rest of us. It only seemed appropriate that we stop here briefly on his final journey to reflect on the time spent here. I even "forgave" him for working with Mom to arrange his Tuesday morning blood draws so that, more often than not, he would miss school Mass, as if he really needed to be forgiven considering the life he had lead. It was a sacred moment in time, shared with family who knew and loved Will well. It brought me some closure knowing that I gave Will a chance to say goodbye to St. Francis Church and to the School.

Later, as the sun climbed higher in the sky, we streamed into St. John's Catholic Church. We needed to use St. John's because of the large crowd anticipated for our beloved son's funeral. Will was lying peacefully in his casket at the end of the gathering space, waiting for the celebration that would send him forth to his final resting place. The church teemed with people. We circulated through the crowd, handing out tight hugs to friends, family and colleagues; it was so uplifting to see so many friends who had traveled from far away to be with us. Shortly before the Mass began, Will's extended family gathered around his casket, saying our final goodbyes before it would be closed and we would no longer lay our eyes on his sweet face. Into the casket went many items to accompany Will on his final journey: his baseball signed by Justin Morneau; his beloved red Twins cap signed by Joe Mauer, Joe's signature just barely visible above the brim after so many loving years of use out in the sun; an orange rose to remember his favorite color; one of his *Diary of a Wimpy Kid* books; photos of Will, Katherine, Liz and me at a Twins game with the Gades. The accumulated memories of a short lifetime. Tears were shed as the lid of the casket was fastened for the last time. Liz, Katherine and I gently unwrapped the pall and spread it over Will's casket, a symbol to recall his Baptismal garment. Fathers McNea and Loomis then processed slowly down the aisle to the altar, followed by Will's pallbearers; Marcia and Jack walked slowly in front of Will's casket, Jack proudly wearing his service jacket with his Green Bay Packer pins, clearing the way for the rest of us, protective of Will and bringing comfort to the end.

The funeral was beautiful and joyful, the church filled to capacity. Will's former classmates gathered *en masse* and watched carefully, just steps away from his casket. Will would have loved it: readings from Timothy about fighting the good fight and winning the race; readings from Corinthians about faith, hope and love and the greatest of these being love; the gospel from the book of Matthew about how you must become like a little child if you wish the enter the kingdom of heaven. These all were words that Will certainly took to heart. The music included the Beatles song, "Let It Be," sung beautifully during the offertory, as well as the hymn at Communion, "You Are Mine," which had meant so much to us throughout Will's journey as a source of comfort in the darkest of days and hope for the future. The eulogies were delivered by Barb Plenge, Will's principal at St. Francis, who spoke about Will's life encouraging us to "become better versions of ourselves;" Mark Arvold, Will's phy ed teacher at St. Francis, telling us about Will packing away racks of ribs and of chats in his office before returning to class; Will's best friend Joey Viggiano, telling us about the time when he and Will were driving a golf cart, did two donuts and lost control on the green, knocking over the pin and nearly upending the cart into a sand trap with Will telling Joey, "Let's do that again with Mr. Arvold next time!"; and Chris Gade reading "A LETTER TO WILL" from Liz and Katherine and me, pouring out the contents of our hearts to the assembled multitude.

Dear Will:

You were born in Rochester on a cold winter day on February 19, 1998, which also happened to be Granny Levy's birthday too. You were welcomed into the world by Mom and Dad and big sister Katherine. You brought us unending joy as you grew from a happy baby with the biggest blue eyes and radiant smile, to a toddler who liked to bite his sister, and finally a proud pre-schooler at St. Francis of Assisi School.

When you were diagnosed with a brain tumor on March 14, 2004, there had been weeks of fatigue, periodic fevers and you were having trouble skating at hockey practice due to balance issues. Cancer never crossed our minds. Thus began your journey. You were so brave and courageous during your 8½ year journey. You had multiple brain surgeries, repeated rounds of radiation and chemo, experimental drugs in hopes it would help you and other children in the future. You were treated by the best surgical and medical teams at Mayo Clinic, Memorial Sloan-Kettering in New York City, and St. Jude, who all worked together in earnest to do everything within their power to cure your cancer.

You touched the lives of many, especially the hundreds of doctors, nurses, nurse practitioners, and other medical personnel who shared in your journey. We are forever grateful for the work they did to help. We could not have made it without the help and support from your grandparents, friends and co-workers at Mayo and Olmsted County, the St. Francis and Lourdes High School communities, parishioners at St. Francis Church, just to mention a few, who so graciously stepped in and helped many times along the way.

There were many others who helped you and our family in other important ways. You and your sister (your parents too) loved the Make-A-Wish trip to Walt Disney World, staying at Give Kids the World Village, where you could eat ice cream 24 hours/day and little gifts awaited you and Katherine each night when we returned to our villa. You told us your favorite trip was to Alaska to "fish for salmon." Hunt of a Lifetime and Whaler's Cove Lodge in Angoon, Alaska made this a reality in June 2007. We'll never forget you reeling in a 41-pound halibut the first day out, with a little help from Dad. We loved going to Camp Sunshine in Casco, Maine and spending a week with 40 other brain tumor families. We remember actors Kirk and Chelsea Cameron and the wonderful staff at Camp Firefly who made it possible for all of us to join the circus for a day and fly from the high trapeze and experience other wonderful adventures at Calloway Gardens Resort in Pine Mountain, Georgia. Mom is so grateful for the 10 days she spent with you at Camp Big Sky Kids in Montana and seeing Old Faithful erupt and fulfilling your wish to see Yellowstone. We're so proud of you for winning the "last comic standing" award at the talent show too!

We know how much you loved sports, especially baseball and the Green Bay Packers. Who will ever forget the night when you, Mom, Uncle David and Aunt Karin were Sloan-Kettering's guests of the Yankees, meeting many notable players, taking that awesome picture with you and Derek Jeter, going into the dugout, and sitting right behind home plate in the last season at old Yankee stadium. And, what a class act those Minnesota Twins have been during your journey. You met Justin Morneau at spring training and your eyes were big as saucers when he whipped out his Sharpie, signed his bat, and handed it over to you. Joe Mauer made time to spend a few precious moments with you at Twinsfest. Only a few weeks ago, the Twins sent you a beautiful bouquet as well as an autographed Joe Mauer jersey and autographed Morneau baseball. Katherine was really hoping that the jersey had been worn by Joe and smelled like Joe. Chris Gade worked his magic and made it a reality to meet Big Papi and other Boston Red Sox players one-on-one during a "closed" spring training practice. And finally, you and Dad got to go to Dallas, Texas to see your favorite football team beat the Pittsburgh Steelers in the Super Bowl in February 2011. This trip became a reality in the course of only a few days by so many caring, generous people. We had great times at the cabin in Colorado – playing golf at Garden of the Gods, even though your Mom threw you out of a golf cart one summer, and playing Rummikube, a strategy game you were so good at playing! There were also great times at Aunt Kathy and Uncle Tom's house on Lake Wissota in Wisconsin – kneeboarding, fishing, campfires.

Will, you packed in a lot of special experiences in your much-too-short life, which was some compensation for the countless hours of pain and suffering you had to endure fighting your cancer for so many years. But you never wanted the focus to be on you. You just wanted to be one of the kids; in the class, on the team, or among friends. You were blessed by many caring teachers and staff at St. Francis School who stood by you every step of the way. Every day when we picked you up after school, you wouldn't be waiting outside but we'd have to ask Mrs. H. to announce on the loud speaker for you to come to the office. We could usually find you in Mr. Arvold's office or Mr. K's room, brightening their days. You were blessed to play on a baseball team with some of your St. Francis classmates and have two of the best coaches and dads around – Brian Cada and Jim Ryan. These coaches knew your story and knew so well what you had to overcome to take the field in a game.

How will we remember you Will? A boy with a radiant smile. A person who did not EVER complain about the extreme difficulties that he had to overcome in his life every day just to do the things others took for granted. Whenever anyone asked you, "How are you today Will?", your response was always, "I'm good." If you were having a bad day, then it was, "I'm pretty good." You were the Lego builder, who could take a box full of tiny pieces and create a masterpiece. You loved to read Dr. Seuss, Diary of a Wimpy Kid and Captain Underpants books. Will, you were the consummate lover of all things baseball, who loved to play shortstop and refused to let cancer define who you were on the baseball field. Will, you knew most all of the names and stats of MLB players and regrettably never got to see your beloved Minnesota Twins win a World Series. You were the boy enthralled with all things Star Wars who also never outgrew your love for Sponge Bob Squarepants. You were Mr. Hood in Du Wop Wed Widing Hood, in your bathrobe and with natural control over the TV remote, who delivered your lines with your dry wit. You were the video game expert who drove your carts in Mario Kart Wii like a crazy man and mowed down Dad on the racetrack. You had strong faith in God, even if you scheduled your Tuesday blood draws during school Mass. ☺ You had a special bond with your Mom, who was such a wonderful caregiver to you.

Will, everyone loved your sense of humor, your sarcasm, your honesty. You loved to tell jokes, your favorite being – "Why did Eeyore stick his head in the toilet? – To find Pooh." A Mayo physician told you this one! You weren't afraid to say what was on your mind when you told a surgeon that you didn't find his jokes funny and you didn't really even like him. You also asked about every doctor and nurse how old they were, by starting the question with, "I know I'm not supposed to ask this, but…" You also were so good at creating nicknames – V-Rod (Dr. Rodriguez) and Djuan (Donna Betcher), to name just a few. You were the most unselfish person – always thinking of others before yourself. When Grandpa came most recently, the first thing you asked was, "How's your broken arm?" Consoling Katherine in those final weeks of your life with a pat on her shoulder saying "it's OK" and ending the conversation with "See ya toots."

You were a young man of few words, but always honest. When we asked you to describe your journey, you simply said, "Cancer Sucks." Nothing more. You showed us how to not let cancer define you. You showed us such bravery, determination, courage and grace. You showed us the importance of a positive attitude and maintaining a sense of humor, in the best of times and on the darkest of days. You will never be here for us to watch you get a driver's license, have a girlfriend and experience that first kiss, grow up, get married and have a family of your own; however, your spirit and legacy will live on. The class of 2016 has begun at Lourdes High School and you were able to join them for two days, a goal we were so proud that you accomplished. We ask your classmates at Lourdes, and former classmates at St. Francis, to carry your memory with them as they move through their high school years and beyond. We ask them to remember your beautiful smile, your sense of humor and your kindness toward others before God called you home. We remember that even death does not does not mean the end, but a new beginning for you in heaven with God. And we will remember your unquenchable determination. When your former classmates conquer difficult obstacles as they live out the rest of their lives, we ask that they think about what you overcame to accomplish in eight years of fighting cancer. And we know that you would want us to remember that as we encounter others fighting cancer, we will do what we can to help. Someday we may be the ones that need the help and once the people you knew have walked in your shoes, they will understand better how your simple acts inspired many.

Will, you loved your sister dearly and affectionately referred to her as

"Fran." You never failed to brighten Katherine's mood. She was the first person to get you to smile and laugh after your initial surgery in 2004. Although she won't miss the hospital stays, she'll miss every time she made you smile. Like when she danced on the fountain in the Children's Hospital, looking like some crazy person. Katherine loved doing anything that could take away the constant reminder of the grueling battle your body was fighting. She is proud to say that she saw some of your biggest smiles, when you were in the most pain. And, she was the only person who got to "pet" your head when you had lost your hair. The scars and bumps referenced the hard hits your body was taking, but the top part of your head was as smooth as baby's skin. The smoothness reminded me of your calmness through it all. You handled everything with such grace. "Please let me stay home from school, Mom! I want to be here with him!" Willy, Katherine always wanted to keep you happy and she did a pretty good job of this. You were the best brother anyone could have. You are a gift only a few people are lucky enough to receive. ☺

Will, we admire you, and we will forever. You have taught us lessons that can never be learned from a book. You help us strive for greater STRENGTH, PERSERVERANCE, AND POSITIVITY – three things that helped you fight this battle. A few weeks ago, Katherine was standing by your bed with Mom and Dad as we shared a sacred moment. While she was crying, memories were racing through her head and reminding me of how lonely it would be once you were gone. She told you, "Will, you're my best friend. I love you so much. And I just don't want you to leave." Then you replied, "Don't cry – [as I began to cry more] – remember the good times," as you gently patted her folded hands. Will, we know that you always will help us remember the good times. As a brother, as a friend, as an inspiration, we will look to you. We will miss you every day for the rest of our lives, but you will always live on in our hearts. We love you and we'll all be together again someday.

Love,
Mom, Dad, and Katherine

After Chris read our goodbye to Will, Father gave the closing blessing and Will's journey to his final resting place began. The heart-rending strains of "Going Home" played as the three of us filed out of the pew into the center aisle; placing our hands on Will's casket, we gently pushed him up the aisle. We made our way through the throng of people, many faces bearing both smiles and traces of tears, as we approached the back of the church. We watched as Will's pallbearers gingerly lifted his casket to carry it to the waiting hearse; the beautiful lilting strains of a Scottish hymn played nearby. My dear friend, bagpiper Charles McKee, stood guard in the small courtyard outside of the church, arrayed in his uniform and kilt, as the pallbearers slowly carried Will past him to the hearse. I held Liz tightly and we watched the sun catch the orange flowers of the blanket of flowers as Will's casket rolled slowly into the hearse. We followed the hearse carrying our son's body on the slow drive to the cemetery. The line of cars in the funeral procession was shown dutiful respect as we stopped traffic momentarily, the funeral home flags gently swaying in the breeze on the car hoods giving us permission to pass. The old stone arch of Oakwood Cemetery was the portal to Will's final resting place. The sun glowed orange through the few maples in the cemetery as we approached the site of his grave and we once again heard the far off sounds of a bagpipe beckoning us to gather. The pallbearers lifted Will's casket out of the hearse and processed slowly through the grass to deposit him gently on the stand over the grave. Prayers from Fathers McNea and Loomis to commit Will's body to the Earth, and the playing of "Amazing Grace" by Charles on the bagpipes were a soothing balm as we remembered the grace that Will showed all of us throughout his days. Katherine released homing pigeons while standing near Will's casket – white symbols of freedom, winging their way above the trees and back home. The look of joy on Katherine's face, with the symbolism of the moment, gave us great peace. Family and close friends lined up for final goodbyes to Will. We placed hands and kissed his casket and whispered the contents of our hearts to be carried from Will's final resting place to the heavens where he could hear them. I wanted so much to take it all in before we departed, forever etched in my mind and heart: the tweeting of the songbirds in the old oak tree above Will's grave; the slight breeze rustling the leaves gathering on the ground; the glimpse of the Mayo buildings in the distance where Will got so much of his care; the sight of Mayo Field, the city baseball stadium, where Will received his Youth Baseball Player of the Year award, through the trees. A fitting place to put him to rest – the places where people who were so passionate about his life, his care and his loves could be seen. I watched Will's casket catching the late afternoon sunlight as we drove away and his grave vanished from sight. It was the perfect end to Will's remarkable life. Happiness at his peace, and the joy he gave people, overpowered the sadness at his passing. We were privileged to be present to share in it.

Chapter 12 – The Holidays and Adjusting to a Life Without Will

**But all endings are also beginnings.
We just don't know it at the time.**
*– Mitch Albom,
The Five People You Meet In Heaven*

November 23, 2012 – Thanksgiving was difficult for the Canan family this year, our first without Will. Liz had purchased a beautiful pot of evergreen boughs to place on Will's grave before gathering at the Viggianos' house for Thanksgiving dinner. We made the slow drive across town and into Oakwood Cemetery before pulling up to Will's special place. It was a cold day, the wind swirling through the treetops and scattering the fallen leaves, as we gathered around Will's grave. We noticed on our arrival that Marcia and Gary Fritzmeier, our friends, had preceded us; Will's grave was now adorned with a small, clear, smiling snowman, keeping watch over him from a small shepherd's hook. We huddled together against the cold as we placed our evergreens and said the "Prayer of St. Francis," which meant so much to our son. Then we went on to the Viggianos' home for dinner. Before our meal, we prepared to say Grace and I thought it was a perfect opportunity to recite a prayer sent to us by our friend Mary DeRuyter, though some tears were shed before the end could be reached:

*Dear God,
there's an empty chair at our table,
an ache in our hearts
and tears upon our faces...
We try to shield one another from our grief
but we cannot hide it from you...
We pray for Will
whose presence we miss in these homecoming days...
Open our eyes and our hearts to the healing, the warmth
and the peace of your presence...
Assure us that those we miss
have a home in your heart as well as in ours
and a place at your table forever...
Open our hearts to joyful memories of the love we shared
with those who have gone before us...*

Help us tell the stories that bring us close to one another
and to the ones we miss so much…
Teach us to lean on you and on each other
for the strength we need
to walk through difficult times…
Give us quiet moments with you, with our thoughts,
with our memories and our prayers…
And in the stillness of the quiet,
give us your consolation and your peace…
Be with us and hold us in your arms
as you hold the ones we miss…
This is the day you have made, O Lord:
help us rejoice and be glad in the peace you've promised
and share with those who've gone before us…
Amen

Thank you to the Viggiano family for hosting us for a delicious meal and for being with us to share our memories of Will on that day when he belonged there with us.

The next day, we headed north to Lake Wissota near Chippewa Falls, Wisconsin to my sister Kathy and brother-in-law Tom's house to join them and my parents for a belated Thanksgiving gathering for part of the extended Canan family. Catching sight of the lake behind the house as we pulled up brought back many memories of happy summer afternoons on the lake all together, skiing, tubing, fishing, swimming and laughing in the warm sunshine. We had a second Thanksgiving meal on Saturday night, though one place at the table was very empty. I spent some time with my nephew Ben showing him one of Will's favorite video game websites on the PC, Miniclip.com, and soon he was as happy playing the many games found there as Will had been. The goodbye hugs were extra tight, recognition that all of them had been with us for many of the highs and lows of the final months of Will's life journey. We are still trying to find our way. The world is moving on, and we are learning a new path, stumbling when grief "boulders" loom unseen in the darkness. I think of Will every night as I climb the stairs and walk past his bedroom where the treasures of his life lay, the sacred place where we tucked him in bed and kissed him goodnight for 14 years, always saying a prayer that we would have another day to share tomorrow. Now his bed lies undisturbed, the energy that made his room alive moved on. I will rest and try again to carry a little piece of him with me tomorrow and, always, to share with someone else when life gives me a chance.

December 1-2 – Liz, Katherine and I had a good weekend. We started it off on Saturday evening when we gathered with several other families for the Christmas party with our Brighter Tomorrows support group for families of kids fighting cancer. We enjoyed a great meal from Ye Olde Butcher Shoppe catering and a great singing performance from Vanessa Gamble and her "Theater for the Thirsty," which was a light-hearted take on the Nativity from the perspective of Mary, Joseph, the shepherds, the Three Wise Men and even one of the cows in the humble stable where Jesus was born. We have shared many triumphs and tears with the families in that group as the cancer wars have been waged. Then on Sunday, Gary and Marcia Fritzmeier, owners of Jack the service dog, came over to help us watch the Green Bay Packers come out victorious over the Viking purple and gold, and we remembered the games we watched together with Will, most especially the time we shared at the Super Bowl on a magical night in 2011 when Will's Packers were the best in the world. The weekend was capped off with a chance to take in the Rochester Honors Choir at their annual Christmas concert. Our good friends, Chris, Marne, Mitch, and Meredith Gade dedicated a song by the Chorale Choir (Meredith is a member of this awesome group) to Will. The song is called "Lost in the Night" by composer Kyle Haugen. The Gades walked Will's journey by our sides, they knew the immense mountains he had to climb along the way, and they know the dark valleys that we have struggled through since he left us. We continue to be blessed by people who have felt our pain and want to help; we're grateful to count all of them as our friends.

Lyrics to "Lost in the Night" by Kyle Haugen

Lost in the night do the people yet languish,
Longing for morning the darkness to vanquish,
Plaintively heaving a sigh full of anguish,
Will day not come soon? Will day not come soon?

Must we be vainly waiting the morrow?
Shall those who have light no light let us borrow,
Giving no heed to our burden of sorrow?
Will you help us soon? Will you help us soon?

Sorrowing wanderers, in darkness yet dwelling,
Dawned has the day of a radiance excelling,
Death's dreaded darkness forever dispelling,
Christ is coming soon. Christ is coming soon!

Will not day come soon?
Come and save us soon.
Christ is coming soon!

December 4 – My co-worker at the County Attorney's Office, Liz LaRoque, has been waging her own battle against cancer for many months. Her friends and co-workers have been working diligently to try to help meet her needs as she lives alone. I have tried to help in my own small way by regularly walking her dogs, Sammy and Pippin, after work. When I showed up last night to walk them, I learned that our friend Liz was no longer there; she had been declining rapidly in recent days and they moved her to a hospice care facility yesterday. It was a quiet walk around her darkened neighborhood, with the electric reds, greens and blues from the blinking Christmas lights on the houses nearby and the distant hum of the city audible in the distance. The dogs were anxious to work off their energy from being cooped up inside all day. I thought about the dogs as I walked them, like our dog Buddy with Will. They would never again know the loving touch of the one that doted on them daily. *Did they know? Would they care? Hard to get inside of a dog's head to watch how it ticks.* I learned this afternoon that Liz passed away. She brought an infectious smile and a can-do positive attitude to the clients we help in the Civil Division at the County Attorney's Office, especially the parents with children deserving regular child support, the folks who go off their meds in their struggles with mental illness, the developmentally disabled who need guardians or conservators appointed. She will be sorely missed by all who knew her.

This evening, I spent the first hour at the Brighter Tomorrows December meeting, gathered with the cancer families at the Ronald McDonald House. I was struck most by a video that our friend Shanna Decker had put together back in November of the kids – cancer fighters and siblings alike – telling about what they were thankful for this Christmas. More than anything, they were thankful for their families. They also mentioned in the video what they would like for Christmas. It's going to be hard for Santa to come up with a real dinosaur for our little friend Miles Gustafson, but, hey anything's possible when you believe!

Then I spent the last half of my evening with Gary and Marcia Fritzmeier at an event, sponsored by Season's Hospice at Christ United Methodist Church, which is a service to remember all those in the Rochester area who have passed away over the past year. It's a room choked with emotion when you enter; every saddened face in every pew has lost someone they love dearly. We entered and lit a candle for Will, joining hundreds of others, flickering intensely in the darkened sanctuary. A heartbreaking reflection on another cancer journey shared by one survivor, several beautiful pieces of music and finally the slow reading of each of the names, including Will Canan, a reminder that each of those souls was a father, mother, husband, wife, son, daughter, brother, sister or friend to one or more in attendance. Will, and now Liz LaRoque, are no doubt in a better place, where cancer haunts them no longer. But when can we stop counting the host of family and friends claimed by cancer and death?

December 9 – Last evening Katherine was gone to an All City Dance and so Liz and I decided to go and take in the movie *Lincoln*. Daniel Day-Lewis did a great job and should be nominated for an Academy Award for Best Actor for his portrayal of Lincoln, fighting for passage of the 13th Amendment to abolish slavery, shortly before his own death in the spring of 1865. There was one scene between Lincoln and his wife, Mary, that had Liz and me on the verge of tears. I had forgotten long ago that the Lincolns had lost their own son named Willie, who died at age 11, just three years younger than our Will. In the movie, Abraham and Mary are in a darkened room. Mary is dressed in a dark purple gown symbolic of mourning. The room contains a bed with a canopy covered with a black veil. There is a toy train engine on the nightstand by the bed and Mary holds a photograph of Willie. They discuss him and are deeply distraught over the recent death of their son; in real life, Lincoln was quoted as saying "My poor boy. He was too good for this earth. God has called him home. I know that he is much better off in heaven, but then we loved him so. It is hard, hard to have him die!" Willie Lincoln was finally buried at Oak Ridge Cemetery in Springfield, Illinois following his father's death. Our sweet Will was buried at Oakwood Cemetery. The parallels stir me deeply. The loss of a child is a universal language of grief throughout the ages, whether that be the Lincoln family or the Canan family. I respect Abraham and

Mary Lincoln even more now, seeing what they went on to accomplish in the throes of war, despite their sorrow after suffering such a blow. *You are always in our thoughts, Will, and reminders of you come at the most unexpected times and places.*

December 16 – My Uncle Pat is my Dad's "little" brother. They have always been close, even though he and his family have lived on the East Coast for decades now, and we have many fond memories of time spent with Uncle Pat and Aunt Loretta and their kids in my Grandma's small town of Darlington when I was little growing up in Wisconsin. Uncle Pat lost his wife Loretta to breast cancer a little over two years ago and I posted about her and her courageous battle on Will's Facebook site while his own fight still raged. Uncle Pat followed Will's struggles closely over the years, despite the miles that separate us. He recently sent us a Christmas card, which included this heartfelt note to his great-nephew Will.

Dear William,
When tomorrow starts without you,
We try to understand,
That an angel called you by your name,
And took you by the hand.
You went to heaven far above,
But we are not that far apart,
For everytime we think of you,
You're right here in our heart,

Love Forever and Always,
Mom, Dad, Katherine and Uncle Pat

To Uncle Pat, and Aunt Loretta and all of your kids and grandkids, you're right here in our hearts as well, always.

December 21 – We woke up yesterday to our first real snowstorm in Rochester in quite a while. Schools are closed, though of course employers still want you to hitch up the family dogsled for the trek into work that is too dangerous for your kids. Will used to love snow days, playing outside in the fluffy, white stuff with Buddy, having a snowball fight and making a stout snowman with a carrot nose and one of my old baseball caps on his noggin. Today was a landmark day. The Mayans foretold that today would be the end of the world. Looks like thankfully they missed the boat on that prediction as we are all still here and looking forward to the promise of a new day tomorrow. There has been plenty of darkness lately, more children gone to heaven from Sandy Hook Elementary in a place called Newtown, Connecticut – unexpected departures from families and friends who were still learning the ways they loved them, just like we loved our Will. But today is also the day of the Winter Solstice, the official beginning of winter, although winter always get underway up here in Minnesota weeks before the first official day dawns, and that means that the days will no longer get shorter. They will grow longer, bit by bit, the light slowly building day by day until the green buds of spring poke through the melting snow and we emerge from our home hibernation caves to get to know our neighbors once again. Perhaps it's a metaphor: emerging from the darkness of Will's death, and creeping toward the light, where we will cultivate only the happy memories that he left in our care.

That's what I hope for in the coming months. But before we leave the holidays behind, I have a gift from Will and a gift from a friend. I saved for last the best picture that Will took with his cell phone before he left us. A close up shot of a giraffe, taken at the Cheyenne Mountain Zoo in Colorado Springs, Colorado in the summer of 2011, another place Will loved. The picture reminds me of Will, the giraffe like Will – curious, playful, content with his life – even though they both lived confined in a way, the giraffe by physical walls, Will by the invisible boundaries created by his illness. The gift from our friend, Janet Rein, is a poem someone had given her years ago, which she shared with us and it felt just right to share it with all of you. *Will, Mom was right, we hope that Christmas is beautiful in heaven. Christmas here will not be the same without your gentle smile beneath our tree. Love you always. Dad.*

I'm Spending Christmas with Jesus Christ this Year

I see the countless Christmas trees,
Around the world below.
With tiny lights, like heaven's stars,
Reflecting on the snow.

The sight is so spectacular,
Please wipe away that tear.
For I'm spending Christmas,
With Jesus Christ this year.

I hear the many Christmas songs,
That people hold so dear.
But the sounds of music can't compare,
With the Christmas choir up here.

For I have no words to tell you,
The joy their voices bring.
For it is beyond description,
To hear the angels sing.

I can't tell you of the splendor,
Or the peace here in this place.
Can you just imagine Christmas,
With our Savior, face to face?

I'll ask Him to light your spirit,
As I tell Him of your love.
So then pray one for another,
As I lift your eyes above.

Please let your hearts be joyful,
And let your spirit sing.
For I'm spending Christmas in Heaven,
And I'm walking with the King.

December 22 – Our thoughts and prayers go out to the Tjossem family of Rochester tonight, as their son Kaden joined Will, and the other kids lost to cancer, in heaven this morning. He fought a gallant battle for 15 months with his parents and his sisters constantly at his side. His courage and spunk moved many. I hope that Will is there to welcome him, and that all of you will keep his family in your thoughts and prayers at this most difficult time just before Christmas.

December 25 – We spent our first Christmas without Will with Liz's extended family in the balmy warmth of Houston, Texas. We did our best to remember Will on Christmas Eve as we gathered at church and on Christmas morning as we opened our presents. Far away from our familiar cold and snowy surroundings and traditions at home in Minnesota, there was a huge void in our gatherings without Will that we could not fill. I missed the shared play time with Will proudly demonstrating his new toys and video games. It made me think briefly about *A Christmas Carol* by Charles Dickens, which I had the opportunity to read on the plane ride down. Will was my Tiny Tim, to my Bob Cratchit – but wishing we did not have the imagined ending where Tiny Tim dies and they huddle on Christmas, mourning his absence taking place, rather the real one where he survives and thrives and ends their perfect Christmas gathering with "God bless us, every one." We were grateful to Liz's niece, Sarah and her husband Scott Hatch for hosting the family, for the delicious meals, and the time shared together.

January 1, 2013 – When Will and Katherine attended Camp Jornada near Rochester, from 2005-2008, for kids fighting cancer and their siblings, the camp staff held an annual New Year's Eve gathering at a small hotel in Preston, Minnesota. We were so blessed to come to know Stacey Hildebrandt and all of the special people that made Camp Jornada unforgettable. The gathering was a chance for the families and the staff to get together, catch up on progress won and lost in the cancer struggles, play some board games, get good and wrinkled up in the motel pool, eat too much junk food and pop, and finally cap off the evening at midnight with fireworks and party horns for the kids to blow to welcome the beginning of another year of life. Katherine and Will joined together for a great photo at midnight on January 1, 2007. Will was not yet halfway through his epic battle then, the future still held promise that the new year could be better than the last.

We've put 2012 behind us now, Will, the last year you shared with us on the Earth, and we've begun a new year.

Will is now in his new home and Liz, Katherine and I are still mapping out where the journey of life will guide us next. I tell myself we no longer have to fear the future as we did for so many years about what it might mean for Will's life, as there is nothing left to fear. And so I resolve to remember to be optimistic about what this new year may hold for all of us and not let fear pin us down any longer.

We will carry the memory of you with us Will, wherever the path will lead to new adventures, and the memory of you will make us strong when the burdens we carry become hard to bear.

Will and Katherine at Camp Jornada New Year's Eve Celebration in Preston, Minnesota – January 2007

Chapter 13 – Postlude – Reflections On The Journey

What a cruel thing is war: to separate and destroy families and friends, and mar the purest joys and happiness God has granted us in this world; to fill our hearts with hatred instead of love for our neighbors, and to devastate the fair face of this beautiful world.
– Robert E. Lee, letter to his wife, 1864

Darkness cannot drive out darkness, only light can do that.
– The Rev. Martin Luther King, Jr.

Will's war is over now, and what a monumental battle it was in so many ways. Why is fighting childhood cancer like a war? Fighting cancer requires soldiers, brave young men and women who are asked to put their bodies on the line against a formidable foe. Fighting cancer requires officers to lead the soldiers in battle, dedicated oncologists like Dr. Wetmore and Dr. Rao, and nurses and staff to help carry out the orders. Fighting cancer requires reconnaissance, reading about your enemy and ways to outfox it with new, more effective treatments than the old methods. Fighting cancer requires logistical support, parents and extended family to transport the patients to and from innumerable medical appointments and treatments, gas for the vehicles, money for the medical bills and the cafeteria food and the parking fees and the antidepressants. And when the child soldiers are joined in battle with cancer, some of them emerge mostly unscathed, some are wounded and some lose their lives.

And as we walk off Will's battlefield after this war has been lost, we try to count the costs to better understand what he endured. The total financial cost for this titanic struggle came to an unbelievable $2,201,090.10, which does not include the care he received at Memorial–Sloan Kettering Medical Center or St. Jude Children's Research Hospital. We are very thankful that Mayo medical insurance helped shoulder much of this burden. The number of hours that Will spent over eight-plus years in his epic battle against cancer are hard to calculate, but it is something on the order of this:

- 80 MRIs of his brain and spine, each one required him to lie perfectly still for anywhere from one-half to an hour at a time and he did this without ever requiring sedation as many patients do.

- Will endured 12 different surgical procedures related to his cancer.
- He weathered 90 different sessions where he received various doses of radiation to his head, including the radioactive antibody therapy given at Memorial-Sloan Kettering.
- He hung on through some 30+ cycles of chemotherapy, which spanned a period of about 50 months – more than a quarter of the years of Will's short life.
- It's impossible to count the number of times Will was stuck with a needle to access the port-a-cath in his chest, except to say that it numbered in the hundreds.
- It's impossible to count the pills of all shapes and sizes Will had to patiently swallow over eight years, except to say it was easily in the thousands.

The list goes on and on. He was absolutely the toughest person I will ever know, possessed of more fortitude than Cal Ripken Jr., Brett Favre or any of the other sports legends he idolized who set endurance records by playing on, game after game, through the pain. Will had nothing left to give when the battle was over and he earned a just reward in heaven. But despite being strong enough to endure all these hardships, Will never wanted to dwell on this. He was so very compassionate and kindhearted, anxious to learn about how the people in his life were doing, loving and respectful to his parents and his sister, a hard worker in school, generous and ready to serve when his body permitted it, always ready for a joke and a smile, passionate about his loves, Legos and baseball, dogs and video games. He showed us all much about how to make the very most of what you have been given in life. I am so very proud of Will. He was the very best son a father could ever have.

What is your legacy, Will? How do we honor you and what lessons do we share with others as we go forward?

1. Take time to enjoy your kids: the time they will be with you is here and gone in the blink of an eye. Don't look back years from now and have regrets about the missed opportunities to shower them with love. Give them your time, and share with them your talents.

2. Remember to enjoy life whenever you can, smile and laugh a little each day; do not dwell on your failures or misfortunes as each day

is a chance to start anew. Do your best every day, whether you are fighting the cancer or trying to comfort the cancer fighter, and let others step in to help when you falter to help you bear the weight on your shoulders.

3. Help others less fortunate than yourself. None of us on this Earth can make it through hard times without a helping hand. The Canan family received a mountain of help during Will's journey; we have a debt of gratitude that we can never fully repay in this lifetime. Paying it forward is the best way we can give back and honor Will's memory.

4. Remember that cancer cannot steal the light that shines from within, your precious memories, your love for your family and friends and their love for you, your faith in your Creator and in the new life that waits for you when your life here on Earth is done, your assurance that your loved ones will be with you again someday.

You were our gift from God, Will. Your life was difficult, but you lit a fire in many hearts while you were here in so many ways you will never fully know. Heaven is surely a little better place since you arrived there. We will love you and remember you always. Dad.

APPENDIX A - SUMMARY OF WILL'S PAST TREATMENTS AND DATES OF TREATMENT

March 14, 2004: Diagnosis of standard risk medulloblastoma

March 15, 2004: Complete re-section surgery to remove visible tumor

April 15, 2004: Port-a-Cath surgically implanted in Will's chest

April 19, 2004 - June, 2004: 31 fractions (sessions) of cranial and spinal radiation

April 20, 2004: Vincristine and Cisplatin chemotherapy weekly – Will undergoes eight six-week cycles, or a total of 48 weeks of chemotherapy, which he completes May 17, 2005

April 21, 2004: Will commences rehabilitation with the staff of the Physical Medicine and Rehabilitation Department at Mayo to counteract the effects of his cancer and original surgery, which is completed December 28, 2004

April 27, 2004: Darbepoetin received to help stimulate Will's red blood cell counts while he undergoes radiation

March 2, 2005: Will contracted form of chicken pox causing shingles on the right side of his face and back of his head. Received anti-viral IV, blood transfusion, and daily shots for three days to stimulate white blood cell production.

First Relapse – April 17, 2006

April 20, 2006: Port-a-Cath surgically implanted in Will's chest again

May 3, 2006: Surgical biopsy of lesion in right ventricle of brain

June 29, 2006: Gamma Knife radiation procedure

August 9, 2006: Attempted stem cell collection

September 5, 2006: Topotecan chemotherapy via IV infusion for four hours each day for five days, followed by a three week break. Will's white blood cell counts dropped so low after a couple of weeks that they had him come into the hospital twice a day for IV antibiotic infusions. Spent six nights in the hospital related to this issue. Received daily GCSF (granulocyte colony-stimulating factor) shots intended to help his bone marrow produce more stem cells. Endured five straight months of chemo with six cycles of topotecan, a total of over 120 hours of treatment and sitting in the Pediatric Infusion Treatment Center through January 31, 2007.

October 16, 2006: Will is admitted to hospital due to bad cough and persistent fever. Low white blood cell counts and the beginnings of pneumonia. Received an IV antibiotic, discharged from the hospital October 19, 2006.

November 10, 2006: Will admitted to hospital due to neutropenia (white blood cell count too low). Developed hives on his face and torso and they itched terribly while receiving red blood cell transfusion. Discharged from hospital on November 13, 2006.

February 12, 2007: Consultation with the complementary medicine staff at Minneapolis Children's Hospital

March 16, 2007: Port-a-Cath surgically removed from Will's Chest

Second Relapse – December 11, 2007

December 21, 2007: Gamma Knife radiation procedure for lesions in both lateral ventricles

January 21, 2008: Port-a-Cath surgically implanted in Will's chest again

January 29, 2008: Surgery at Memorial-Sloan Kettering (MSK) to surgically implant the Ommaya reservoir in Will's head

February 6, February 14, February 28, June 11 and June 24, 2008: I3F8 antibody therapy injections into the Ommaya reservoir in Will's head at MSK

April 2, 2008: Temodar Chemotherapy – five days, 28-day cycle

April 30, 2008: Dosage of Temodar chemotherapy increased

July 29, 2008: Hearing tests show significant low and high frequency hearing loss in Will's right ear as a side effect of the treatments.

August 22, 2008: Temozolomide and Isotretinoin/Accutane Chemotherapy – 5 days, then off for 23 days in a 28-day cycle – total of five cycles, which did not end until February 12, 2009.

November 21, 2008: Will is lymphopenic (low lymphocyte levels). His immune system was compromised in its ability to fight fungal infections like pneumonia. Bactrim prescription begun.

Third Relapse – January 27, 2009

February 12, 2009: Commenced Avastin and Irinotecan chemotherapy through infusions at Pediatric Infusion Treatment Center at Mayo on Days 1 and 15 of cycle; six cycles through July 28, 2009

September 3, 2009: Gamma Knife radiation procedure at Mayo on right ventricular lesions

October 8, 2009: Sonic Hedgehog pathway inhibitor clinical trial – Begun at St. Jude Children's Research Hospital; remained on drug until March 5, 2010. Stopped due to continued tumor growth.

November 5, 2009: After Will injures his left ankle, his left leg starts twitching/shaking involuntarily; neurologic tests are normal; determined to be related to injury, not to tumor growth.

November 20, 2009: Took Will to ER with persistent fever of between

100 and 102 degrees, sore throat. Gave him an IV antibiotic to cover any other potential infections.

February 5, 2010: Surgery at Mayo to remove tumor in left frontal horn of left ventricle

March 29, 2010: Ara-C/DepoCyt chemotherapy drug via infusion every two weeks at Pediatric Infusion Treatment Center; remained on drug until April 28, 2010

May 12, 2010: VP-16/Etoposide chemotherapy drug taken orally, 21 days on/seven days off until October 10, 2010

July 14, 2010: Will spiked a high temp of 102, his counts are low, we head off to the ER in Eau Claire, WI; they give him some fluids, IV dose of antibiotics.

October 14, 2010: Will starts on a new chemo drug, SAHA with retinoic acid/Accutane, which dries out his nose and lips, continues until January 14, 2011 when it's learned that SAHA drug is not working so Will is taken off SAHA/retinoic acid

February 10, 2011: Surgery to remove frontal lobe tumors in left and right ventricles at LeBonheur Children's Hospital in Memphis, TN

March 9, 2011: Will begins five weeks (Monday-Friday) of re-radiation to the anterior parts of the upper left and right ventricles only, two treatments per day, finishing on April 12, 2011.

June 28, 2011: Will has Gamma Knife procedure to tumors in posterior horn and posterior fossa near the brain stem at Mayo

July 18, 2011: Will has serious "cradle cap" on his scalp with dead skin cell buildup from radiation treatments; had his hair washed numerous times with special shampoo to soften the "plaque" build up, then comb his hair gently, removing pieces of plaque.

September 2, 2011: Will ends up in the ER with hives from his head to his knees in some areas and large, irregular shaped areas of very red skin on his torso area. He also itched terribly, had difficulty swallowing, gave him Benadryl and also prescribed steroids for five days.

September 7, 2011: Will had his first symptoms attributable to the spinal tumors, significant pain in his back and tingling in his left foot; takes Celebrex and Tylenol for the pain.

September 8, 2011: Will starts the Kieran Metronomic Chemotherapy Protocol, includes drugs VP-16 and Cytoxan, statins, an NSAID (pain reliever), thalidomide and Avastin, a drug that works to cut off the blood supply to tumors. All of the drugs will be taken orally except the Avastin, which will be infused through his Port-a-Cath every two weeks in the Pediatric Infusion Treatment Center. Discontinued May 15, 2012 due to continued tumor growth.

November 22, 2011: Will learns that the metronomic protocol is working and the tumors are shrinking in size for the first time in several years.

January 24, 2012: Will had been out walking Buddy, our dog, and had fallen and hit his head hard on the sidewalk (slippery after an ice storm). Took him to the ER, neuro exam and a CT scan two hours later showed that he had no signs of internal bleeding, but most likely got a concussion; the tremor in his left hand is a little stronger than usual.

March 6, 2012: Will receives two other chemo drugs intrathecally, through the Ommaya reservoir in his head; had to take three days of steroids, which is standard protocol when taking this drug intrathecally. March 14 administration of the drugs intrathecally is halted when he has episode where he is unable to think or speak, but continues to take Avastin via IV.

April 2, 2012: Will starts receiving VP-16-etoposide intrathecally once again

May 15, 2012: Will starts receiving valproic acid, an anti-seizure medication, which has shown some promise in fighting cancer.

June 29, 2012: Will visits the ER in Bozeman, MT, while at Camp Big Sky when his balance becomes precarious. They checked Will's counts, which were fine, and gave him a dose of antibiotics and fluids and dismissed him.

June 30, 2012: Upon return from Montana, Will had 3-4 vomiting spells; needed to hold on to him to steady him when he walked, and was having some confusion too; called 911 for the ambulance to come and transport Will to the ER. The CT scan showed that ventricles were enlarged due to excess fluid on brain, known as hydrocephalus; drained 24cc of CSF using Will's Ommaya; showed some bacterial growth in his CSF, started him on antibiotics. Then surgically removed the Ommaya, the suspected source of the infection, and put in a temporary external ventricular drain to continuously drain off excess CSF that was being generated.

July 24, 2012: Will's balance grows steadily worse again, he begins vomiting repeatedly and his short-term memory declines further. CT scan shows that his hydrocephalus had returned. Dr. Wetjen decides it would be best to install permanent shunt; Will released to return home on July 25.

August 3, 2012: Will falls while on a family trip to Lambeau Field in Green Bay, WI and ends up reopening the surgical wound on his head from July 1 surgery. Trip to ER in Green Bay where wound is irrigated and covered for trip back to Rochester.

August 8, 2012: Will's wound is surgically stitched closed, using an inflated breast implant under his skin to stretch it just enough so they can close the wound; the stitches will remain in; Will is released from the hospital on August 9.

September 29, 2012: Will goes on oxygen for the first time.

October 11, 2012: Will passes away.

APPENDIX B - REMINISCENCES OF WILL BY FRIENDS AND FAMILY

Shanna Decker – Osteogenic Sarcoma Survivor and Long Time Friend of Will

I am sitting in the Francis Tower at Saint Marys, enjoying an acoustic concert and thinking about you guys. :) One evening when Katherine, Will, and I went out for ice cream, he and I sat down in the Apache Mall to "people watch." A moment shared between two fighters, though we'd rarely acknowledge that to others because our families fight too. We were just chatting. Sports and chemo and surgery. He stopped me while we were chatting and we looked out at the people bustling by. One sentence is all he said to me, "They move so fast." "Yeah they do," I said in real appreciation of my own thoughts. "They need to slow down," he finished with. He's right, and it's beautiful that he has always moved slowly enough to appreciate life. :) Those are the parts of anyone's struggle I appreciate – not the struggle, but the expression of knowledge, wisdom, and compassion that changes us always for the better in the midst of a simple life. Love you all. :)

Nicole Hines – Mother of other students at St. Francis of Assisi School

Hello Liz and Tom, I've been thinking about you and your family many times throughout every day these past few months.

I believe I've shared this story about Will with you before, but it's always nice to hear it again. I think it was two years ago when the kids were doing the mile run for Presidential fitness that I came upon Will's class running the course Mr. Arvold set up in the St. Francis parking lot. I'm always fascinated by the mile run as it brings back many memories of when Mr. Arvold was my gym teacher, and my classmates and I endured the yearly torturous rite of passage. Pretty much every kid, regardless of running ability, devised some elaborate excuse why he/she couldn't possibly run that day. Just witnessing today's kids lining up to run makes my stomach turn somersaults.

As Will and his group approached the starting line, he exhibited a definite look of determination and quiet confidence. I watched the entire time as Will persevered. As he passed some classmates, and he was passed by others, Will's determination grew with every step. I stood in awe and admiration until Will crossed the finish line. Your son has set an example for us all. When we face struggles in our lives and excuses are readily available, perseverance and determination are what will get us through the day.

Thinking of you all – Nicole

Kathy Chase – **Mother of Alice Chase, a classmate of Will's at St. Francis School**
Dearest Will,
You have been a walking miracle in my life and in the lives of my whole family. We have watched you fight and struggle and get better and fight and struggle and get better and fight and struggle again and again ... but you never complain ... you only move forward with your contagious smile and unswerving spirit. We are all inspired by you and are awed by your strength and tenacity. You are a remarkable young man who has blessed our lives ever so deeply.

Your parents are two of the strongest people I have ever known. God definitely knew what he was doing when he picked them to be your parents, and you to be their kid. They are selfless in their love for you and I know that either one of them would change places with you in a second to not have you endure all that you have. They love you like crazy and will miss you in ways that you will never have the chance to fully understand. I don't think I ever truly understood how much my own parents loved me until I had children of my own. My heart aches for your mom and dad, Will. Your sister will miss her best friend too. You will be so missed in this world. I hope and pray that somehow we all will find some comfort in knowing that you are going to a better place ... a place where cancer does not exist ... the next place where love beyond understanding will prevail. I am so sad for all of us, but so happy for you that you will be whole, healthy, without pain and struggle.
I wrote a similar letter to Axel (Johnson) before he left us. I think this image is especially appropriate for you, the baseball player. When you hit your last home run here on earth, I know that the gates of Heaven

Photos

Get Well Card to Will from Classmate Matthew Ryan – Spring 2004

Get Well Card to Will from Classmate Victoria Woodward – Spring 2004

Will and Katherine – On the beach near Mackinac Island, Michigan – Summer 2004

Will and Uncle Tom and the big fish Will caught at Lake Wissota, Wisconsin – Christmas 2004

Will, Liz, Katherine, Marcia Fritzmeier and "Dr. Jack" in Will's 1st grade class at St. Francis of Assisi School, Rochester – April 2005

Will – Picking out his pumpkin at Tweite's Pumpkin Patch – October 2004

When He Stands Beside his giant sunflower that he planted in kindergarten
last spring and then transplanted at
home, 6-year-old Tom Canan feels somewhat like Jack and his famous beanstalk.
The sunflower now towers roof-high.
Tom is the son of Dr. and Mrs. Michael
E. Canan, 322 S. Helen St., Kimberly.

Will, and Dad at Will's age – "Two Generations of Young
Sunflower Growers" – August 2004 and August 1970

Will and his first canine best friend, "Thoreau" – Spring 2005

Will's Make-A-Wish trip to Walt Disney World, Orlando, Florida – December 2005

Will, Katherine, Liz, Tom and "Roxie" the Dolphin – Discovery Cove, Orlando, Florida – December 2005

Will, Katherine, Liz and Tom – Will's Cub Scout Pinewood Derby, St. Francis School Gym – Spring 2006

Will and our new
Sheltie puppy
"Scout," Rochester
– April 2006

Will in his first baseball uniform
with Rochester Youth Baseball –
the "Grasshoppers" – Spring 2006

Will and Family –
American Cancer Society
Relay for Life, University
Center Rochester –
Summer 2006

Will – Arrival of Care Package from the Green Bay Packers, Rochester – Summer 2006

Will and friend Cate Arendt at Minnesota Twins Playoff Game – Metrodome, Minneapolis – Fall 2006

Will as Darth Vader, Katherine, friends Anna Sutherland, Ben, Joey and Gracie Viggiano, Rochester – Halloween 2006

Will, Marcia and "Dr. Jack" – St. Francis Christmas Concert, Lourdes High School, Rochester – December 2006

Will and Katherine prepare for Pep Fest Dress Up Day at school, Rochester - December 2006

Will and ski instructor Al Southwick at Welch Village Ski Resort, Welch, Minnesota – February 2007

Will, Mom and Dad at YMCA basketball practice, Rochester – February 2007

Will and his second canine best friend "Buddy" – Spring 2007

Will, Katherine, Mom and Dad with Will's big halibut at Whaler's Cove Lodge, Angoon, Alaska – Summer 2007

Will's drawing selected for the Children's Brain Tumor Association Calendar – August 2007

Will, Katherine, Mom and Dad – On the National Mall in Washington D.C. – January 2008

Will, Katherine and Twins Catcher Joe Mauer at Twinsfest – Metrodome, Minneapolis – February 2008

Will and contestant at Westminster Kennel Club Dog Show – Madison Square Garden, New York City – February 2008

Will's 10th birthday celebration at home in Rochester – February 2008

Will, Katherine and Liz on a New York Harbor Cruise, New York City – June 2008

Will and kids racing their boats at the Ronald McDonald House, New York City – June 2008

Will and New
York Yankees
Star Derek
Jeter, Yankees
Stadium, New
York City –
June 2008

Will and family –
Black Hills, South
Dakota, August 2008

Will and family and
his new horse friend
– Black Hills, South
Dakota, August 2008

Will, Katherine, Mom and Dad at "Will Weekend" Benefit at St. Francis Catholic Church, Rochester – September 2008

Will and Minnesota Twins players Justin Morneau and Carlos Gomez at Twins Spring Training, Ft. Myers, Florida – February 2009

Will, Katherine, Boston Red Sox Star "Big Papi" David Ortiz and the Canan family, Ft. Myers, Florida – February 2009

Canan family, Ft. Myers and Sanibel Island, Florida – February 2009

Will and his best friend Joey Viggiano at Kid's Cup Benefit Golf Tournament, The Links of Byron, Byron, Minnesota – Spring 2009

Will With "V is for Vomet" Poster at St. Jude's Children Research Center in Memphis, Tennessee – October 2009

Will dressed as a hobo for trick or treating at home in Rochester – Halloween 2009

Will dressed up for "Community Worker Day" at St. Francis School, Rochester – February 2010

Will and Katherine at Will's 12th Birthday Party at Home in Rochester – February 2010

First Visit to the
Minnesota Twins
Target Field in
Minneapolis –
Mother's Day 2010

Will's Surprise VIP
Visit to Target Field,
made possible by
Chris, Marne, Mitch
and Meredith Gade –
May 2010

Will and family
and Hawaiian
dance troupe at
Camp Firefly near
Pine Mountain,
Georgia – June
2010

Will and family and
Kirk and Chelsea
Cameron and their
family at Camp
Firefly near Pine
Mountain, Georgia –
June 2010

Will and his 6th
Grade baseball
team show off their
tournament 2nd
Place trophies,
RYBA Baseball
Complex, Rochester
– July 2010

Will with his "Player of the Year"
Award for Good Sportsmanship
from Rochester Youth Baseball
Association, Mayo Field,
Rochester – August 2010

Will in the only game he ever got to pitch for RYBA Baseball, Soldier's Field Park, Rochester – September 2010

Will channeling his "Inner King of Rock and Roll" with Mom and Dad – Sun Studios – Memphis, Tennessee – January 2011

Will and Katherine with the members of the band "Rascal Flatts" before the concert – Xcel Energy Center, St. Paul, Minnesota – January 2011

Will and Dad at
Super Bowl XLV
– Texas Stadium,
Irving, Texas –
February 2011

Will, Dad, Gary
and Marcia
Fritzmeier at the
NFL Experience
Expo – Dallas
Convention
Center, Dallas,
Texas – February
2011

Will rings the bell
at Desk R to signal
the end of radiation
treatments – Mayo
Clinic – April 2011

Will and Dad at the Kid's Cup Golf Tournament, Little Willow Creek Golf Course, Rochester – May 2011

Will and friend Lenn Brown at Camp Sunshine near Casco, Maine – July 2011

Will launching his "Wish Boat" at sunset on the Pond at Camp Sunshine near Casco, Maine – July 2011

Will and Katherine at Lake Wissota near Chippewa Falls, Wisconsin – July 2011

Photo Will took himself at Lake Wissota near Chippewa Falls, Wisconsin – July 2011

Will and buddy Tom Ryan – "Camp Out" at Oxbow Park, near Byron, Minnesota – September 2011

"Go Team Will" 8th grade class event at St. Francis School, Rochester – September 2011

Will and Katherine – Lourdes High School Homecoming Night, Victoria's Restaurant, Rochester – October 2011

Will, Katherine. Mom, Dad, and Grandma and Grandpa Canan – "Brains Together for a Cure" Benefit Walk, University Center Rochester – October 2011

Will and Hannah greeting the King and Queen of Norway at Mayo Clinic, Rochester – October 2011

Will and Uncle Steve and Grandpa Canan at the Green Bay Packer Hall of Fame, Lambeau Field, Green Bay, Wisconsin – December 2011

Will at the Green Bay Packer Hall of Fame, Lambeau Field, Green Bay, Wisconsin – December 2011

Will, Katherine, Mom and Dad and "Salvador" the Dolphin at the Blue Lagoon Dolphin Encounter, Bahamas – February 2012

Will and Mom – University of Kansas Basketball Game, Allen Field House, Lawrence, Kansas - February 2012

Will and his extended family – Du Wop Wed Widing Hood, St. Francis School Play – April 2012

Will and members of 8th grade Lourdes High School golf team, Soldier's Field Golf Course, Rochester – April 2012

Will and a friendly turtle at Quarry Hill Nature Center, Rochester, Minnesota – May 2012

Will and classmates Riley Orr and Matthew Chestolowski at class trip to Valleyfair Amusement Park, Shakopee, Minnesota – May 2012

Will and the 8th Grade Graduating Class of St. Francis of Assisi School, Rochester – May 2012

Will, Katherine, Mom, Dad and their extended families on Graduation Night, St. Francis School, Rochester – May 2012

Will, Mom, the campers and camp counselor, Camp Big Sky, Eagle Mount, near Bozeman, Montana – June 2012

Will and his 8th grade baseball team at the last regular season game, RYBA Complex, Rochester – July 2012

Will and his baseball coaches, Jim Ryan and Brian Cada, following the final tournament game, RYBA Complex, Rochester – July 2012

Will, Katherine, Mom and Dad following the final tournament game – July 2012

Will and "Dr. Jack" before Packer Family Night at Lambeau Field, Green Bay, Wisconsin – August 2012

Confirmation for Will with Father Mark McNea and Will's sponsor, St. Francis School Principal Barb Plenge, at our home – August 2012

Will, Katherine, Mom and Dad on visit to Oxbow Park Zoo near Byron, Minnesota – August 2012

Will and 9th grade classmates Miranda Hawkinson, Skylar Drefcinski, Abigail Thompson, and Nora Haas start the "Go Blue for Will" phenomenon at our home – August 2012

Will, Mom, Dad and Katherine on Will's first day of high school at Lourdes High School, Rochester – August 2012

Will and part of the Lourdes High School football team at our home – September 2012

Will, Katherine, Mom and Dad at final family photo session at home – Labor Day Weekend 2012

Will with final gift from the Minnesota Twins, a Joe Mauer jersey and a Justin Morneau signed baseball at our home – September 2012

The wonderful Pediatric Oncology Staff on the 16th Floor of the Mayo Building at Mayo Clinic and the rock band "Paul Revere and the Raiders" Go Blue for Will – September 2012

Will and his new Guardian
Angel from the Dearani family
at our home – September 2012

300 Students at
Mayo High School
in Rochester
Gather to Go Blue
for Will, initiated
by Will's friend,
Ben Viggiano –
September 2012

Will and "Dr. Jack"
together for one
last time at our
home – October
2012

Will's visitation at Macken Funeral Home Chapel, Rochester – October 2012

Will's final resting place at Oakwood Cemetery, Rochester – October 2012

Porcelain angel unearthed from our garden while planting Will's memorial tree at our home – October 2012

Photo Will took of giraffe at Cheyenne Mountain Zoo, Colorado Springs, Colorado – August 2011

Will and His Best Pal "Buddy" – September 2012

Photo of butterflies shot by photographer friend, Randy Ziegler, in Texas when Will passed away – October 2012